Healthcare Architecture as Infrastructure

Architects and healthcare clients are increasingly coming to recognize that, once built, healthcare facilities are almost immediately subject to physical alterations which both respond to and affect healthcare practices. This calls into question the traditional ways in which these facilities are designed. If functions and practices are subject to alteration, the standard approach of defining required functions and practices before acquiring facilities is obsolete. We need other starting points, working methods, and ways of collaborating.

Healthcare Architecture as Infrastructure presents these new approaches. Advocating an infrastructure theory of built environment transformation in which design and investment decisions are organized hierarchically and transcend short-term use, the book draws on the practice and research of a number of architects from around the world. Written by experts with experience in policy making, designing, building, and managing complex healthcare environments, it shows professionals in architecture, engineering, healthcare and facilities management how to enhance the long-term usefulness of their campuses and their building stock and how to strengthen their physical assets with the capacity to accommodate a quickly evolving healthcare sector.

Stephen H. Kendall, PhD, RA is Emeritus Professor of Architecture at Ball State University and co-director of the Council on Open Building. Dr Kendall's career in architectural practice, research, and education spans more than 35 years. His research focuses on the Open Building approach, needed to make buildings more adaptable, easier to customize to meet changing preferences and thus more sustainable. His work recognizes the increasing size and complexity of projects and the dynamics of living environments, the workplace, and the marketplace where design must go beyond short-term uses and where control is distributed not only during initial planning but also over time.

Healthcare Architecture as Infrastructure

Open Building in Practice

EDITED BY STEPHEN H. KENDALL

LONDON AND NEW YORK

First published 2019
by Routledge
2 Park Square, Milton Park, Abingdon, Oxon OX14 4RN

and by Routledge
52 Vanderbilt Avenue, New York, NY 10017

Routledge is an imprint of the Taylor & Francis Group, an informa business

© 2019 selection and editorial matter, Stephen H. Kendall; individual chapters, the contributors

The right of Stephen H. Kendall to be identified as the author of the editorial material, and of the authors for their individual chapters, has been asserted in accordance with sections 77 and 78 of the Copyright, Designs and Patents Act 1988.

All rights reserved. No part of this book may be reprinted or reproduced or utilised in any form or by any electronic, mechanical, or other means, now known or hereafter invented, including photocopying and recording, or in any information storage or retrieval system, without permission in writing from the publishers.

Trademark notice: Product or corporate names may be trademarks or registered trademarks, and are used only for identification and explanation without intent to infringe.

British Library Cataloguing-in-Publication Data
A catalogue record for this book is available from the British Library

Library of Congress Cataloging-in-Publication Data
Names: Kendall, Stephen H., editor.
Title: Healthcare architecture as infrastructure : open building in practice / edited by Stephen H. Kendall.
Description: Milton Park, Abingdon, Oxon ;
New York, NY : Routledge, 2019. |
Includes bibliographical references and index.
Identifiers: LCCN 2018030306| ISBN 9780815367840
(hb : alk. paper) | ISBN 9780815367857 (pb : alk. paper) |
ISBN 9781351256407 (ebook)
Subjects: LCSH: Hospital architecture. |
Health facilities--Design and construction.
Classification: LCC RA967 .H395 2019 | DDC 725/.51--dc23
LC record available at https://lccn.loc.gov/2018030306

ISBN: 978-0-815-36784-0 (hbk)
ISBN: 978-0-815-36785-7 (pbk)
ISBN: 978-1-351-25640-7 (ebk)

Typeset in Univers LT Std
by Integra Software Services Pvt. Ltd.

 Printed in the United Kingdom by Henry Ling Limited

"We should not try to forecast what will happen, but try to make provisions for what cannot be foreseen."

John Habraken

Dedicated to John Habraken, mentor and friend, whose body of work over more than 50 years has helped lead to a deeper understanding of change and the distribution of control in the making of built environment, and who has pioneered the development of architectural design methods needed to cultivate the built field in all its wonder and complexity.

Contents

List of figures	ix
List of tables	xiv
Preface	xvi
List of contributors	xviii
Introduction	xxii
Summary of the chapters	xxvi

1 An infrastructure model of the building stock 1
  Stephen H. Kendall

2 System Separation: A strategy for preventive building design 13
  Giorgio Macchi

3 A dynamic steering instrument for the development of the Inselspital University healthcare campus 32
  Martin Henn

4 Dynamic facilities development: A client perspective on managing change 54
  David Hanitchak and Malaina Bowker

5 Planning for change: Banner Estrella Medical Center, Phoenix, Arizona 71
  John Pangrazio, Ryan Hullinger, Mark Patterson, and Anne Friedrich Bilsbarrow

6 The evolution of a hospital planned for change 91
  Nirit Putievsky Pilosof

7 Finding shared ambitions to design for change: Building the AZ Groeninge hospital 108
  Waldo Galle and Pieter Herthogs

8	Transformation of an existing hospital building to a hospice: Open Building as strategy for process and product *Karel Dekker*	125
9	Simulation: Tools for planning for change *William Fawcett*	140
10	The growth and change of hospital buildings *Kazuhiko Okamoto*	164
	Index	196

Figures

1.1	A levels of infrastructure model of the built environment	5
2.1	Mind opening bottle crate – (a) combined; (b) crate; (c) bottles; (d) liquid	16
2.2	The three levels of System Separation	16
2.3	The three principles of System Separation	17
2.4	INO: (a) Primary System Competition entry; (b) Primary System external view; (c) Secondary System Circulation zone; (d) Primary System under construction	23
2.5	(a) vonRoll Primary System external view; (b) vonRoll Floor Plan; (c) vonRoll Interior Access Zone; (d) vonRoll Interior view of the Library	24
2.6	Ancient and medieval road systems of a European city	27
3.1	Arial View Inselspital 2010	33
3.2	Competition Model of the Master plan: HENN Architects	33
3.3	Inselspital – Historical Illustration 1884	34
3.4	Site Development	34
3.5	Competition Key Ideas	37
3.6	Master plan 2060	38
3.7	Rulebook	40
3.8	Key Ideas	42
3.9	Rules	44
3.10	Organizational Master plan	47
3.11	Connecting Space and Organization	48
3.12	Workshop Sketches	50
3.13	Zoning Plan	52
3.14	Master plan Model with Spatial Frame and Example of Possible Building Bulk and Massing	53
4.1	Campus growth by decade	57
5.1	Circulation and Infrastructure Systems – the three-dimensional framework which organizes	

	and integrates the structural skeleton, with pathways for the distribution of building systems (heating, cooling, ventilation, plumbing, medical gasses, electrical, communications) and major circulation systems (vertical and horizontal systems of movement of supplies, patients, staff, visitors)	72
5.2	The space field (column grid and floor-to-floor heights indicated) accommodates all clinical and procedural services; HVAC systems, mechanical shafts, electrical/IT rooms, elevator cores, and stairs are excluded from the space field zone	73
5.3	Infrastructure – the building is organized along a central spine sized with capacity to furnish all mechanical, electrical, and plumbing needs for patient care and support spaces up to the maximum projected campus build-out	74
5.4	Phase I was completed in 2005 and houses one patient tower with 172 beds and one diagnostic and treatment wing	75
5.5	Phase II added a second patient tower, for a total of approximately 400 beds, and was designed by SmithGroup and constructed without disrupting hospital operations	76
5.6	Phase III was projected to expand diagnostic and treatment services; the fully expanded hospital would have three patient towers, 600 beds and a total of 1.2 million sf (111,483 m^2)	76
5.7	A sublevel links the utility plant to the main hospital along the central infrastructure spine.	77
5.8	Phase I/Built Concept/Floor Level 1	78
5.9	Final Phase/Full Build-out Concept (not yet implemented)/Floor Level 1	80
5.10	Capacity studies of the site considering new development	83
5.11	The original Emergency Department layout limited the future growth of the department because of site constraints, and created a significant challenge in renovating without disrupting emergency services	86
5.12	Emergency Department renovations included the displacement of unrelated "soft spaces" and a small addition on the west to accommodate a new ED walk-in entrance/lobby. This allowed for the relocation and replacement of ED "front-end" program spaces without disrupting emergency services. Additionally, by moving the walk-in entrance to the west, it	

	allowed for future grown of the department to the east	87
5.13	The second floor (left image) of the nursing tower was adapted to house expanded diagnostic and treatment (D&T) functions. All remaining upper floors (right image) house acuity-ADA (Americans with Disabilities Act) patient rooms. A bridge was added to provide a dedicated patient/staff connection from the new tower to the existing D&T block	88
6.1	Design illustrations of the Sammy Ofer Heart Building, 2006	94
6.2	Preliminary study of schematic design options of the hospital typical floor, 2005	96
6.3	Analysis of the design of the hospital medical unit by the three system levels	97
6.4	Section of the building illustrates the five phases of construction and the hospital's dynamic program	101
6.5	Architecture floor plans of the variety of medical programs	103
7.1	AZ Groeninge has five interconnected blocks, either three or four levels high; introducing interior courtyards of 20 x 60 m created spaces closer to human scale, despite the large site	111
7.2	Precast facade elements and two rows of concrete columns, alternated with staircases, technical shafts, and patios, form the structure of every hospital wing	114
7.3	A well-considered building layout of the hospital wings, implemented in the first construction phase, allowed the first wings to remain operational during the subsequent construction phase	116
7.4	The prefabrication and on-site assembly of the facade reduced construction costs and enabled the designers to allocate more of the budget towards other aspects to improve the building's generality	117
7.5	The columns of the facade elements are angled, serving as permanent sun blinds while providing the building its serene appearance	118
7.6	This typical section shows how a series of ducts has been integrated in the concrete structure: by providing placeholder ducts at regular intervals in the structure, the framework for technical services adds generality to the support	119
8.1	Original and new location of the Hospice as part of the total Hospital facility. A Heath Centre adjacent to the new Hospice was created in a building previously housing another function	126

xi

8.2	One of several iterations of the capacity analysis process using the raster method	127
8.3	The definitive layout of the hospice	128
8.4	Quick Scan Refurb costs, used for defining first budgets for Base Building and Fit-out	131
8.5	Comparing selection results for the short-list of 7 contractors. The white bar is for the Hospice building and the light grey bar for the Health Centre. The dark grey bar shows the cumulative result of this selection phase	132
8.6	Hospice "Het Vliethuis"	134
8.7, 8.8, 8.9	CableStud installation in metal stud interior non-load-bearing walls, ready for electrical and data wiring installation; Wieland's "Gesis" quick-connect cabling system (www.wieland-electric.com/en/products/building-installation-systems)	136
8.10, 8.11, 8.12	The garden and interior semi-public areas	137
9.1	The McMaster University Health Sciences Centre (MHSC) at Hamilton, Canada, by Eberhard Zeidler of Craig Zeidler & Strong was opened in 1972. It incorporates elaborate and expensive strategies for adaptation	143
9.2	Northwick Park Hospital by John Weeks of Llewelyn-Davies Weeks was built in 1965–1972. It incorporated Weeks's loose-fit and indeterminacy strategies for adaptation. The corrugated panels indicate an "open end" for extension that was never used	145
9.3	Northwick Park Hospital site plan, showing the original construction of 1965–1972, the extensions added up to 2004 (including the replacement of the residential accommodation at the southeast of the site), and extensions added between 2004 and 2014. The "open ends" for extensions that have been left unused are shown with arrows. The viewpoint of the photo in Figure 9.2 is marked with an asterisk	146
9.4	The structural system for Northwick Park as shown in the 1973 prospective evaluation exercise (identified as Hospital E)	149
9.5	The structural system for best performing strategy in the 1973 prospective evaluation exercise (identified as Hospital F)	150
9.6	Results from the 1973 prospective evaluation of seven alternative hospital structures, showing the rankings for construction and cumulative costs (data from Table 9.2). The rankings vary with the number of adaptations. Hospitals A and G with high	

	construction cost and low adaptation cost are shown with broken lines; Hospitals D and B/C with lower construction cost and higher adaptation cost are shown with dotted lines. Hospital E represents Northwick Park Hospital; Hospital F performed best in this exercise	152
9.7	Graphs showing departmental growth and shrinkage over the service life of the hypothetical hospital in two contrasting "life history" scenarios, for the medium rate of growth and change	156
9.8	Graph of growth and shrinkage over the service life in Department D3 in the hypothetical hospital, for one "life history" scenario for the medium rate of growth and change, showing the year-to-year variation in: (i) the floor area demand (broken line), and (ii) the floor area provision where adaptations in 1,000 m^2 increments respond to changes in demand (solid line)	157
9.9	Scattergram of results for 1,000 simulated "life history" scenarios for hospital H (reference), medium rate of growth and change and no discounting. The average cumulative cost over 50 years is £315 m (including £119 m initial construction cost) and the average number of adaptations is 20, but there is wide variation between scenarios; and there are a few extreme outliers	158
10.1	Illustrations of types of methodologies	171
10.2	Illustrations of types of methodologies	172
10.3	Hospital site at each era	193

Tables

4.1	Chronology of inpatient building characteristics	59
4.2	Chronology of the characteristics of diagnostic, treatment and procedure floors	60
4.3	Chronology of the characteristics of outpatient buildings	61
4.4	Yawkey's Nine Commandments	62
6.1	Change in practice 2005–2018	99
9.1	Indexed cost data for the 1973 prospective evaluation of seven alternative hospital structures (with the lowest costs set to 100), showing the construction cost and the cost of adaptation for changes of use. Blank entries indicate that the hospital did not have the relevant departments. Alternative A is Greenwich Hospital and alternative E is Northwick Park Hospital. The range of adaptation costs is much narrower than the range of construction costs	151
9.2	Indexed cost data for the 1973 prospective evaluation of seven alternative hospital structures, showing the cumulative cost of construction and adaptations for 20, 40, 60, and 80 changes of use. The range of values for cumulative costs is narrow	151
9.3	The five departments in the hypothetical hospital	154
9.4	The construction and running costs for the three space grades in the hypothetical hospital, for the reference case ($£/m^2$)	154
9.5	The adaptation cost when floor space is exchanged between departments in the hypothetical hospital, for the reference case ($£/m^2$)	154
9.6	The five alternative design specifications for the hypothetical hospital, defined by cost adjustments compared to the reference case (H)	155
9.7	Average life cycle costs for the hypothetical hospital (initial construction plus 50-year service life, in £m) for 1,000 simulated "life history" scenarios, for five alternative design specifications (H-M) and three rates of growth and change (σ), with no discounting (top), 3.5% discount rate (centre) and 7%	

	discount rate (bottom). In each line the lowest cost alternative is boxed and the higher cost alternatives are toned	159
10.1	Number of hospitals according to hospital administration	165
10.2	Number of beds according to hospital administration	165
10.3	Hospital site at each era	168
10.4	Types of methodologies	169
10.5	Types of hospital administrations	170
10.6	Applied methodologies in domestic/overseas hospitals	173
10.7	Applied methodologies according to domestic hospital administration	174
10.8	Number of methodologies according to hospital size	176
10.9	Number of applied methodologies in domestic/overseas hospitals	178
10.10	Number of applied methodologies according to hospital administration	178
10.11	Number of applied methodologies according to hospital size	178
10.12	Number of hospitals in year of completion	179
10.13	Number of domestic hospitals according to completion year and methodologies applied	179
10.14	Number of overseas hospitals according to completion year and methodologies applied	179
10.15	Number of domestic hospitals according to completion year and methodologies applied	180
10.16	Number of overseas hospitals according to completion year and methodologies applied	181
10.17	Type of hospital building and site	182
10.18	Results of type of building	183
10.19	Results of type of site	183
10.20	Results of type of growth and change	183
10.21	Hospital type in city/local area	184
10.22	Hospital type according to building age	185
10.23	Hospital type according to completion year of old building	186

Preface

When I was a student of architecture in the late 1960s, I worked at a coop job at The Architects Collaborative in Cambridge, Massachusetts. One of my assignments was to design the laundry department on the basement level of a new building to be constructed on the Tufts New England Medical Center campus in downtown Boston. Someone else designed the building; I was tasked with the design of a small part of it. Later, when I joined the Christner Partnership in St. Louis, and became a registered architect, I also worked on healthcare facilities, both new projects and renovation/additions to older buildings, in addition to schools and houses. After I entered the academic field in the early 1980s – in large part to pursue my interest in John Habraken's work and others practicing "Open Building" on the international stage – I focused on teaching, studying, and writing about residential Open Building. During this period I completed a PhD in Design Theory and Methods at the Massachusetts Institute of Technology under Professor Habraken's direction, in which I came to understand that even the most brilliant technical innovations developed by architects would never come to fruition without equivalent changes in the ecology – the social structure or patterns of control – of the building industry.

My attempt to understand the ecology of production in the built environment came into sharper focus and brought me back to the healthcare architecture field when, on a trip to Europe in 2000, I visited the architectural office of Peter Kamm, in Zug, Switzerland. Kamm had done residential Open Building projects in the 1960s. His office had recently won the competition to design what was called the Primary System of a major new building (the INO project) on the campus of the Inselspital, a large public teaching hospital in Bern. I subsequently met Giorgio Macchi, the chief architect of the Canton Bern Office for Real Estate and Public Buildings, who had initiated an entirely new approach to facilities acquisition called System Separation. Over the years since it was implemented, it has, at this writing, guided more than 20 public projects of all kinds to fruition. This was a remarkable example of public policy akin to Open Building, aimed at assuring long-term value of public assets. In 2006, Mr Macchi hosted an international seminar in Bern, to discuss System Separation, resulting in a published report (Macchi et al., 2008).

System Separation and the resultant INO project were a revelation; I had discovered a rich field for investigation that connected my earliest years in practice and my interest in developments toward Open Building, not only in housing but also in all project types. I subsequently learned that "planning for change" in healthcare facility design was being explored by other pioneering researchers, practitioners, and clients in many countries. This led to participation in numerous conferences, followed by published papers, and, between 2011 and 2014, participation in several research contracts for the National Institute of Building Sciences addressing healthcare facilities designed for flexibility in the portfolio of the Defense Health Agency, part of the US Department of Defense. (Kendall et al., 2014).

The concept of an infrastructure model of the built environment underlying this book is not new. It was first articulated and worked out in practical design tools for housing in the Netherlands in the 1960s. But even then, the extension of this way of working into the healthcare sector was hinted at. In 2011, a subgroup of the international network "Open Building Implementation" – a commission in the CIB (The International Council for Research and Innovation in Building and Construction) – began to focus on the application of the Open Building approach to the healthcare sector. Then, in 2017, the Council on Open Building was formed in the US, with members from many prominent architecture and engineering offices, to advocate for planning for change.

This book has been inspired by many hard working practitioners, pioneering clients, and diligent researchers, many of whom go unrecognized. As such, it is just one effort to add to the literature on long-lasting architecture planned for change under conditions of distributed control. While this collection focuses on healthcare architecture, the same issues face the building stock generally, across project types. Let us hope that, for the sake of a resilient and sustainable built field, these issues continue to be taken seriously.

References

Macchi, G, S Kendall, and M Voeglin (Eds.) (2008). *System Separation: Open Building at the Inselspital Bern, INO Project*. Bern, Switzerland: Stämpfli Verlag AG.

Kendall, S, T Kurmel, K Dekker, and J Becker (2014). Healthcare Facilities Designed for Flexibility the Challenge of Culture Change in a Large U.S. Public Agency. In *Proceedings, International Union of Architects Congress*. Durban, South Africa.

Contributors

Stephen H. Kendall, PhD, RA *Emeritus Professor of Architecture, Ball State University, Council on Open Building, Philadelphia, USA.* Dr Kendall's career in architectural practice, research and education spans more than 35 years. His research focuses on the Open Building approach, needed to make buildings more adaptable, easier to customize to meet changing preferences and thus more sustainable. His work recognizes the increasing size and complexity of projects and the dynamics of living environments, the workplace and the marketplace where design must go beyond short-term uses and where control is distributed not only during initial planning but also over time.

Anne Friedrich Bilsbarrow, AIA, ACHA, AICP, LEED AP *Corporate Director of Planning, SmithGroup, Phoenix, Arizona, USA.* Anne's work has focused on the early stages of project planning, with an emphasis on developing innovative programmatic responses to client needs. Her recent work has concentrated on looking beyond standard healthcare planning approaches, to integrate best practices from the wider design community.

Malaina Bowker *Associate Director, Real Estate & Facilities, Brigham Health, Boston, USA.* Malaina Bowker is an urban planner with extensive healthcare planning experience. Since 2004, she has focused on master planning and campus renewal at two of Boston's largest academic medical centers, where she has led master planning efforts. She is currently the Associate Director of Real Estate and Facilities at Brigham Health. She holds a Masters of Public Affairs and Urban and Regional Planning from the Woodrow Wilson School for Public and International Affairs at Princeton University, and a Bachelor of Arts from Williams College.

Karel Dekker *KD/Consultants BV, Voorburg, The Netherlands.* Karel Dekker is an architect and researcher in the Netherlands. He has managed his own architecture and consultancy office since 1973. His career has focused on sustainability and the Open Building approach, emphasizing building process innovation and decision-making tools for architects and building owners, taking into account flexibility strategies and return on investment. He has served on the Board of the Stichting Architecten

Research (Foundation for Architects Research), the Foundation of Open Building, as a senior researcher in TNO Building and Construction, and as Senior Researcher in the Center for People and Buildings.

William Fawcett, PhD *Chair, Cambridge Architectural Research Ltd, Cambridge, the United Kingdom.* William Fawcett is an architect and trained at Cambridge University Department of Architecture. He continued with PhD research on 'A mathematical approach to adaptability in buildings' at the Martin Centre, the Department's research division. He worked in an architectural practice and held a lectureship at Hong Kong University Department of Architecture, before joining Cambridge Architectural Research Ltd, a private consultancy, as a founder-director in 1987. At CAR he has focused on studies of buildings in use and new methods of life-cycle evaluation, as well as conservation policy for historic buildings. In 2005–2010 he held the Chadwick Fellowship in Architecture at Pembroke College, Cambridge, leading the Activity-Space Research initiative. Since 2016 he has been the Chair of CAR.

Waldo Galle, PhD, MSc *Postdoctoral Researcher, Department of Architectural Engineering, Vrije Universiteit Brussels, Belgium.* Dr Galle is a postdoctoral researcher for the European Regional Development Fund ERDF and the Flemish Institute for Technological Research VITO at the department of Architectural Engineering of Vrije Universiteit Brussel, Belgium. He holds a BSc and MSc in architectural engineering (Ghent University, 2009 and 2011) and a PhD in engineering (Vrije Universiteit Brussel, 2016). Dr Galle's doctoral research focused on Scenario-based Life Cycle Costing, a financial evaluation method that analyzes a building's changing and uncertain specifications. This method empowers designers to promote and implement open and transformable building in an informed way. As a member of the TRANSFORM research team, chaired by Professor Niels De Temmerman, Dr Galle studies the financial and technical feasibility of designing for change.

David Hanitchak *Vice President for Real Estate & Facilities, Massachusetts General Hospital, Boston, USA.* David is Vice President for Real Estate & Facilities at Massachusetts General Hospital (MGH) in Boston, where, from 1985 to 2011, he was Architect, Project Manager, Director of Planning and Construction, and Executive Director for major building projects. From 2011 to 2016 he was a Principal at the architecture and planning firm NBBJ working on a range of complex healthcare projects after which he returned to his current role at MGH. He is a registered architect, master planner, and strategist, and has focused on healthcare for over 35 years. He has a Masters of Architecture with Honors from the Graduate School of Design at Harvard University.

Martin Henn, Dipl.-Arch. ETH & M.S. AAD *Managing Director, Head of Design, Henn Architects, Berlin and Beijing.* Martin Henn undertook his architectural studies at the University of Stuttgart and ETH Zurich, where he obtained his masters degree in 2006. In 2008 he received a Master of Advanced Architectural Design at Columbia University in New York. Prior to joining HENN he was employed at Zaha Hadid Architects in London and Asymptote Architecture in New York. Martin Henn has worked for the HENN office since 2008. In 2012 he was named a partner and serves as Head of Design, directing the design studios in Berlin, Munich, and Beijing. He is also the global partner in charge of the firm's high-rise buildings sector.

Pieter Herthogs, PhD, MSc *Postdoctoral Researcher, Future Cities Laboratory, Department of Architecture, ETH Zürich, Switzerland.* Pieter Herthogs has an MSc and BSc in architectural engineering (Vrije Universiteit Brussel, 2009 and 2007) and a PhD in engineering sciences (Vrije Universiteit Brussel, 2016). Dr Herthogs is a postdoctoral researcher at ETH Zürich's Future Cities Laboratory in Singapore. As a member of the Big Data Informed Urban Design and Governance project, he develops models to estimate the liveliness and qualities of public spaces. He is also a member of the Informed Design Lab of Professor Bige Tunçer at the Singapore University of Technology and Design (SUTD). For over ten years, his research has focused on various aspects of Open Building and Design for Change; during his doctoral research, Dr Herthogs developed a methodology to integrate Design for Change in sustainable urban planning. His research interests include Design for Change and Open Building, evidence-based urban and architectural design, graph-based assessment models, big data informed urban design, parametric design, and transdisciplinary urban research approaches.

Ryan Hullinger, AIA, NCARB *Partner, NBBJ, Columbus, Ohio, USA.* With a specific focus on enhanced clinical performance and adaptable hospital design, Ryan works to ensure that research-driven methodologies are at the center of NBBJ's design process. His projects have been widely published, and his pioneering work in hospital prefabrication has repeatedly been the focus of published academic research.

Giorgio Macchi, Architect *Former Director of the Office for Real Estate and Public Buildings of the Swiss Canton of Bern, Switzerland.* Giorgio Macchi is the former chief architect and Director of the Office for Real Estate and Public Buildings of the Swiss Canton of Bern (OPB). As a client he was responsible for structuring the perspectives of users' requirements and for commissioning architects and engineers to carry out public building projects for the Canton that prioritize the System Separation Strategy developed by the OPB. He studied architecture at the ETH Zurich and graduated with a diploma. In 1977/78 he lectured at the Bern University of Applied Sciences and in 1990/91 he assisted the chair of Architecture and Planning at the ETH Zurich. He joined the building department of the Canton of Bern in 1974, where he headed various organizational developments, planning procedures, and large projects, and worked on numerous competitions and awards.

Kazuhiko Okamoto, Dr. Eng., 1st class architect of Japan, AIJ, JIHA, HEAJ, GUPHA *Associate Professor, Department of Architecture, Toyo University, Japan.* Kazuhiko Okamoto received a Doctor of Engineering Degree from the University of Tokyo in 2000 on "A Study on Architectural Environment for Psychiatric Patients." He worked at Okada and Associates in Tokyo from 2000 to 2003 and was involved in the design of several hospital projects. In 2003, he joined the Department of Architecture at the University of Tokyo and was promoted to Assistant Professor in 2007. He has served as a consultant to the World Health Organization for examining hospital endurance and preparedness against natural disasters including earthquakes, in Mongolia and Japan. He was a visiting scholar at Texas A&M University from 2008 to 2010, conducted research at London South Bank University in 2012 and moved to Toyo University in 2014.

John Pangrazio, FAIA, FACHA *Consulting Partner, NBBJ, Seattle, Washington, USA.* In a 40-year career devoted to designing buildings that promote health and healing, John has been instrumental in shaping NBBJ's internationally recognized healthcare practice. He has designed more than 100 healthcare projects, establishing precedents for quality and innovation. He is a former president of the AIA American Academy of Healthcare and the American College of Healthcare Architects (ACHA) and a recipient of the ACHA Lifetime Achievement Award.

Mark Patterson, AIA, ACHA, EDAC *Health Practice Leader, SmithGroup, Phoenix, Arizona, USA.* For 30 years, Mark devoted his career to healthcare architecture. His dedication to improving the patient experience still inspires us. Although he was unable to finish this project, it bears his influence and is dedicated to his memory.

Nirit Putievsky Pilosof, Architect *Tel Aviv, Israel.* Nirit Putievsky Pilosof is a registered architect and a PhD candidate at the Faculty of Architecture and Town Planning at the Technion – Israel Institute of Technology. Nirit holds a Post-Professional Masters of Architecture from McGill University and a B.Arch and B.SC from the University of Wales. Nirit practiced architecture as a design project manager at leading architecture firms in Israel and in Canada, specializing in healthcare design, as well as researching and teaching in academic architecture programs. She has gained international awards including the prestigious AIA Academy of Architects for Health award, the American Hospital Association (AHA) graduate fellowship, the McGill University major fellowship, and the Azrieli Foundation fellowship.

Introduction

Healthcare architecture planned for change is the main theme of the essays collected here. The book's broader proposition is, however, that the architecture of today's and tomorrow's building stock can and should inspire, be prepared for and open to developments not imaginable in a specific moment. This encompasses all project types – housing, educational and healthcare facilities, places of work and commerce.

The chapters, in diverse fashion, touch on two assumptions about how healthcare facilities – and built environment more broadly – come into being and transform: 1) the acquisition of buildings and building complexes – to be resilient, culturally grounded and prepared for change – must recognize the distribution rather than unification of decision-making control, initially and over time, and 2) new design skills are needed, suited to this reality, to assure excellence and readiness for change in both architectural and urban design.

There can really be no question that buildings and built environments that remain vital, coherent, and resilient transform part-by-part, not once, but over and over. This is a long view, an admittedly elusive view in cultures in a rush. Too often, we architects fall into the trap of thinking that once a project is "done" under our watch, that it will never change again. Certainly this ideology is at the center of architectural education world-wide, thus planting seeds that must be overcome in practice, without much of a supportive theoretical or methodological discourse. This short-sighted perspective serves no-one and certainly not the sustainability and coherence of built environment as such and certainly doesn't correspond with reality. After all, we are often called back to change a building we designed earlier, but more frequently we add to or modify a building designed by someone else. Our practices depend on it.

How are we doing at this work? What attitudes – and policies – are needed as we rethink our endeavors? How are our skills adjusting to this more dynamic and long-term way of seeing architecture and urban design? How do we "hand-off" a project to other architects who follow us in cultivating a particular building site? Will "big data" help as we employ simulation tools to support multi-disciplined decision-making? How will increased computational power assist distributed control? What can history teach us? Are we producing coherence with variety, or simply confusion, conflict and waste?

My hope is that readers of these chapters will come away sharing the recognition that we are in a hopeful transition phase in learning the skills needed to steer incremental change in the built environment – at whatever level we are working. The "we" I refer to includes the design professions, certainly, but also our clients, their financiers, and those operating in the regulatory / policy-making sector. This transition is not smooth, but is inevitable. The rough sailing should not be particularly surprising given the fact that decision-making is increasingly dispersed and unfolds over time, that building users are increasingly individualized, and that our technical repertoire and technical mastery have expanded with incredible rapidity in the last 50 years. Apart from important questions on matters of style or architectural quality, this is a confusing and contentious – and often litigious – time in the building and real property industries. New players enter the stage and frequently display the hubris of believing that they can remake the stage itself with little or no deep understanding of what happened before or without sending out thought probes into the future. It is as if the breathless rush of invention and innovation, rather than cultivation, was key to success. Aversion to risk and new approaches are high, and yet at the same time pressures are strong to find better ways of building and managing divided control of complex real property assets over time.

While planning our building stock for constant adjustment and transformation is not a settled process, there are signs of hopeful new approaches that do in fact suggest effective departures from past methods – and the belief systems that gave rise to those methods. In selecting authors to contribute to this book, I found myself asking why we should expect the process of built environment transformation to be less riddled with conflict, waste, and disruption than it is. Perhaps expecting otherwise is naive, given how multifaceted and never-ending the process is, how rapidly standards of building performance change, how quickly user preferences shift, and recognizing how deeply entangled decision-making is among parties with competing and conflicting interests.

Naive or not, such a vision of doing a better job drives those whose work is collected in this book. Their voices are varied, and are not alone. Their work is mirrored by many other building professionals, researchers, and managers around the world (for example: Capolongo, 2012) who haven't capitulated to cynicism or ignorance, but who work with their feet on the ground and their minds in a constant learning mode. We should hope for a sustainable and resilient building stock less burdened by incessant and tiresome conflict and difficulty. This requires us to develop new methods to make building stock transformation effective, equitable, and conventional in practice – as well as producing excellent if not delightful architecture. In moving toward this goal, we need to work very hard to recreate the knowledge that has undergirded built environments around the world that have sustained themselves for hundreds of years, and adjust and augment that knowledge so that it is compatible with contemporary realities. The authors in this collection are part of this search.

While technical issues are discussed in these chapters, the core challenges, not surprisingly, are essentially non-technical. They reside in the ecology of decision-making and in changing minds. Moving beyond detailed programming and fixed floor plans as a necessary precursor of designing and procuring complex buildings is clearly not easy for clients, users, financial institutions, regulators, or design service providers who seek certainty and to avoid risk. So what comes first: changing skills (habits) or changing minds? Is it worthwhile learning new skills and attitudes if those who we think need them and must eventually demand them have not changed their minds? My experience in teaching architecture students is that it is not difficult to teach new skills associated with the Open Building approach. But what good is it if an architect has shifted attitudes and has learned a new set of design skills if their client has not recognized the need to ask for them? Then what? What is the dance that designers engage in with the actors that they exist to serve? Between the lines, and sometimes explicitly, the chapters in this book hint at these questions and the problem of changing attitudes and minds – our own and others. There is a very large and deep literature on changing minds – see, for example, Howard Gardner's writings (2006), or that of Adam Grant (2016), but too little of this work focuses on the field we operate in – the built environment.

Functions (healthcare and otherwise) and practices are changing, and we really should stop scraping buildings and neighborhoods and rebuilding anew from scratch at the current feverish and wasteful pace. We need other starting points, other working methods, other ways of collaborating, and other ways of seeing architecture, ways that recognize continuous cultivation as a value. Perhaps the needed transition is happening because reality is drawing us there. The book's title suggests that an infrastructure model of built facilities makes sense as a guiding principle in the design of healthcare facilities – and other project types as well. This is implicit in the recognition by both clients and the architecture/engineering communities that once built, healthcare facilities are almost immediately subject to physical alterations, at several levels, that respond to – and also have an impact on – medical practices, human wellbeing, governmental policies, and professional techniques. Changes both large-scope and fine-grained occur even before the construction of new buildings is completed, and often occur during the design process, not to mention on the time axis well into the future. The infrastructure model for buildings helps clarify how to manage these complex systems. This perspective is further developed in Chapter 1 and those that follow.

References

Capolongo, S (2012). *Architecture for Flexibility in Healthcare*. Milano, Italy: FrancoAngeli s.r.l.

Gardner, H (2006). *Changing Minds – The Art and Science of Changing Our Own and Other People's Minds*. Cambridge: Harvard Business School Press.

Grant, A (2016). *Originals – How Non-Conformists Move the World*. New York: Viking – Imprint of Penguin-Random House.

Summary of the chapters

I decided to invite these particular authors to write chapters knowing their varied backgrounds, points of view and experiences. The authors are all architects, whether in practice, doing research, in policy-making, or a combination of these roles. With this shared professional background, they currently hold diverse positions – representing building owners, as architects in private practice, or as researchers. They have experience across scales: from healthcare campus complexes to buildings, to interior fit-out and technical subsystems.

In Chapter 1, I introduce the infrastructure model of design decision-making, referring to the broader definitions of infrastructure familiar in transport and utility system and how they use levels of intervention to work effectively. I discuss how this model is already conventional in some project types, how it can be useful in the design of healthcare facilities planned for change, and the challenges it makes us face as we move toward a new architecture based on these principles.

Chapter 2, by Giorgio Macchi, discusses the theory and principles of System Separation, the strategy he pioneered in the Canton Bern's Office of Properties and Buildings in the 1990s for their large public real estate portfolio. This policy has guided more than 20 projects, two of which he describes, as well as the master plan for a major healthcare campus in Bern.

Chapter 3, by Martin Henn, discusses the Inselspital Teaching Hospital Campus master plan in Bern. He discusses its historic origins, its principles and how the competition entry, which Henn's firm won, evolved into a detailed steering instrument to guide the campus' development over 50 years.

Chapter 4, by David Hanitchak and Malaina Bowker, offers an historical overview and discussion, from the client's perspective, of an urban academic healthcare campus in downtown Boston undergoing dynamic change. They identify the challenges of managing facility planning and acquisition under the pressure of evolving investment priorities, medical practices, and demographics.

Chapter 5 is the story of the design of a large healthcare facility in Phoenix, Arizona, in which Phase I was designed by NBBJ (John Pangrazio and Ryan Hullinger) and Phase II was designed by a team from another office – the SmithGroup (Mark Patterson and Anne Friedrich Bilsbarrow). NBBJ established site planning and building design principles that they believed would assure the facilities' capacity to accommodate growth and change. The SmithGroup discusses their work building on and adjusting the master plan and adding additional space to the existing facility.

Chapter 6, by the Israeli architect and researcher Nirit Putievsky Pilosof, is the story of the 12-year evolution of a large hospital project in Tel Aviv, in which the architect and client cooperated in making decisions to assure that the building was prepared for and eventually did accommodate change.

Chapter 7, written by Waldo Galle and Pieter Herthogs, discusses a major healthcare project in Belgium. The hospital client was acutely aware that the healthcare field was undergoing change, and thus hired an architectural team which understood the importance of creating a healing environment in a building prepared for growth and change, and which offered the potential for changes in use in the future.

Chapter 8, written Karel Dekker, is the story of the decision-making process leading to the acquisition and renovation of an existing building in the Netherlands, for a hospice organization. He describes how the Open Building approach was key to exploring alternative design scenarios, linked to economic issues; how the separation of Base Building and Fit-Out helped resolve financing issues, and eventually led to the successful realization of the hospice facility.

Chapter 9 written by William Fawcett, discusses both retrospective and prospective approaches to the design of healthcare facilities planned for change, citing several case studies. He then presents and discusses a simulation decision-support tool to aid clients and design teams map out alternative approaches to building in adaptability strategies, and discusses both its advantages and limitations.

Chapter 10, by Kazuhiko Okamoto, presents a unique and extensive literature survey of Japanese architecture publications over a century that focused on issues of growth and change in healthcare facility site and building design. The literature review highlights the early influence on Japanese architects by Western architects. His chapter also offers a case study of healthcare facility growth and change at the University of Tokyo Medical Center.

Chapter 1

An infrastructure model of the building stock

Stephen H. Kendall

A significant literature exists in many fields – including economics, business and engineering – addressing infrastructure in the built environment (Ainger and Fenner, 2014). Road networks at different scales, railway lines and irrigation systems come to mind, as do potable water and sewer systems and communication networks. They all serve multiple users and frame physical conditions for inhabitation and use. These are large capital assets whose design and use stretch over large territories and continue in operation over long periods of time, and whose parts are incrementally upgraded while the whole system remains in operation. Control of their design, construction, use and adjustment is distributed and guided by both deep cultural conventions and coercive regulations. Governmental entities as well as private parties and, in recent years, public-private partnerships are involved in complex and changing patterns of initiative, financing and management of such infrastructure.

From the perspective of design, construction, management and use, infrastructure depends on the use of a hierarchy of "levels" of intervention. These levels are related to each other in a particular way. That is, a "higher level" constrains "lower levels" which can change or be replaced without causing higher levels to shut down or be altered (Habraken, 1998, 2002). In a transportation system, a highway is such a "higher level" offering capacity for "lower level" physical systems – i.e. vehicles of certain kinds. There are other relations between levels. For instance, highways are located in and funded by political jurisdictions, with all the negotiations and evolving standards we are familiar with, but are then occupied by private vehicles, new versions of which are regularly introduced. Highway construction and automotive standards and regulations are also distinguished according to levels, as are the specialists designing, financing, building and maintaining them. The clarity of these "levels," their interfaces and disentanglement lends infrastructures longevity at the same time that they enable incremental renewal.

Increasingly, large buildings serving multiple and changing users show similar characteristics by offering space for customized user settlement. Shopping centers and office buildings, for instance, have behaved this way for more than a half-century. We also see residential buildings (Kendall,

2017; Kendall and Teicher, 2000), hospitals (Kendall et al., 2014), and educational facilities (Dale and Kendall, 2018) shifting toward this mode. For everyday users, such buildings are experienced as "whole" artifacts – the building as entirety or the space occupied as a unity – yet the processes by which they come to be and transform follow a levels or infrastructure model.

Aside from important questions of architectural quality and the enduring and deep resonance of a building or place with its local culture, the implications for regulation, financing, policy making and for innovation in the building industry are important.

Base Buildings: a new infrastructure

In large buildings, we are seeing a tendency to separate a "Base Building" from "Fit-Out" and "Fit-Out" from "FF&E" (fixtures, finishes and equipment). This separation into three "levels" is also known by other names, but whatever the words used, the distinctions are increasingly conventional – internationally – and are mirrored in the real property and building industries' practices, methods and incentive systems.

For example, commercial office buildings use these distinctions, internationally. Tenants lease space in buildings in which the layout for each is custom designed and individually adaptable over time, and in which furnishings and equipment are updated frequently. Private and governmental institutions owning (or leasing) large buildings likewise make these separations to accommodate ongoing relocation, reconfiguration and re-equipping of functional units. Large architecture, engineering, construction and product manufacturing companies have distinct divisions to service the design and construction of Base Buildings. Other companies operate exclusively at the level of the Fit-Out; some design, produce and install proprietary product service solutions (Morelli et al., 2018; Yu and Sangiorgi, 2017); still others concentrate on equipment and furnishings. Tenants own or lease Fit-Out partitioning and equipment, and if they own it, can sell it to the next users, or may clear out the space when they leave, increasingly aided by parts prepared for disassembly or recycling, or sold into a secondary market as part of a circular economy (McDonough and Braungart, 2002), leaving spaces to be fitted out anew by the next occupant.

Another example is shopping malls, either free-standing or incorporated into mixed use developments, including airports. Developers – public, private or public-private partnerships – build large structures giving attention to public or common space and functions (such as parking and public facilities, etc.) and shared utility systems. Retail space is left empty. Overall architectural, technical, space and signage standards are established and documented in detailed tenant handbooks that themselves are periodically updated. This enables retail chains to lease space and bring in their own designers and Fit-Out services in a process that enables rapid turnaround of space for new occupancies, without disturbing the longer-lasting and shared infrastructure, public space or neighboring users.

This way of constructing and using built space constitutes a substantial market, which, in turn, has given rise to increasingly profitable and well-organized supply chains serving the demands for tenant "Fit-Out" (Kendall, 2013). All decision levels include finance companies, product manufacturers, design and engineering firms, construction companies, equipment suppliers and a host of others.

There is good reason to believe that innovation in services, products, finance and management has flowered because of this model, because it is easier to innovate on parts of a complex system when the "whole" system is disaggregated or "de-integrated" (but held together by smart agreements and interfaces), as in any well-functioning infrastructure.

Why has this trend emerged?

The emergence of this phenomenon lies in a convergence of three dominant characteristics of everyday contemporary built environment. First is the increasing size of buildings, sometimes serving thousands. Second is the dynamics of the workplace and the marketplace where use is increasingly varied and changing. Third is the availability of, and demand for, an increasing array of equipment and facilities serving the inhabitant user. In that convergence, large-scale real estate interventions make simultaneous or unified design of the Base Building and the user level impractical. User-level decisions are effectively deferred and inevitably change over time in any case, in big and small ways. This is what drives the very large and growing remodeling and renovation sector of the building industry, which now includes vertically integrated companies. Social trends towards individualization of use make functional specification increasingly personalized and changing. Greater complexity and variety of places of work, healing, commerce, dwelling and education demand adaptation by way of architectural components with shorter use-life, such as partitioning, ceilings, bathroom and kitchen facilities, specialized equipment, and so on.

This separation of Base Building from Fit-Out, and Fit-Out from equipment – observable everywhere in the world while using diverse terminology – includes utility systems as well. Adaptable and accessible piping, air handling and wiring systems on the equipment and Fit-Out levels, for example, connect to their counterpart and more fixed ("higher level") main lines in the Base Building, many of which connect to the next higher level infrastructure serving a district, an entire city or region. Here again, control is distributed hierarchically, not unified; for practical – if not political – reasons it would be very unusual for one party to control all levels. In this process we see a significant contrast between what is to be done on the user level on the one hand and what is understood to be part of the traditional long-term investment and functionality of the building on the other.

This is the reason for the emergence of the Base Building as a new kind of architectural infrastructure.

The distinction here is best understood as happening between "levels of intervention" as is always the case when we compare infrastructure with what it is serving. In the case of buildings, the comparison has multiple dimensions, including the following:

BASE BUILDING	INFILL or FIT-OUT
Longer-term use	Shorter-term use
Shared-service related design	User-related design
Heavy construction	Lightweight components
Long-term investment	Short-term investment
Equivalent to real estate	Equivalent to durable consumer goods
Long-term financing	Short-term financing

Hospitals are evolving in similar ways

Application of this distinction is now evident internationally in healthcare facility construction, as the chapters that follow show. More than any other building type, hospitals are functionally diverse and technically complex. Changes in demographics, diseases and their treatment, equipment, doctors' insights and preferences and regulations are forcing the emergence of a shorter use-life Fit-Out level, corresponding directly to healthcare functions which are the basis for the fiscal management of healthcare organizations. The Fit-Out level is again usefully distinguished from the even shorter life of equipment and furnishings.

When this distinction is recognized, construction of medical Base Buildings can start before detailed Fit-Out design has been finalized, allowing a substantial shortening of the project critical path. Currently, it is not exceptional that a five- to seven-year period elapses between initiating the planning process for a large medical facility and start of operations. Much of that time is normally spent determining the specifics of what we can call Fit-Out and equipment, during which time overall design is typically on hold. The evidence is that departmental requirements (e.g. surgery, pediatrics, laboratories) and equipment specifics evolve during the design phase in any case, and are to some extent obsolete when the building is first occupied. If a Base Building is conceived of as a project by itself, construction can commence and functional layouts and equipment acquisition can be deferred, without disturbing the construction schedule of the Base Building. There is already a distinction of this kind in the procurement of healthcare facilities for the United States Defense Health Agency called Initial Outfitting and Transition (Initial Outfitting and Transition) (US Army Corps of Engineers, 2017).

Some hospital clients also build "shell" or "soft" space which they later Fit-Out or leave empty for use when the building must be changed and functional units redistributed or resized. In such cases, it is not uncommon that different firms are hired to design the Base Building and the Fit-Out of the building and still others to specify and install the equipment. While commencing a complex project without having all of the details known might appear to increase risk, the opposite is evident: using infrastructure principles helps manage uncertainty, and reduce risk to investors, users, and service providers designing, building and managing complex medical facilities.

Some implications of adopting an infrastructure model of buildings

In the literature on real property and real estate, real property assets including healthcare facilities are usually described as what I would call "lumpy" assets (Geltner and de Neufville, 2017). They are seen as largely indivisible or unitary economic entities, to be juggled and moved as "wholes." The adoption of an infrastructure or "levels of intervention" model of the building stock reveals the actual granularity – or deeper hierarchy of "wholes within wholes" – of built environments. (Habraken, 1998, 2002) (See Figure 1.1).

The use of levels, evincing territorial/hierarchical depth, can, but need not, result in a shift from unified to divided control. A single party may still control all or several levels in this model, with the consequence of centralizing risk and expanding the management responsibility of the single party. For instance, one party can control the Base Building, Fit-Out, and furnishings. Frank Lloyd Wright was not alone in demonstrating a propensity for an architecture of unified control.

But using levels also enables control distribution to be managed, rather than avoided. This is evident when the design control of an urban tissue belongs to an urban design firm, while design of individual buildings is

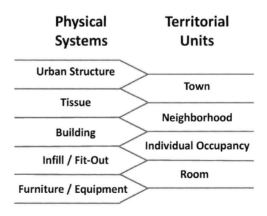

Figure 1.1
A levels of infrastructure model of the built environment.

distributed to different design firms. Another example is when part of a real property asset is owned by one party (or the collective of individual owners), and the many spaces served by it (or that occupy it) are each controlled by independent parties. This can happen either through distributed ownership as in condominiums, through leasing or "granted rights" agreements, or in the case of individual departments of an organization such as an academic medical center, when each functional unit may serve as a decision unit or profit center.

Divided or distributed control – either through separated contracts or in unified contracts mandating clear separation of activities – produces interfaces and the need for clear agreements (Emmitt and Gorse, 2009). But tacit interfaces exist in any case, even in situations of "integrated" control, between designer and builder, or between client and designer where a handshake often suffices. The presence of interfaces can result in boundary frictions even if such boundaries are conventional, but are more likely to cause problems when they are not explicitly recognized, which can happen with new players, with unconventional practices, or in uncertain, litigious times. The addition of decision-makers distributes risk but also adds organizational complexity. Divided control also effects design processes, construction cost accounting and schedule, facility management, investor risk, financing, building regulations, and many other aspects of the behavior of the building stock.

None of this is new, but at the same time this ecology remains obscure. An infrastructure model, however, when explicitly adopted and normalized, should encourage the development of industry-wide interface standards, product innovation and new kinds of skills. These are slow to evolve in what are now excessively entangled and overlapping relations among the players in the building sector and the parts controlled by each agent (Kendall, 1990).

In fact, improving communication and technical interfaces between levels of intervention is critically important. This is probably one of the most important aspects of the infrastructure model and the open building approach, requiring an exploration of new conceptual, management and technical solutions, and new design skills.

Autonomy of individual units of occupancy in an infrastructure model

When control is distributed, situations of conflict can naturally arise as already noted. This is most evident when autonomous action is sought at each level, as happens when an occupant of a multistory building wants to rearrange their space and doing so causes disturbance of those occupying space beside or below them. These conflicts have greater clarity in multi-occupant buildings since 3D property demarcation came to be formally used (Paulson, 2007). But even when clear accounting of 3D property is in effect in legal documents, technical entanglement persists, particularly in respect to "who controls what" with the utility systems that cut across territorial boundaries, despite the use of "easements" (Easements, n.d.).

There are examples of technical solutions to these situations of conflict. For example, in electrical utility (and communication) systems, the introduction of standard power outlets and plugs enabled equipment to be disentangled and achieve autonomy, and with it a new distribution control. Liberating electrical equipment (refrigerators, computers, surgical equipment, etc.) from the electrical circuitry that powers them – by developing "plug-in" connections with standards governing interfaces and products – stimulated the development of many hardware solutions, which proliferated once standards associated with them were established. Developments in wireless and battery-powered technology may further mitigate entanglement problems.

Far less advanced are drainage piping systems that carry both black and gray water from individual plumbing fixtures to the "higher level" parts of these drainage systems – the "public" infrastructure elements (both in buildings and at the urban level) and waste treatment facilities. In buildings with multiple occupants, several territorial boundaries are typically crossed between the individual fixture and the pipes in the street: problems easily arise when drainage pipes serving a dwelling unit or medical department's fixture pass through another territory (i.e. in the ceiling of another unit of occupancy) before entering the "common" piping in the Base Building. This technical/territorial entanglement, while conventional, is counterproductive, leads to decision-making rigidity during design, and legal/social conflict and waste of resources during transformation.

But, despite the availability of an increasing array of technical solutions, the most important first step is recognition of the territorial hierarchy implicit in the infrastructure model. When that recognition informs decision-making, technical solutions can be found to enable autonomy of each level.

Legal implications of the infrastructure model

It is clear that there are legal implications of the infrastructure model in real estate transactions. These will be undoubtedly different from the legal implications of, for example, a highway system and the vehicles using it; or in a public utility. In the infrastructure model of buildings, as explained earlier, we understand the distinction of a permanent part (Base Building) from the more changeable part (the Fit-Out) and finally the even more mutable FF&E. What is the legal status of a part of the whole (e.g. the Fit-Out or Equipment) that can be altered, removed and replaced without disturbing the Base Building? In respect to the healthcare building stock and the building stock in general, these questions deserve much more careful scrutiny than is possible here, and are certainly going to vary depending on the legal tradition in force. But some basic issues can be discussed briefly.

Real property vs. real estate
A passage quoted here explains the dilemma faced by decision-makers, designers and policy makers in setting up real estate developments of all kinds for inevitable change.

> Real estate professionals, investors, and even homeowners need to be able understand and differentiate between types of property that may be involved in a real estate transaction. The first big distinction ... is the difference between real property and real estate.
>
> You can think of **real estate** as land, the natural resources that are on or under it, and any man-made structure that is permanently attached to it ... any type of development on land that changes its original state and increases its economic value is considered an improvement. **Real property is a broader concept than real estate**. Real property is a concept that not only includes real estate but also a bundle of rights related to the real estate. In other words, real estate is a term that defines a set of physical things, while real property is a concept that includes those things plus the legal rights attached to it. Some common real property rights include ownership, possession, and use and enjoyment.
>
> Real property vs. personal property
> If a piece of property (e.g. a chair, a car, etc.) is not real property (real estate is real property), it is personal property. In other words, personal property is all property that is not real property. If it's not land and the natural resources on or under it or the man-made stuff **permanently affixed** to the land, the property is personal property. Sometimes movable personal property is called a "chattel."
>
> When personal property becomes real property
> Sometimes personal property can become real property and real property can become personal property. Let's consider ... a house to see how a piece of personal property can become real property. Let's say that ... a new Jacuzzi bathtub has been installed in a bathroom. The tub has become a **fixture**, which is a piece of personal property that has been permanently attached to real property and becomes part of it. **We call this transformative process of personal property becoming part of real property annexation**. Fixtures may not be removed before closing a sale because they are considered an improvement to the real property.
>
> Now, let's take a moment to **distinguish between fixtures and trade fixtures**. In commercial real estate, trade fixtures are fixtures that are used in a trade or business. Unlike regular fixtures, it's generally lawful for a trade fixture to be removed, or severed, from the real property. For example, a bookstore's bookcases affixed to the walls of retail space rented in a mall is a trade fixture. The business may remove the

bookcases after the lease is up, but it will have to compensate the landlord for any damaged caused to the retail space by removing the trade fixtures.

(Study.com, n.d.)

A number of questions arise from this "lesson" that relate to the infrastructure model. How is it determined which parts are to be classified as "real property," as "fixtures" and as "trade fixtures?" How has this determination changed and why? Commercial real estate has a classification called "trade fixtures" but apparently residential properties do not, at least in the United States. This suggests that if a healthcare facility is classified as commercial, then the autonomy of the various levels in the infrastructure model can be legally justified. But the literature shows that definitions of what is a fixture and a trade fixture are confusing, as the citation below indicates.

To understand the law of fixtures, one must know its origins. The history of the law of fixtures involves several theories. English law follows the maxim "quicquid plantatur solo, solo credit" (whatever is fixed to the earth goes to the earth), whereas American law uses several different tests to determine whether an object should be classified as a fixture. These tests are vague and subjective, and result in inconsistencies when applied to substantially similar fact patterns. It is therefore understandable that one commentator has observed that "to attempt to discover an all-inclusive definition for a 'fixture' or to posit tests for fixtures in all circumstances is not a profitable undertaking".

(Squillante, 1987)

Clearly, much remains to be clarified in respect to the legal basis for implementing an infrastructure model in the building stock. These brief quotations only begin to reveal the extent to which legal definitions and precedents help to shape the social conditions for implementing an infrastructure model. Further analysis is clearly called for.

Summary
In healthcare projects, there is always pressure to assure short-term return on investment (ROI). Public agencies face pressures not unlike private enterprise or public-private partnerships in this respect. But it can reasonably be argued that long-term ROI must become an important criteria for evaluation in the built environment across all project types as we move toward a sustainable circular economy. But it is also clear that this is a very difficult goal to achieve, because of the high degree of uncertainty in the mid to long-term future (de Neufville and Scholtes, 2011).

This produces a dilemma. A central tenet of facility planning for at least a half-century has been the proposition that "user participation" is vitally important. Engaging "user requirements" in front-end decision-making in all building types is stressful, however, even when the client demands it as is conventional in healthcare facility design. This difficulty arises because users come and go, change their minds, make choices based on different conceptual schema, disagree on priorities, and there are usually simply too many participants. Many methods of eliciting consensus among users and their requirements have nevertheless been put to use in programming building projects, including healthcare facilities. But in an effort to reduce uncertainty, the "end user" is one of the first to be excluded. As a result, attempts at early specification of "user-level requirements" has become the Achilles heel in planning large projects. On the other hand, data shows that buildings begin to change as soon as they are occupied, often driven by changing user requirements, if not changing regulations and performance requirements.

In real estate projects, including healthcare facilities, investors and developers need to acquire land, seek financing, deal with local regulations and site/climate constraints and construction in all kinds of weather and labor conditions. These processes will likely become more complex and more constrained by regulations, and face material and skilled labor shortages.

Given the already arduous path to developing sites and constructing buildings, investors wanting to build for the long haul should consider adopting an infrastructure model as one helpful tool. It also happens that advanced off-site production of various kinds – what may be called prefabrication, kitting or product bundling – can offer new levels of quality and cost control, and just-in-time customized solutions for what goes into buildings to make space habitable – across project types (Kendall, 2013). This suggests the emergence of a certified Fit-Out industry. With such a service industry, with many competitors, we should reasonably expect clients to learn the benefits of deferring decisions about functional specificity and floor plans for as long as possible, recognizing that they no longer need to drive overall project investment. They can now demand high-quality architectural Base Buildings awaiting user initiative, across project types, to be outfitted again and again. No longer tied to arranging floor plans, architects can return to what they love to do – shaping the commons, at the same time building long-lasting and living environments.

This is what an infrastructure model makes possible. Using levels of intervention to guide collaboration is the future. The opportunities for the infrastructure model to inspire a new architecture and urbanism in which evolving healthcare functions finds their place are of the most profound significance and await further study, elaboration and discussion. The opportunities in an infrastructure model are also auspicious for those who initiate projects – both private and public – and for those that regulate, finance, build and manage them. These too await more systematic study and evaluation.

References

Ainger, C and R Fenner (2014). *Sustainable Infrastructure: Principles into Practice*. London: ICE Publishing.

Barton, C (2014). Civilian Hospitals Increasingly Taking Tips From Military Projects on Equipment Planning. www.hoar.com/civilian-hospitals-increasingly-taking-tips-from-military-projects-on-equipment-planning/.

Dale, J and Kendall, S (2018). An Open Building Approach to School Design. AIA Knowledge Community Committee on Architecture for Education. In *Learning by Design*, pp. 6–8. www.learningbydesign.biz.

de Neufville, R and S Scholtes (2011). *Flexibility in Engineering Design*. Cambridge: MIT Press.

Easements. (n.d.). https://real-estate-law.freeadvice.com/real-estate-law/zoning/easement.htm (sourced April 28, 2018).

Emmitt, S and C Gorse (2009). *Construction Communication*. New York: John Wiley and Sons.

Geltner, D and R de Neufville (2017). *Flexibility and Real Estate Valuation Under Uncertainty: A Practical Guide for Developers*. London: Wiley Blackwell.

Habraken, NJ (1998). *The Structure of the Ordinary: Form and Control in the Built Environment*. Cambridge: MIT Press.

Habraken, NJ (2002). The Uses of Levels. *Openhouse International*, 7(2), pp. 9–20.

Kendall, S (2013). The Next Wave in Housing Personalization: Customized Residential Fit-Out. In PAE Piroozfar and FT Piller (Eds.), *Mass Customization and Personalization in Architecture and Construction* (pp. 42–52). London: Taylor & Francis.

Kendall, S (2017). Four Decades of Open Building Implementation. *Loose-Fit Architecture: Designing Buildings for Change*, 87(5), pp. 54–61. (guest edited by A Lifschutz).

Kendall, S, T Kurmel, K Dekker and J Becker (2014). Healthcare Facilities Designed for Flexibility the Challenge of Culture Change in a Large U.S. Public Agency. *Proceedings, International Union of Architects Congress*, Durban, South Africa.

Kendall, S and J Teicher (2000). *Residential Open Building*. London: Spon Press.

Kendall, SH (1990). *Control of Parts: Parts Making in the Building Industry*. Unpublished PhD Dissertation, MIT Department of Architecture.

Levy, M and R Panchyk (2000). *Engineering the City: How Infrastructure Works, Projects and Principles for Beginners*. Chicago: Chicago Review Press.

McDonough, W and M Braungart (2002). *Cradle to Cradle: Remaking the Way We Make Things*. New York: North Point Press.

Morelli, N et al. (2018). Bringing Service Design to Manufacturing Companies: Integrating PSS and Service Design Approaches. *Design Studies*, 55(March), pp. 112–145.

Paulson, J (2007). *3D Property Rights – An Analysis of Key Factors Based on International Experience*. Doctoral Thesis in Real Estate Planning Real Estate Planning and Land Law, Department of Real Estate and Construction Management, School of Architecture and the Built Environment, Royal Institute of Technology (KTH), Stockholm, Sweden.

Squillante, AM (1987). The Law of Fixtures: Common Law and the Uniform Commercial Code-Part I: Common Law of Fixtures. *Hofstra Law Review*, 15(2), Article 2.

Study.com (n.d.). Real Estate vs. Real Property: Differences & Terms. https://study.com/academy/lesson/real-estate-vs-real-property-differences-terms.html

US Army Core of Engineers (2017). Medical Division – Medical Outfitting and Transition. www.hnc.usace.army.mil/Media/Fact-Sheets/Fact-Sheet-Article-View/Article/482098/medical-division-initial-outfitting-and-transition/.

Yu, E and D Sangiorgi (2017). Service Design as an Approach to Implement the Value Cocreation Perspective in New Service Development. *Journal of Service Research*, 21(1), pp. 40–58. doi:10.1177/109467051770935.

Chapter 2

System Separation

A strategy for preventive building design

Giorgio Macchi

A paradigm shift

The only thing that lasts is change. That's not really breaking news. Every day we are repeatedly required to rethink our habits and change our minds. However, when this touches on crucial things we must be concerned. How we conceive and perceive architecture is one such crucial thing.

Answers span a large field from approaches fostering anything goes, haphazardness and wild shots, on the one hand, to approaches aiming at planning security and certainty by means of limiting regulations and analytical data, on the other hand. A back and forth between "non-plan license" and "data-focused determination" create stress within planning procedures that persists in the use over time of what has been built at a specific time.

All built environment is subject to the question of what should have priority: performance or permanence, readiness or steadiness, change or stability, function or form, present or future. Nevertheless, planning should avoid that limiting "either/or" trap, and support an "as-well-as" openness.

Healthcare buildings are especially affected by this dilemma. In this expensive and dynamic domain, change and factual developments have led to built environments over time that can hardly be perceived as pleasant. Nobody would disagree that a therapeutic environment is a key factor that any healthcare environment has to offer to patients, staff, and the urban context. Nevertheless, hospital areas have architectonic black holes.

Instead of being refined over time, what was built at a specific time, to a large extent, conflicts more and more with what ought to be. Dealing with change should become a fundamental aspect of how we perceive architecture, and consequently also how we conceive it. As long as time is not a guiding factor the planning processes will be dominated by stress.

This chapter offers insights into a strategy for overcoming this basic dilemma. The strategy was developed, and is applied, in the field of the built environment. But its underlying ideas go far beyond architecture. As a result, the strategy is resilient in that it resists many counterarguments; it has an inner adaptability to specific cases; and its potential to prompt innovative thinking is great. The strategy can be cooked gently – that's what many projects do; or it can become hot stuff – which some projects did and do thanks to highly committed key players with a changed mindset about what the purpose of architecture should be.

The strategy is called System Separation (SYS). The core principle of this strategy for designing buildings is: fix few things, to keep flexibility, but fix them firmly, to achieve reliability. What emerges is high utility value. Buildings of high utility value remain useful over a very long time, are effectively renewable, convertible, and developable, and generate a growing cultural identity. SYS fosters sustainability and facilitates change necessitated by technical life cycles or by life spans of use.

The Office for Real Estate and Public Buildings of the Swiss Canton of Bern (OPB) started developing the strategy 20 years ago. It has since become a binding guideline for all projects.[1] The portfolio includes approximately 2,000 public buildings worth five billion Swiss Francs, as well as annual investments of 150–200 million.

SYS separates both requirement planning and building design into three levels, referring to long-, medium-, and short-term perspectives. Divide and rule, allocate and delegate – that is the managerial backbone of SYS. Components and steps are well-defined and manageable. The whole maintains complexity at a specific time as well as over time. Architecture – conceived and perceived in this way – emerges through its use.

SYS doubles the challenge to "rethink habits and change one's mindset," first when bringing the planning process in line with the principles of SYS, and second, when the preventively installed openness enables rethinking and change over a very long time of use. That's when breaking news will happen – again and again.

The key players' roles

In all planning procedures, one thing is uncontested: the completion line. The rest appears to be a question of management and stress. This widespread method functions quite effectively. Deadlines are respected, and maybe even the budget. However, at the same time, problems start. Much of what was planned no longer meets the needs. Rejected ideas reappear; new people and modified circumstances enter the stage.

SYS addresses these constraints. Proceeding according to SYS, decisions are allocated to three levels; planning procedures are arranged sequentially; implementation starts before discussions about details are brought to an end; and last but not least, the strategy makes clear that a good investment never ends.

Implementing such an approach is not easy. That's why smart clients have a clear idea of who has to do what and when. Smart clients and architects create a pre-architectural scene. They brief the key players and activate long-term reflections, preventing a future that is hurried on by short-term reflexes. They anticipate openness for the unexpected. Smart clients and architects create high utility value. They practice SYS. Smart clients and architects create a culture of use. They coach users to behave as actors. An interactive performance in use over time brings a real payback, going beyond a simple payback of what was planned at a specific time.

The common thread connecting these three aspects of cleverness is: Nothing changes unless one's mindset changes. Without well-briefed planners and decision-makers, no building of high utility value will be conceived, and without trained users, the potential of such buildings will not be perceived. The nub of the matter is: Who briefs whom? SYS is well-reflected and has been applied in numerous projects. Still, each project has its own story. A team of strictly committed leaders must form the hub of all procedures. SYS makes it possible to integrate contributions coming from traditional understandings of planning procedures and to cooperate with the existing building industry, assembling traditional products and facilities in a new way – under one condition: The leaders must keep the project on course, and to do so, they must communicate using incisive and compelling metaphors.

Decision-makers generally dislike openness and particularly uncertainty. Their job is to eliminate openness and uncertainty by means of decisions. However, they are accessible to priorities and especially to hierarchies. These are entry points for bringing them on board. You may find other analogies to convey the idea of SYS appropriately to others; in our case, the comparison with a bottle-crate helped us cut many mental knots.

In Figure 2.1, the crate stands for the long term, the bottles for the medium term, and the drinks for the short term. Crate, bottles, and drinks are a useful, reliable, and proven product and procedure. That's what SYS will deliver.

The strategy's structure: three concepts, three systems, three principles

Requirement planning and building design are each separated into three levels, representing the long-, medium-, and short-term perspectives. Each level is linked to level-specific cost planning. This well-structured approach with only loosely coupled levels applies to both planning decisions and physical components. The interface of one level to the other respects the uppermost independence of one from the other. In this way, SYS supports the optimization of the whole over time. Ultimately, the idea of separation unifies over time.

The three levels for requirement planning are the Process Concept, the Organizational Concept, and the Operating Concept (see Figure 2.2). The Process Concept is the level where strategic priorities and overall functional aspects are decided, such as the number of sites to run and the global budget. The Organizational Concept is the level where structuring decisions are taken, such as what units are concerned, and general total of space requirements. The Operating Concept is the level where requirements are specified in a very detailed way, including rooms, technical equipment, and human resources.

Figure 2.1 Mind opening bottle crate – (a) combined; (b) crate; (c) bottles; (d) liquid.

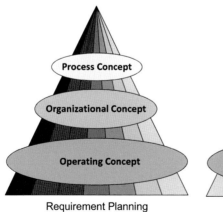

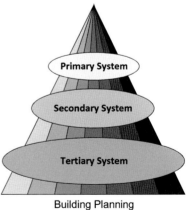

Figure 2.2 The three levels of System Separation.

Requirement Planning

Building Planning

This approach to understanding how a building will function contrasts with the widespread practice of technical briefs that are based on very large, highly detailed datasets specifying requirements – which are generally outdated even before the building, whose shape they have determined, is complete. Strict application of SYS, separating the three levels of the Process, Organization, and Operating Concepts, shifts this fatal paradigm.

The three levels for building design are the Primary System (PS), the Secondary System (SS), and the Tertiary System (TS). The PS is oriented on the long-term and concerns the building structure, including the facades and the area availability. The SS is oriented on the medium term and concerns the internal building construction, the fit-out, the engineering with technical installations and mechanical systems. The TS is oriented on the short term and concerns the building facilities, devices, equipment, and furnishings. Designing and managing the planning and building procedure respecting this hierarchy of life spans means that replacement or modification of shorter-life elements does not affect or damage those of greater durability or longer use.

Handling these system levels in a strategic way generates the three main principles of SYS (see Figure 2.3): **the partition of building components** – limiting all entanglements on or across the three levels to a minimum; **flexibility** – above all ensured by the structural capacity and geometries of the PS and appropriate SSs, and **area availability** – ensured by appropriate PSs in order to develop the building site densely over time.

Fix few things, but fix them firmly means, above all, designing a resilient PS. A resilient PS has no structural complications, a minimum of structural barriers, high net loads, high floor heights, and stated reserves for installations, and it strictly respects the partition of building components. No pipes or conduits in PSs. The precautions for area availability, besides guaranteeing a general openness, are justified by the fact that all traffic and transport to and from a building has almost the same impact on the environment as the building's operation. The potential of well-connected areas must therefore be built up to the maximum, whether at the time of construction or in the future, even if current building regulations do not yet allow this. Time will tell. PSs must therefore enable vertical and horizontal expansions.

Partition of Building Components

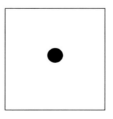
Flexibility

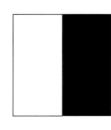
Area Availability

Figure 2.3
The three principles of System Separation.

The design of resilient PSs, as an urban and architectonically reliable form, as a kind of well-shaped, well-placed pedestal – firm but open to fine-grained adjustment and development – is architects' supreme task.

Tasks and mandates have to be aligned with the principles of SYS from the very beginning. Planning in line with SYS is not just an additional planning criterion. It is a radical new way to do things. To keep all procedures aligned with SYS, it may be helpful to consider frequent reservations about it.

SYS does not compromise the completion line, but it gives priority to what has to be decided first and what can wait. The three loosely coupled systems are planned and realized in sequence. First, the PS is determined. During its realization, the SS is planned. The TS follows just in time, benefiting from up-to-date data.

SYS is not just another design fashion; rather, it fosters a historical view. Some old buildings teach us what advantages non-customized constructions offer. They have proved to be transformable and have retained high urban relevance. They have shaped sites through their history. A closer look shows that they respect even many of the purely technical parameters that SYS imposes: high floor heights, high net load capacity, robust base building construction. We must be aware that the good old world was not confronted with today's complex entanglement of engineering components. Buildings were composed of PSs and TSs only. The SS with its engineering is a product of the modern world and its future. When applying SYS, the SS and the TS are designed as tailored suits that are changeable and never become "straitjackets"; and the PS provides a lasting stage for customized "ready-to-wears."

SYS does not favor anything goes, but it supports future claims. It imposes a strict differentiation between long-, medium-, and short-term components. Complexity is ensured in what will develop over time and not merely in how present requirements are solved, however complicated these might be. And yet, change is not a must. The must is to provide possibilities for change. The strategic precautions can be made quite radical. Nevertheless, the physical and cost implications are absolutely within the range of current and accepted decision-making standards.

SYS does not assure innovation, but it is a precondition to enable it. Imagine that a user's brainchild concerning an innovative functional solution to a controversial problem has been disputed at length and eventually decided, although remaining severely contested. Put into structural concrete, this innovative solution is definitively fixed. By contrast, SYS will never nail down innovation. Decisions made at a specific time may be reconsidered later, as often as necessary. However, as a German saying goes: "Where there's choice, there's torment" – that is a fact key players have to be actively alert on.

SYS does not mean substituting proven data with the unknown; but it prevents data from blocking future developments or rethinking. Appropriate structuring of the requirement planning on the three defined levels is mandatory. Experience shows that this is where the greatest backlog tends to accumulate. Professional clients should try to advance this work; otherwise designing for openness will be mistaken for designing for plausibility or probability. Achieving openness requires firm and deliberate decisions that keep strategic room for maneuver as large as possible rather than predicting the future. Nobody is able predict the future. How sophisticated the technics may be they merely can extrapolate the present. Although it's absolutely mandatory to apply the current knowledge, it would be far from smart to limit an investment on resulting perspectives. TS and to a great extend the SS will mirror the current knowledge, but SYS has to go beyond installing openness for the future.

SYS is not complicated, but it allocates planning tasks with a view to creating high utility value. If the managerial power of decision-makers and the design creativity of planners are aligned with SYS, the logic of the new procedure will enable and motivate those involved to cooperate in this new way. Nevertheless, ideas will arise to simplify things. Why not reduce the number of levels to two instead of three – wouldn't they be easier to manage? The SS has a very important guiding effect. With only two levels, the PS permanently risks being compromised, and openness tends to shrink to a predefined flexibility. Compared to decision-making on the level of the TS, the new perspectives for the PS and the SS indeed demand rethinking of habits and a change of mindset. The resulting change of priorities cannot be achieved as a side effect. Traditional planning procedures are focused on an Operating Concept, which is vaguely embedded in informal reflections on the level of the Organizational Concept. The tendency to replace "as-well-as" openness with the traditional "either/or" simplification is omnipresent and deeply rooted. Using three levels instead of two has an essential preventive effect to eliminate the entanglement of long-, medium-, and short-term parts – both physical parts and managerial horizons.

SYS does not lead to faceless boxes, but fosters well-shaped PSs that serve as platforms for a continuous cultural dialogue between use and contextual development. What else can we learn from history? What else could be a better matrix for inclusivity? What else could be more economical? What else could be more environmentally friendly? What is planned and built is merely an initial act in the creation of a whole that will emerge over time through use and change. The challenge of transcending individual biographies by giving space and a face to social biographies is huge. What else could be the purpose of architecture?

SYS does not result in a pretentious display of multiple choices, but it brings what is built into a new balance with implicit capacities. Some of the preventions designed for this purpose have a more tacit character. They may be hidden, not expressly defining the spatial shape and atmosphere of the planned building. "Hidden design" is not really architects' ambition; hence the shifted emphasis has to be well embedded in the new view of planners' tasks. Structural precautions in the foundations for future vertical expansion may represent one of such hidden preventions.

SYS is not risk-free, but it clarifies which risks should be eliminated from the very beginning. The greatest risk is that things will turn out to be different than expected because of wrong decisions, shifted priorities, or changed contexts. Instead of trying to eliminate these facts with great effort, it is much smarter to cooperate – by planning buildings that are capable of learning. The separation into three levels compartmentalizes the risks. A problem or need for change on one level will not upset the whole. Difficult but important decisions are no longer hidden behind a mass of well-known but minor problems.

SYS does not violate current legislation, but it has a professedly anarchist component. Legal constraints are always the result of political decisions at a given time. The principle of area availability does not deny existing constraints, but buildings designed according to SYS will always retain an openness for developments in this domain as well. The tension between what is actually realized and what needs to be assured as future options is very challenging. Therefore, decision-makers must explicitly consider different stages when deciding on the current project. Their successors will be grateful.

SYS does not triple planning efforts, but it clearly demands more rigorous discipline in decision-making and consistency of planning. Planning on three levels that are largely autonomous and only loosely coupled is more difficult than planning overall solutions. The PS has to transcend the accumulated current requirements. The SS has to keep open options for medium-term change. Only in handling the TS will the traditional planning procedure mentality not really come to harm, because appropriate SSs and resilient PSs will not be affected by these short-term views. At the end of the day, the increased planning efforts reduce the lasting efforts over time, and that's what counts.

SYS is not obstructing the building industry, but it allocates the performances of the companies in a way that is in accordance with the life cycles of the three systems. What part belongs to which system (PS/SS/TS) is given by the rules of SYS. Consequently, tendering and contracting have to be in accordance with the three levels. With regard to specific product constellations that exceptionally may be composed by building components of two levels appropriate contracting solutions are required. For example, the operating theaters are delivered as a whole, including the walls that normally belong to the SS unlike the equipment and devices as parts of the TS. However the managerial solution will be, the short-, medium-, and long-term demarcation lines should never be compromised for momentary simplifications of tendering or contracting.

SYS does not cut synergies, but potentiates capacities. Separated planning mandates for each level may appear to create gaps. However, SYS deals with these gaps in a way that installs transparency. Loosely coupled levels are the guarantors of openness and flexibility. The increased challenge at the planning stage delivers its payback in the building's use over time. Planning of the short-term components is merely a first step in a long series of decisions over time at that level. Moreover, short-term requirements differ significantly from the decisions required in planning the long-term components. In other domains, the dialogue between specified responsibilities is much more widespread. Nobody would expect a tennis champion to win a professional table tennis final. A building planned by specific teams for each of the three levels disentangles them from the very beginning. An "all-in-one" mandate makes the gaps between the levels easier to manage; but at the same time, it also masks them, opening the back door to entanglements. The gap that really needs to be prevented is the gap between the plan and reality over time. Preventing this gap is equal to potentiating a building's capacities.

You will encounter many more aspects and opinions that appear to contradict what SYS imposes, be it in politics, technology, management, architecture, finance, or elsewhere. SYS will not change the world, but the buildings will come closer to what they ought to be – a built environment of sustained and sustainable relevance.

SYS promotes all the three dimensions of sustainability – ecology, society, and the economy. The openness of SYS buildings encourages inclusivity, appropriation, and continuing social development. Independent and autonomous elements of their construction can be retained and redundant elements removed with minimal waste, avoiding wholesale demolition and thereby preserving precious stored carbon. With reduced operating costs over their whole life, these buildings are not only environmentally but also economically viable. Finally, and importantly, components with long-use lives retain references to historical change, preserving the patina and memory of our heritage and our ever-changing cultural identity.

Selected results: INO: a masterpiece; vonRoll: an example to imitate; and MAS: really hot stuff

Out of the many projects realized in the last 20 years following the SYS strategy, three are presented here. The healthcare project *INO* is the first, ground-breaking project. The university building *vonRoll* represents the state of the art, integrating lessons learned over the years. The *MAS* master plan for the urban area of Bern's University Hospital, finally, is quite programmatic.

INO

The INO project was launched in the mid-1990s. It was the first project guided by SYS. As part of the University Hospital of Bern (see Figures 2.4a and 2.4b), it has to fulfil high-tech requirements in a comprehensive academic medical center. INO mainly involves the intensive care units, emergencies, surgeries, and laboratories. Substantial changes took place during the planning and realization phases. The first intensive transformation in use, which has already been quickly accomplished, concerned the laboratories.

The PS was the result of an international competition (typical for Swiss public projects) and was designed by architects without specific experience in hospital planning. Fittingly, the project was called "Time-Space," showing that the authors had caught on to the essential idea of the architectural task that SYS imposed.

The subsequent competition for the SS was open exclusively to highly experienced hospital planners (see Figure 2.4c). The possibility to compare very different solutions for SSs within the same PS was a paradigm shift in decision-making. The team for the TS was selected based on its experience, as was the team for project management.

The PS has a characteristic shape and comprises 51,000 m^2 (550,000 ft^2) on very spacious floors for flexible use. The framework is of concrete construction with a column grid of 8.4 x 8.4 m (27.5 x 27.5 ft). The stabilizing components are limited to four cross-shaped elements. Statically, each field of the column grid allows for an opening of 3.6 x 3.6 m (11.8 x 11.8 ft) to be cut out of the floor slab. These "knock-out fields" can be used on the level of the SS to enable daylight, visual contact, and vertical access, during the planning as well as later on for transformations. All technical installations supplying a given floor are installed on that same floor, including drainage and other piping and air handling duct works. Each column head has four block outs completing the concept of vertical outlets for drainage pipes. The concrete floor structure is strictly free of installations, in line with the principle of the partition of building components (see Figure 2.4d).

That said, it is important to note that openness must not be mistaken for inconclusiveness. On the contrary, openness demands consolidated and qualified decisions – always respecting the hierarchy defined by the three levels.

INO has become a trendsetting medical institution and will persist as a building with high utility value.

VonRoll

VonRoll was completed in 2013 and benefited from lessons learned in other projects over the years (see Figure 2.5a). As a university building for teacher education and human sciences, it has to fulfil comparably low technological requirements. However, thanks to its robust simplicity and a number of systematic preventions, it can be transformed into a high-tech building for laboratories without any significant cost impact if the need arises.

A well-briefed jury selected a very resilient PS as the result of an international competition. The first stage of the project had to adhere to the building regulations then in force. According to the principle of area availability, proposed future stages were free to exceed the current restrictions.

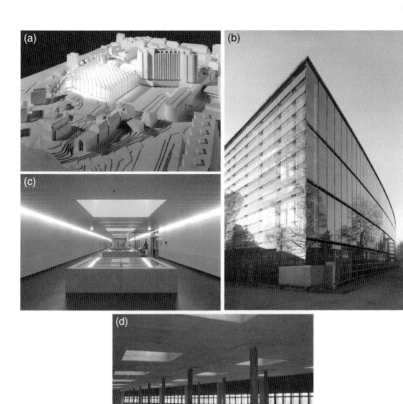

Figures 2.4
INO: (a) Primary System Competition entry; (b) Primary System external view; (c) Secondary System Circulation zone; (d) Primary System under construction.

Before the planners began to work on the SS, the government decided that the building should house the university's department of education (see Figure 2.5b) rather than the chemistry department, as had initially been planned. Given the lower engineering requirements, the new future users promptly proposed to add a floor and reduce the average floor height. However, based on the principle "Fix few things, but fix them firmly," the original floor heights were retained, thus safeguarding the openness that the PS offered. Nobody knows what decisions might be made at a later stage in a context of increasing competition between universities.

The PS is rather ordinary on the outside and spatially quite thrilling on the inside (see Figures 2.5c and 2.5d). It measures 100 x 80 m (328ft x 262 ft) and comprises 56,000 m^2 (602,700 ft^2) of floor surface in total. The framework consists of a concrete structure. All engineering installations (SS elements) are accessible and visible. All preventive measures taken to enable an upgrade to a high-tech building are well documented, and the possibility of vertical and horizontal extensions is assured.

Figure 2.5
(a) vonRoll Primary System external view; (b) vonRoll Floor Plan; (c) vonRoll Interior Access Zone; (d) vonRoll Interior view of the Library.

VonRoll has become a branding showpiece example of a high utility value building, representing a perfect union of contemporary university business and assured openness for future decisions that neither the university nor politicians can predict today. The fairly calm and humble building is the result of a powerful superposition of an explicit present with an eventful appropriation by the users and an implicit potential for future developments.

MAS

MAS is the master plan for the future development of Bern's University Hospital area. This innovative work was only possible thanks to the trained minds of all key players who had become familiar with the open-ended thinking required by SYS. The main topics of the international competition were area availability at quite a large scale and best conditions for the hospital's operation and future development. Chapter 3 reports on this master plan in detail.

Four things make the result striking. First: Few believed that the area could be further developed, as it was already built up. Second: The traditional understanding of a master plan as a kind of overall project was deeply rooted in the minds of authorities and planners. This traditional understanding demands decisions by the client that nobody can honestly make. Still, such decisions are requested again and again in order to be able to determine whether the plan fits predictions. Considering the complexity of healthcare development and a time horizon of 50 years, such a procedure would mean setting the cart before the horse. Third: The pre-architectural phase on the client's side was quite challenging and required two years of intensive work. The big question was: Would the participants in the competition get the message? Would they follow the pioneering track of SYS? The jury was prepared for the possibility of finding none of the projects convincing. This proved its resoluteness in advance. The payback of the thorough elaboration of constraints and requirements was excellent, however, because the results of the international competition were surprisingly conclusive. One team made the big step forward. Their proposal was pioneering. That's why the fourth point became quite important: The client's jury was smart enough not to fall in love with more traditional and much more comprehensible urban proposals. It selected the innovative master plan, although it was quite bewildering. Looking back, all four points were important, but one was crucial: Real innovation only happens when tasks are formulated anew.

The SYS spirit formed a reliable basis, and communication by the key players demanded perseverance. The formula "fix few things, but fix them firmly" set the agenda, resulting in the challenge that the master plan had to be at all times defined, but at no time definite.

Thanks to the client's firm commitment, the new understanding of a master plan gained support from the authorities, who backed both the international competition as well as the master plan's adoption in a public vote.

Suitable analogies and comparisons had been developed to convey the idea of area availability. The comparison with the significantly higher building densities of other well-known urban situations showed that quantity is only half the story, and quality is decisive. The question was through which steps a maximum density could be reached. Above all, the area is a running hospital and not primarily a building site. One helpful analogy was the historical agricultural three-field system, where one field was always left fallow. Translated into master plan language, defined "fallow" zones would become the building zones that were temporarily unavailable for hospital use. Historical urban development principles, whether from the Romans or from the House of Zähringen – the latter imposed the historic and emotionally uncontested master plan of Bern – provided intellectual support for the application of "fix few things, but fix them firmly" (see Figure 2.6).

The authors of the winning master plan made a determined step to a new interpretation of an old instrument of urban planning. The spirit that the client invoked took command, and that was for the best. The MAS has the character of a real steering instrument, bringing together stability and dynamic **reality** for a very large area and a very long period.

The master plan defines rules but not definite spatial shapes. What is fixed are axes; building fields, each defined by a total volume and its boundaries; and characteristic open spaces between the volumes. The volumes in the different building fields can be shaped as needed, as long as the total is respected. The rules are simple but firm, and have a radical structuring effect on the area's complex and dynamic processes and future development.

To prove in advance that the master plan was capable of responding to the hospital's current requirements and future developments, two alternative scenarios were tested. Their simulation promptly demonstrated the master plan's resilience.

In a sense the MAS has to be an immaterial vision of how contradictory and changing requirement of space, time, and behaviors can be brought in a synergy that makes sense, again and again. In the 2010 program of the international competition for the MAS, the superposition of the ancient and the medieval road systems of a European city symbolized this challenge: At one time a fixed grid; point to point connections later on; today common chaos; and in future? The crux of the matter is that the vision will have material impacts. That's why the really thrilling part of the challenge any good MAS has to meet is to avoid becoming the contradiction of itself over time. Hierarchic levels, flexibility, and availability will always be crucial principles for all decisions made at any time.

The spirit of the matter

What is built at a given time will always be amid a broad spectrum of human life and its complexity over time. A building should never become

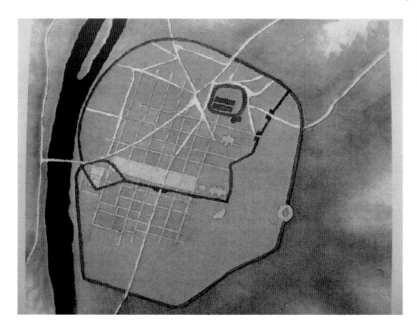

Figure 2.6
Ancient and medieval road systems of a European city.

the tomb of what has defined its plan. Rather it ought to be a kind of womb, giving birth to architecture through its use.

There are many parallels outside architecture that support the spirit of SYS. Such mental links help to rethink habits and will strengthen commitment to implementing the strategy.

The author of *Creating Capabilities, The Human Development Approach*, US professor of Law and Ethics Martha Nussbaum, is advocating intensively for strengthening citizens' capabilities, which she regards as a fundamental precondition for social development and cultural coexistence. SYS focuses on actors. What is built, has capacity for change. Capabilities develop by passing a kind of cultural evaluation. Buildings have to be platforms for potential spaces and uncommitted flexibility. Users must be able to test roles and options, interact, and develop empathy and reciprocity. Time and people will bring what is built to new ends. And these ends will never end. The linkage to Nussbaum stands for the question of whether it is worth doing SYS. Will openness meet actors? It's a basic responsibility to create such opportunities. Perhaps it will take time until the opportunities are taken.

The author of *Counter Clockwise, The Power of Possibility*, US psychologist Ellen Langer, has scientifically proved that people who have less defined information are mentally much more alert compared to people who have more definite information. Keeping their minds open, they live healthier and longer. Five points she suggests are akin to the spirit of SYS. Be actively alert to the present – in consequence you will plan fewer illusions; be open to new and different information – in consequence you will ensure capacity for change; be able to devise new categories when processing information – in consequence you will build resilience; be aware of multiple perspectives – in consequence you will cooperate with uncertainty; pay attention to progress rather than outcomes – in consequence you will accept that a building is never finished. The link to Langer lies in the fact that handling uncertainty in an open-minded way leads to saner behaviors and probably also better buildings. Without a structured separation into levels, it is a mission impossible to effectively separate strategic perspectives from present needs.

The German sociologist Dirk Baecker states in *Organization und Management* that the strategy of an organization consists in structuring its knowledge and communicating it appropriately to others in a way that enables the definition of a space of possibilities which can be imposed and maintained; if necessary – that is, under circumstances of uncertainty – by means of power. SYS is apt to define spaces of possibilities, provided that leadership skills are available and that spirit and purpose are transmitted appropriately. The linkage to Baecker emphasizes the relevance of managerial guidance in bringing "as-well-as" procedures to successful fruition.

Planning efforts should never compromise the building's purpose. That means to support life's diversity and dynamic. If the German playwright and poet Bertolt Brecht in *Flüchtlingsgespräche* declares that the need to create order is a kind of deficiency symptom, or if US sociologist Richard Sennett in *The Uses of Disorder: Personal Identity and City Life* argues that planning which puts primary emphasis on creating order runs the risk of suffocating people – we should be alert. The Swedish geographer Sara Westin, in *The Paradoxes of Planning*, investigates the gap between what architects conceive and what users perceive. Architects seem to judge themselves competent or sometimes even forced by professional "self-image" to pre-plan "right" behaviors. SYS is a way to get out of this unhealthy dilemma.

The Swiss system scientist and psychiatrist Gottlieb Guntern, in *The Spirit of Creativity: Basic Mechanisms for Creative Achievements*, reflects on chaos and order, and on the difference between a farmer, who works with the life cycles of seed and harvest, and a cook, who produces just in time. When planning buildings, architects and users have to be both. However, the architects' creativity must not suppress users' creativity, and what is built, must guarantee openness. Therefore, the role of architects is to determine, creating firmness, as well as to moderate, delegating creativity and initiative.

What is built at a given time does not matter in itself. What matters is that it supports progress over time – whether concerning technical parameters, operative procedures, social behaviors, or users' emotions.

A mental agenda

Buildings that respect the technical and managerial impacts the SYS produce will be better prepared for their use, change, and development. However, this paradigm shift will only succeed based on a firm commitment. To be committed means to support consequently the spirit the strategy is rooted in and aimed at in order to respect the time-oriented hierarchy of priorities within all the countless tasks, questions, contradictions, and critics.

It would be wrong to think that the benefits of SYS can be installed simply by imposing the strategy. To bring the project to its destination requires a permanent and adequate steering. SYS is an imperturbable compass. However, the specific challenges have to be addressed within the particular client's context, the dynamics of decision-making and a conclusive mandating of the planners.

Clients operate within a context of governing authorities used to handle a building project as a final whole. To get a building permit for a PS specifying the inside only in general demands appropriate negotiations. There is a risk that the authority could refuse the later permit for the SS. However, smart clients know that the real risk would be to complete the request based on decisions that may restrict taking into account, later on, updated information and new developments. Basically authorities are interested that buildings last. That's why negotiations make sense. INO, vonRoll and MAS were welcomed by the Bernese authorities.

As SYS requires, PSs are designed for openness and for supporting innovation. However, that openness does not mean progress per se, nor does it exclude the implementation of not really upgraded solutions on level SS and TS. But it gives the chance to make progress. Sometimes innovative solutions are on the table but the time is not right for change and traditional solutions are applied. That does not contradict the flexibility SYS requires. On the other hand, sometimes it happens that a plan without openness may enforce innovation and its fixed structural walls can become welcome arguments for forcing through the new solution against opposing opinions. However, such a fait accompli tactic obviously would be in contradiction with the spirit of SYS and would be risky. What will happen when the opposing opinions increase and require change? That can happen during the planning phase or later on when the building is in use. The responsibility of how the building has to be used is no longer an initial creative act of architecture but over the time of use becomes the ongoing story decision-making will write. The surgeries in the INO in the initial planning phase had an innovative layout in the form of clusters. Eventually, the traditional linear layout has been realized. Therefore, the SYS management has to be actively alert during both stages: the requirement planning with its concept levels and the building planning with its system levels. Convincing arguments are better than structural barriers.

Planners including architects, structural engineers, engineers for technical installations, and experts for operation domains have to cooperate, optimizing the whole. Because SYS differentiates the whole into long-, middle-, and short-term perspectives the organizational structure of the planners' cooperation must be in compliance with this paradigm shift. The strategy of separation defines new starting positions for all parties involved and for all components to be built and installed. The project MAS proved that even on a large scale the SYS spirit works. Good planners are motivated to be challenged by new tasks. However, despite their enthusiasm, what counts is cool judgment, if what is planned is to keep its openness and to maintain respect for all the three perspectives SYS is claiming: the long, the middle, and the short termed. If not, change. Do not ruin the chance.

Each project reaches an explicit physical reality at a certain time. But the more this reality includes an implicit openness, the better for the present and for the future of both the users and the built environment. SYS shows you the way with its big line, its comprehensive view and its specific challenges.

The following six rules may be helpful when initiating the required paradigm shift. They activate the mental overhead.

- Don't decide, but if you do, be firm: The separation of long-, medium-, and short-term parameters will focus decisions on what is important. We tend to decide where data is available rather than where relevance would justify it. Often a huge stock of short-term decisions are merely embedded in a kind of general context without making truly firm decisions at the strategic level.
- Don't ask, but bring people on stage: Many good ideas are not realized for lack of appropriate questions. Participation ought to be collaboration and must go beyond the planning stage to become an inclusive performance in use over time.
- Don't address the whole, but play a good part: It's by separation that parts achieve their particular guiding and competitive impact. Separation installs transparency, replacing managerial and technical black boxes. Contradictions and ambiguities are essential to the new paradigm.
- Don't finish, but simply take breaks: We are used to finalizing things and to award what has been built. That's human, but rethought habits and changed minds will attest excellency to buildings only if they prove apt for progress. Quality control will assess what has been built at a certain point in time, but it should include an assessment of its openness.
- Do not fall in love, but bring happiness: When falling in love with a plan, consider that things may change. With this in mind, take pleasure in facilitating modifications. If happiness persists, there is little risk; otherwise it would be a dangerous liaison.
- And what about rule six? To implement SYS successfully, the key players ought to add their personal spice. SYS is a proven strategy for creating high utility value, but it also demands thinking further. The potential for developing the benefits of SYS is great, in all you will build.

Note

1 Current SYS Guidelines (In German) can be found at the website of the Office of Properties and Buildings (www.bve.be.ch) by following: Amt für Grundstücke und Gebäude, Fachstellen, Nachhaltiges Bauen und Bewirtschaften, Systemtrennung.

References

Baecker, D (2003). *Organization und Management*. Frankfurt am Main: Suhrkamp.
Brecht, B (2000). *Flüchtlingsgespräche*. Frankfurt am Main: Suhrkamp.
Guntern, G (2010). *The Spirit of Creativity: Basic Mechanisms for Creative Achievements*. Lanham, MD: Lanham University Press of America.
Langer, E (2009). *Counter Clockwise, The Power of Possibility*. New York: Ballantine Books.
Macchi, G (2000). Reflexiones Y Cambios. InJF Isasi, A Pieltain, and JL Paniagua (Eds.), *Hospitales, La Architectura del Insalud 1986–2000*. (Vol. 2, pp. 184–189). Insalud.
Nussbaum, M (2013). *Creating Capabilities, The Human Development Approach*. Cambridge, MA: Harvard University Press.
Schweizerische Bauzeitung, espazium (2016). Gemeinsame Wege – Getrennte Systeme. *TEC21*, 43.
Sennett, R (1970). *The Uses of Disorder: Personal Identity and City Life*. New York: Knopf.
Westin, S (2014). *The Paradoxes of Planning; A Psychoanalytical Perspective*. London: Routledge.

Chapter 3

A dynamic steering instrument for the development of the Inselspital University healthcare campus

Martin Henn

Introduction
The Inselspital University Hospital is among the oldest hospitals in Switzerland and today assumes a key role in the Swiss healthcare system (see Figure 3.1). The Inselspital enjoys an international reputation as an academic center of medical excellence, high-technology and science. Over the years, the hospital has grown beyond its task as a place of recovery, into one of the most important drivers of economic and educational development for Bern and the surrounding region.

Hospital campuses like the Inselspital stand out through their various and complex requirements regarding architecture and functionality. They are undergoing a state of permanent change as a result of the constant challenge to foresee and understand future demands. A hospital of this kind needs to excel in both its national and international reputation, as much as keeping focused on the needs of the singular patient. But while in medicine it is all about *reacting* to a certain disease pattern, a hospital master plan is about *acting*, in order to prevent a spatial "disease" to develop in the first place.

This chapter reports on a new master plan, developed by HENN Architects, to guide the campus' development over the next 50 years (see Figure 3.2).

History
The Inselspital Bern reflects on a long history in its development. Today the site presents itself as a mature environment with buildings ranging from listed historical ones to newly constructed state-of-the-art facilities. From its inception (see Figure 3.3), the Inselspital has continually gone through change. This makes it a vivid example of how healthcare infrastructure has constantly met and reacted to new challenges over the course of time.

The Inselspital site today is a closely knit conglomerate of buildings with a highly heterogeneous appearance. There is no recognizable structure or site concept. On the other hand, the site features high-quality public spaces and acts as an integral part of the Bernese urban fabric. Around

Figure 3.1
Arial View Inselspital 2010.
Source: Google Earth

Figure 3.2
Competition Model of the Master plan: HENN Architects.

44,000 inpatients per year receive their treatment in facilities of roughly 280,000 m^2 (3,013,900 ft^2) (Inselspital Universitätsspital Bern, 2015). The number of employees totals about 6,400, in addition to roughly 900 students of medicine and dentistry. The organization sees a constant rise in numbers of patients, staff, and students (see Figure 3.4).

Figure 3.3
Inselspital – Historical Illustration 1884.
Source: Author/copyright unknown

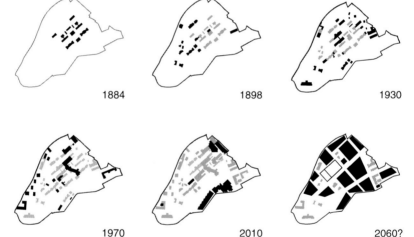

Figure 3.4
Site Development.
Source: HENN Architects

Initially the hospital had been named "Seilerin-Spital" after Anna Seiler, who founded the facility in 1354. In her last will she decreed "that the hospital is to remain after my order forever and without contradiction (…), however changes are to be possible at all times and forever" (Last Will of Mrs Anna Seiler, 1354). In 1532 the hospital relocated to a new site next to the River Aare and thus obtained its name "Inselspital". In 1713, the building was completely destroyed by a fire. Five years later, the construction of a new hospital commenced and was completed in 1724. In 1841 the Inselspital acquired its new function as a university hospital educating medical students.

Already at that time, the constant rise in numbers of patients triggered a significant step in development – the relocation of the Inselspital to a new, larger site. The first strategic design of a coherent complex of buildings from 1867 to 1884 can be called a first master plan for the Inselspital. This master plan had a life cycle of roughly 50 years (1884–1931). During this time, further buildings were added to the campus at its periphery and some buildings of the initial pavilion structure were replaced by new facilities.

A new "master plan 1957" was initiated in 1954, in order to renew the partially obsolete building infrastructure. Based on this second master plan, significant construction activity happened between 1965 and 1970, generating buildings like the current landmark inpatient tower.

Within 20 years it became obvious that the existing infrastructure would not be able to keep up with the rapidly progressing requirements in medicine. Subsequently, an Accident and Emergency and Surgical Center "INO" was built and completed in 2012 to act as a new center of gravity for the Inselspital site (The INO is reported on in Chapter 2).

At this time, new facilities were built largely without consideration of the site structure as a whole, which led to a certain fragmentation of functions. Existing process related and organizational restrictions made adjustments to the changing functional requirements of the new buildings impossible. As a result of this geographical and functional fragmentation, organizational processes became inefficient and insufficient for the qualitative requirements of a modern university hospital in both medical and operational terms. Due to this, the national and international position of the Inselspital was threatened. Significant drivers of success, such as interdisciplinary cooperation, impromptu exchange of knowledge and a high degree of interconnection appeared impossible to realize within the existing infrastructure.

In 2010, the head of Inselspital started to seek suitable planning solutions in order to meet the changing operational requirements in the short term, as well as to enable positive responses to new strategic developments with structured growth in the future. Consequently, a new step to further develop the site had to be taken. In 2010 an international urban planning competition was held to design a 'Master plan 2060' of the Inselspital.

Competition design – objectives and key ideas
HENN'S competition entry aimed at creating a basis for structured growth as well as offering readily available, flexible space to realize new buildings. The new master plan created a strategic planning tool to steer development of the site up to 2060. Acting as a rulebook guiding all future development activities, the master plan enables rapid planning decisions. It allows for various forms of functional organization while additionally leaving space for flexible operational decisions. In addition,

it supports sustainable values for urban planning and facilitates high density building on the site.

Single construction projects were to be facilitated step by step, without impacting the ongoing hospital functions. It was required to strengthen the local identity as a healthcare campus and its positive characteristics. Generally, the requirement of ecological, economic, and social sustainability was set. However, the biggest challenge of the competition was the requirement to develop a planning tool that remained meaningful and usable for the next generation.

A fundamental quantitative requirement of the competition was to provide above ground floor area (GFA) of up to 600,000 m^2 (6,458,300 ft^2), with currently existing areas of roughly 280,000m^2 (3,013,900 ft^2). Floor areas of protected listed buildings were to be included. To nearly double the total floor area within a fixed site boundary seemed to be almost impossible, considering aspects of sustainability and urban scale. Hence it was important to understand that this requirement did not mean to literally build all this space before 2060. Rather, the aim of the requirement was to strategically prescribe an urban density, in order to offer the highest possible potential for future long-term development beyond 2060.

Based on all the above, the competition master plan proposed three key ideas (see Figure 3.5):

Topography

The site's exposed topographic position offered itself as a starting point for the conception of the master plan. The bulk and massing densifies towards the center of the site and thus elevates the existing topography. As a result, the massing increases its significance in its external appearance within the urban context. Towards the site periphery, the building volume, and height reduces to facilitate a connection to the scale of the neighboring buildings.

Forming urban quarters

The urban structure of the master plan derives from the idea to form small urban quarters within the site. Listed buildings form the center of each quarter, each arranged on a new urban square.

Kneading dough

The required floor area per plot serves as the so-called "Dough", which can be "kneaded" freely within the limits of a volumetric frame. Hence, various volumetric forms can emerge within a set three-dimensional boundary. This idea ensures the freedom to newly interpret and realize future functional, economic, and architectural demands.

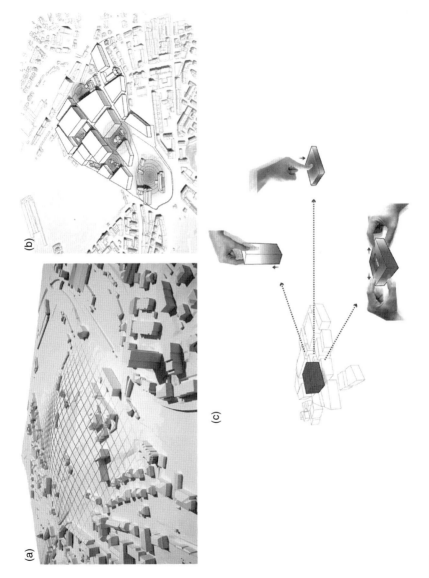

Figure 3.5
Competition Key Ideas.
Source: HENN Architects

Master plan

Having won the competition, HENN was asked to continue developing the 'Master plan 2060' up to a stage at which it could be transferred into a legally binding document. Therefore, the three key ideas: topography, urban quarters, and kneading dough, continued to build the foundation of the 'Master plan 2060' (see Figure 3.6).

During a time span of two generations, the master plan not only has to fulfill social, economic, and ecological requirements through urban planning, it also has to hold up to unforeseeable future requirements of a medical campus. Hence, the master plan cannot be a rigid planning document that will lose its relevance over the course of time due to changing requirements. On the contrary, this master plan is to be a strategic spatial planning tool: It defines a frame for structured urban development, but does not prescribe function or architecture of single building projects. This way, an open-scenario structure emerges, where varying organizational and functional concepts can be realized on each plot, e.g. the arrangement of medical centers or alternatively the arrangement of functional centers.

All central plots have dimensions designed to accommodate various kinds of clinical functions. A largely orthogonal grid supports flexibility and neutrality of use. Moreover, the plots were arranged to maintain existing buildings such as the newly built INO so that they remain fully operational and functionally integrated within the master plan until they finish their life cycle.

Today many university hospitals of comparable size are built as large, interconnected blocks of buildings, detached from their urban context. In

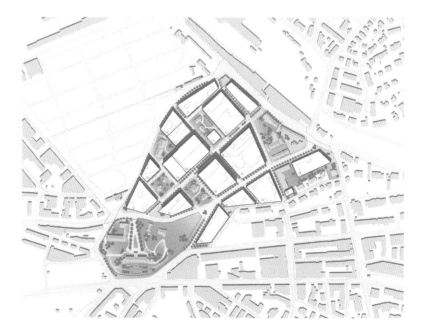

Figure 3.6
Master plan 2060.
Source: HENN Architects

contrast, the Inselspital master plan intends for the site to form a permeable, integral part of the urban fabric and to serve as an attractive public space. Simultaneously, the Inselspital has to exude the positive air of a healthcare campus, not just a place to cure sickness. Obviously, this places high demands on external spaces with regards to atmospheric quality, wayfinding, and spatial permeability. Nevertheless, it has to be possible to connect buildings in a way to facilitate easy transport of persons and goods.

Currently, the Inselspital site offers diversified spatial experiences ranging between busy hospital life at its core and nearly bucolic landscape gardens on the so-called "Englaenderhubel" towards the western end of the site. The master plan therefore intends to not only strengthen these characteristics but also to create a connection between these contrasting elements. In this way, the Inselspital is to become a space that proudly shows its historical past, while also presenting itself as an innovative center of medical excellence.

Master plan objectives

Technically, the master plan's legal document consists of a graphic plan of the site and a written rulebook. The graphic plan defines the urban structure, i.e. future plots, listed buildings, landscaping etc. and quantifies floor area requirements and volumetric limits. Additionally, the rulebook describes in a qualitative manner the overriding objectives and key ideas including tangible rules.

The question remains: how to leave a planning document for the next generation, describing ideas in an easily retraceable way, thus eliminating the need for the author to be present for explanations? The rulebook tries to develop a framework that shows how ideas derive from objectives, and how these ideas then generate rules. This framework, establishing overarching abstract objectives which further define the finer details within the master plan, has proved to be highly effective in the development process.

In detail, the rulebook defines five primary objectives. These objectives originated from requirements during the competition (see Figure 3.7).

Identity
The Inselspital site should be strengthened in its uniqueness and identity. Preserving and integrating listed historical buildings plays a central role.

Structure
The aim is to create an urban quarter with the character of a healthcare campus. This puts a focus on the quality of external space and landscaping. Hierarchies in the new part of urban fabric should be clearly legible and thus enhance orientation and wayfinding on the site and within buildings.

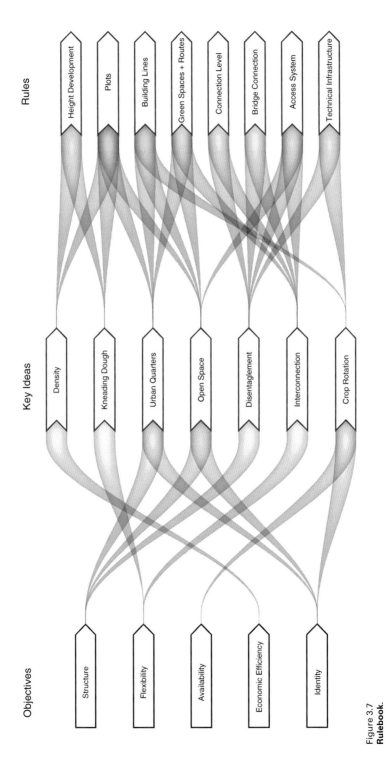

Figure 3.7
Rulebook.
Source: HENN Architects

Flexibility
This means keeping development perspectives open in the long run. Various forms of functional organization should be possible as and when required. A further consideration is to facilitate change of use and temporary usability of buildings, which requires floor layouts to be functionally neutral to a high degree.

Economic efficiency
A prerequisite of all planning activity is to make built space economically efficient to use. Part of this objective therefore is to extend the life cycle of buildings in a sense of sustainability. It should also be possible to offer spaces for external businesses with medicine-related purpose, e.g. med-tech startups emerging from research departments.

Availability of building plots
At any time, there should be a free plot of land available for new buildings in the sense of "crop rotation", in order to start new building projects easily and quickly, depending on the situation and demands at any point in time.

Key ideas
Based on the above five objectives, seven key ideas were formulated. Subsequently, these key ideas became the basis for a set of rules. As mentioned above, three key ideas had been the heart of the competition design: "Topography", "Urban Quarters", and "Kneading Dough". They were then amended and extended, so that the rulebook now defines seven key ideas (see Figure 3.8).

Forming urban quarters
Like the competition design, the Master plan 2060 aims to create urban quarters on the site. A single or group of listed historical buildings defines the center of each new quarter. The building is located centrally on a new urban square or pocket park. This square or park is defined at its boundaries through new building fronts. Pedestrian routes and visual connections connect single quarters with each other. This supports orientation and wayfinding, but also strengthens the cultural and historical identity of the Inselspital site.

Open space
A central axis connects the new urban squares and makes it possible to experience a series of varying ambient atmospheres from the busy

Figure 3.8
Key Ideas.
Source:
HENN
Architects

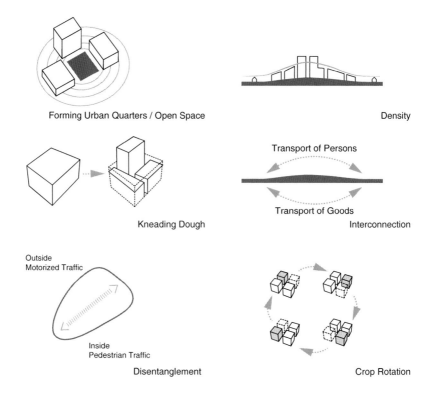

Murtenstrasse high street through to the "Englaenderhubel" landscape garden. This again supports and enhances the local identity of the Inselspital site. The appearance and quality of the open space significantly influences the perceived amenity of the whole site, and as such plays a leading role for the whole master plan.

Density
The density of mass increases towards the center of the site. Along the site boundaries, the massing adjusts to match its context and to ensure a seamless connection with the overall urban fabric.

Kneading dough
As opposed to the usual approach, the Inselspital master plan neither defines nor locates buildings on plots. A given total floor area per plot can be freely formed within a certain volumetric limit, depending on the functional and architectural requirements of each building. This allows each building to individually adapt to future requirements determined at the time of its development and realization.

Interconnection
Neighboring plots on the site should be well connected with each other, in order to ensure maximum capacity as well as functional variability. Through linking elements above and below ground, functional areas can be connected and extended horizontally across separate buildings.

Disentanglement
The aim is to separate motorized and pedestrian traffic as well as transport of patients and transport of goods across the site and within the buildings. Introducing priorities and hierarchies for traffic and transport aims to improve the experience of wayfinding for patients, visitors, and all other users.

Crop rotation
The principle of "crop rotation" intends to offer empty plots for fast but nevertheless sustainable development, while keeping all existing hospital processes intact. This requires available empty plots, so-called "fallow land", for the next step of development. As soon as a construction project is planned for an existing fallow plot, a new empty plot must be located. In case a plot is too large for the intended building, it can be divided into sub-plots with the prerequisite to achieve the required floor area once all sub-plots have been built.

Rules
In the third and final step, rules are derived from the defined key ideas (see Figure 3.9). These can be found at a lower position in the framework, becoming rather precise urban planning requirements.

Green spaces and routes
As the bulk and massing of future buildings is unknown, it is essential that all greenery serves the wayfinding on the site. Therefore, all primary and secondary routes in the master plan are lined by alley trees and linear parks. All linear greenery is interrupted where the route meets an adjacent square, in order to open up the views towards the square. This also helps to interconnect and weave routes into squares.

Building lines
According to the master plan, each urban quarter has a square at its center. However, only certain building proportions provide the right structure to generate the sense of an urban square. Even if form and location of new buildings on plots surrounding the square are still unknown, it has to be ensured that the volume of adjacent buildings helps to form this square. Therefore, building lines were introduced to define the requirement for

Martin Henn

Figure 3.9
Rules.
Source:
HENN
Architects

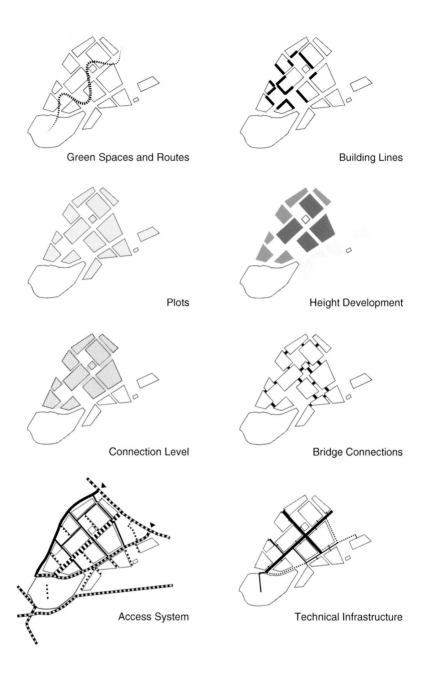

closed building fronts on boundary lines surrounding each square. To avoid towering buildings which suffocate a square by their sheer vertical dimension, the requirement for a closed perimeter only applies to the plinth of each building. The building mass above should be set back from the plinth. The height of the plinth is not set in absolute terms. Instead, the height of

A dynamic steering instrument

the plinth of each building adjacent to a square is defined to range between a minimum and a maximum relative to a set level for each square. There are two variables on each building plot: 1) ground floor location relative to topography and 2) free choice of floor-to-floor dimension. Because the highest point of the site is 35 m (115 ft) above the lowest point, the possible number of stories for each building plinth can vary. The objective is to achieve a consistent edge line of building plinths around each square.

Plots

By their set dimensions, plots define the space where new buildings can be constructed on the site. Buildings can be shaped according to project requirements within the extent of a volumetric spatial frame. In order to determine the shape and appearance of the buildings, a separate competition is to be held for each plot. The "Plot" rule is amended by the "Building Line" rule around squares, requirements of total floor area per plot and maximum possible height requirements.

Height development

One of the three competition ideas, "Topography", can be found again here. By increasing the density and thus building height towards the center of the site, which is already located on a hill, a super-elevation of the topography is achieved. This has significant impact on the physical appearance of the site within the urban context. Today, the inpatient tower is the Inselspital's landmark, as it can be seen from most points in the city and its surroundings. As soon as it is replaced, new high buildings at the site's core will take over this role.

Connection level

Setting a fixed reference level for all plots enables the horizontal connection of new buildings at the site's core. This rule only refers to one floor per plot, so that ceiling heights above and below the connection level remain unaffected. Therefore, functional and organizational connections across buildings become possible.

Bridge connections

A connection between buildings or plots is possible via bridges. This adds an efficient system of internal routes to the already existing transport tunnels below ground. By this means, patients no longer need to be transferred through an unwelcoming logistics tunnel, but can be moved above ground. In addition, internal visitor routes can now be offered between buildings. The rulebook requires these bridges to be designed and proportioned in a way that leaves the buildings legible as autonomous architectural elements.

Access system

The main aim of the traffic and infrastructure concept is to disentangle traffic flows by prioritizing routes and developing a concept of route hierarchies. In the future, all motorized traffic, especially emergency ambulance traffic and logistics traffic, is to access the site directly from both main roads around the site and one historical main road that crosses through the Inselspital campus. All further internal routes are reserved for pedestrian and bicycle traffic. A new main pedestrian alley from east to west will become an important feature of the Inselspital as a healthcare campus.

Technical infrastructure

The aim of this concept is to simplify the infrastructure network on the site by introducing two primary media and infrastructure tunnels below ground. In order to guarantee maximum flexibility for the plots, all technical infrastructures including the two main tunnels are to be run parallel to plots beneath the roads.

Through all the above objectives, key ideas, and rules, the rulebook tries to detail the master plan's intent. Qualitative descriptions have been chosen over quantitative prescriptions (exceptions being the total floor area per plot and maximum height per plot), in order to give the master plan "space to breathe" in the future.

Spatial/organizational/sustainable master plan

Which development, then, triggers the first step in realizing the master plan? Which plot is the right one for the first construction project? Here is where the "Organizational Master plan" essentially comes into play (see Figure 3.10).

While HENN developed a master plan that refers to all things urban and architectural, a team of operational specialists developed a master plan that mainly refers to organizational functions. Both of these master plans were then additionally amended by a third element, the Master plan for "Ecology and Sustainability". While the "Spatial Master plan" provides a stable urban planning tool to ensure structured spatial development through the next decades, the "Organizational Master plan" depicts current and acute requirements of a complex hospital organization within a highly dynamic context. The idea to build a master plan out of three components (spatial, organizational, and sustainability) emerged during the process of shaping the spatial master plan. Both the organizational and sustainability master plans were then mainly developed by the client (i.e. the Inselspital).

A dynamic steering instrument

Figure 3.10
Organizational Master plan.
Source: HENN Architects

To start the Organizational Master plan, an intense quantitative analysis of medical data had to be undertaken. The aim was to visualize patient routes in order to determine the functional dependencies and physical proximity between clinical departments.

But how should these clinical departments relate spatially to each other in the future? The Inselspital's mission statement puts the patient as the central focus. Therefore, an executive decision was made to make the patient process the key driver for future functional structures. The new core idea is interdisciplinary collaboration. This, however, means in the future, that clinical departments cannot constitute spatially independent centers for specialists and thus a new organizational form had to be found for the Inselspital.

In the next step of the modelling process, the existing organizational structure was dissolved and replaced by a new model of "gravitation". The model simulated how closely different units approach each other when patient movements between them amplify the attraction. The result was a clear, but not exactly surprising picture. The A&E, radiology and diagnostics units and operating rooms are medical core functions, which are strongly connected with most other disciplines. Consequently, these core functions need to be centrally located.

In 2012 the newly opened Accident, Emergency and Surgery Center "INO" with radiology and laboratory medicine housed the above core functions. There was now a new requirement recognized for three medical centers: three other medical centers, i.e. the Comprehensive Cancer, Comprehensive Neuroscience and Comprehensive Cardiovascular Center should be sited in immediate adjacency of the INO. This pragmatic proposal, which reflects the day-to-day necessities of clinical process, found fast and broad approval among the hospital management. Thus, the first steps to develop the Inselspital site were set.

Connecting space and organization

What solution does the "Spatial Master plan" offer for the requirements resulting from the "Organizational Master plan"? (See Figure 3.11).

The Accident, Emergency and Surgical Center "INO" is a large, compact building. A few years after it opened, it became evident that the building would soon reach its capacity limits. In order to be able to grow, the INO would need to grow horizontally into the adjacent plots (its structure does not allow it to expand vertically). Through its "Connection Level" and "Bridge Connection" rules, the Spatial Master plan offers the possibility to connect buildings on one specific floor at the same elevation (no sloping bridges). New operating rooms, for example, could be connected to existing

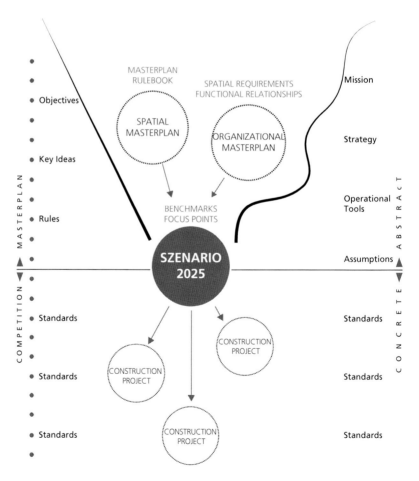

Figure 3.11
Connecting Space and Organization.
Source: HENN Architects

theaters functionally and spatially, even though being located in adjacent buildings. Adding associated processes of acute medicine like intensive care and intermediate-care spaces in the same new building, would create an opportunity for optimized processes.

Subsequently, for the plots adjacent to the "INO" building the following vertical functional structure emerged: High-volume outpatient clinics will be located at ground level. There will be a direct connection to the diagnostic center with centralized radiology. As mentioned, emergency and operation room functions can spill over from the INO into the new neighboring buildings on the bridge connection level. The levels above house patient care, with intensive care most closely connected to the operating rooms. Any additional space available in floors above can be used for administrative functions as well as research and medical startups. This staggering of functions allows compact buildings, interconnection of processes, and flexible reactions to changing future requirements.

Two plots adjacent to the existing INO will accommodate the new Swiss Comprehensive Cardiovascular Center and the Tumor and Organ Center. In the Comprehensive Cardiovascular Center specialists of interventional medicine will have the opportunity of interdisciplinary collaboration on a single floor at an extent of approximately 4,500 m^2 (48,437 ft^2). For patients, this means not only faster treatment and avoiding stressful transfers, but also the highest possible availability of cumulated expertise and state-of-the-art technology. Staff benefit from short distances to walk as well as from the interdisciplinary collaboration. Also in organizational terms, this structure promises an increase in efficiency.

Additionally, the new Tumor and Organ Center aspires to become an interdisciplinary oncology center through its proximity to the INO. The center will offer functions of cancer diagnosis, treatment as well as specialized patient care and therapy. On this plot, the flexibility of the master plan proves its practicality for the first time. The construction of the building will happen in two phases. During the first phase, the building will temporarily house gynecology and neonatology. During the second phase, the building will have stories added to then serve as the intended Organ and Tumor Center.

At the same time, the old inpatient tower will be demolished and leave space for a first plot of fallow land. Thus, the key idea of "crop rotation" will become reality.

Developing the spatial master plan

The Master Plan 2060 was not created at a drawing desk or on a computer screen. Starting with the basic ideas from the competition design, the master plan was developed in intense dialogue with clients and members of all stakeholder groups.

This process took approximately two years. Design team workshops took place at regular intervals involving clients, authorities, architects, and planners. Together the team exchanged ideas and sketched (see Figure 3.12).

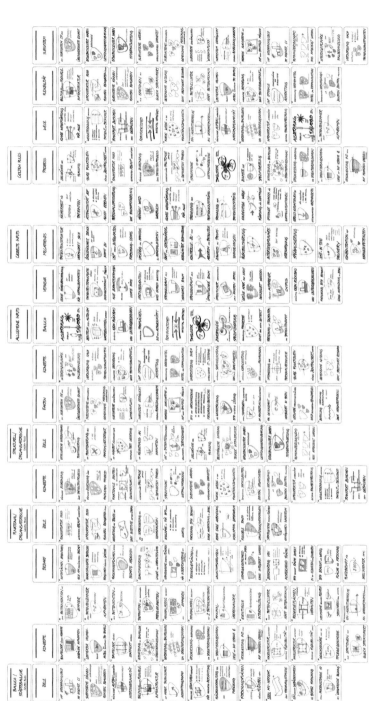

Figure 3.12
Workshop Sketches.

Numerous interviews were held with key persons representing clinical departments, research, medical education, patient care and third-party medtech companies. Only through the knowledge gained in these interviews could the master plan be developed.

Specialist consultants were involved to develop concepts for traffic, infrastructure, and ecological sustainability as a part of the rulebook. Many times, the unusual task to create concepts, which guide structured development without obstructing it through requirements with excessively short life spans, proved a challenge. For example, quantitative prescriptions of energy efficiency will lose their validity in the foreseeable future. Therefore, the team tried to focus on qualitative, descriptive rules.

But not only members of all hospital-related stakeholder groups were involved. The planning authorities of the City of Bern and Canton of Bern contributed significantly to the master plan. A "High-Rise Buildings Commission" discussed the appearance of the planned massing and its impact on the landscape. The hospital administration organized guided tours and citizen informational events. Via press statements, the public was informed about milestones in the development of the master plan.

The process of developing the master plan reached its final destination by transferring it into a legally binding document, a Swiss equivalent of a zoning plan. In March 2015, an eagerly awaited vote took place about the master plan. With a remarkably positive vote of 86.6%, the people of Bern approved the new zoning plan for the Inselspital. Now the most important strategic course was set for the future of Bern as a beacon of medical excellence.

A living master plan

"The masterplan is at any time defined but at no time definite" (Giorgio Macchi, Chief Architect of the Office for Real Estate and Public Buildings, Canton Bern, 2015).

The Inselspital took its first steps towards a structured development immediately after the approval of the zoning plan in March 2015 (see Figure 3.13).

Within two years, there were three large projects under construction. On two core plots, the Organ and Tumor Center as well as the Swiss Comprehensive Cardiovascular Center were being built. A new Center for Translational Research will form the face towards the city center on a plot close to the main entry route to the Inselspital site.

But despite the transfer from master plan to legally binding zoning plan, the planning process still continued. As the zoning plan requires an architectural competition for each plot and the open space of the Inselspital site, three project competitions have already taken place at the time of this writing, with additional competitions planned in the future (see Figure 3.14).

Each of these project competitions will deal with a variety of architectural and organizational requirements for a huge, technically complex building project. Each of these competitions will see new participants and new jury members, selecting a winner based on different criteria. So not only context

Figure 3.13
Zoning Plan.
Source: Stadtplanungsamt Bern (Bern City Council Planning Department)

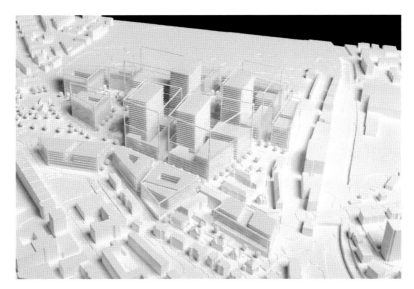

Figure 3.14 Master plan Model with Spatial Frame and Example of Possible Building Bulk and Massing.

but also the actors will vary from project to project. Due to this variability, the question arises "How will it be possible to keep in mind the bigger picture, i.e. the qualitative aspirations of the master plan?"

This is why an advisory board was introduced, consisting of highest-ranking members of the Inselspital, University of Bern, planning authorities of the City and the Canton of Bern and the master planning office HENN. The advisory board aims to continue the story of the master plan by making strategic decisions together and by establishing a common position for all parties. The board obligates itself to subordinate interests of single parties to a common position.

As before in the Inselspital's long history, the site will continue to evolve and develop. Part of this process is to continue "curating" the master plan in the long term.

References

Inselspital Universitätsspital Bern (2015). (Ed.), Jahresbericht 2015. www.insel.ch/de/das-inselspital/publikationen/.

Last Will of Mrs Anna Seiler (1354) Testament Der Frau Anna Seiler. Inselspital Universitätsspital Bern (Ed.). www.inselgruppe.ch/de/die-insel-gruppe/organisation/inselspital-stiftung/.

Macchi, G (2015). Chief Architect of the Office for Real Estate and Public Buildings, Canton Bern: Keynote lecture at the International Conference The Future of Open Building, ETH Wohnforum, ETH Zurich, September 9–11.

Chapter 4

Dynamic facilities development

A client perspective on managing change

David Hanitchak and Malaina Bowker

Introduction

Healthcare in the United States is complex and dynamic. Academic Medical Centers (AMCs) that combine education and research with medical care face unique challenges in responding to change that is constant but at varying cycles. Despite the demands for frequent organizational and facility adjustments in response to changes in the healthcare environment, AMCs need high reliability and minimal disruption for their facilities to effectively support their mission. Physical adjustments that do occur therefore must be tightly planned and managed to send as few "ripple effects" as possible into the healthcare facility.

Massachusetts General Hospital (MGH), a premier US academic medical center, has its main campus in a dense aggregation of 25 buildings in Boston, built over the last 196 years on 18 acres (7.28 ha). The main buildings comprise 4.6 million square feet (428,000 m^2) and support 1.1 million outpatient visits, 54,000 inpatient visits, and approximately 110,000 emergency department visits per year. To manage its portfolio, MGH has a 35-person facilities planning and engineering department responsible for 200 renovation projects per year, plus a major new building approximately every eight years.

This chapter presents a survey and comparison of basic elements of MGH's existing facilities by clinical function throughout their lives. The analysis provides insights regarding expectations placed on the initial design of the buildings, whether and how our buildings have adapted to change, and at what point they have limited clinical functionality and require replacement.

Healthcare facilities are different from other kinds of real estate
Healthcare facilities must accommodate rapidly changing and unique demands on space in response to numerous and complex forces:

- **Science and technology:** Advances in genetics and genomics, nanotechnology and translational research improve the identification of

new diseases as well as the ability to successfully intervene; rapidly changing interventional technologies, demand for cross-collaborations, and pervasive computers place additional demands on facilities, connections and electrical, mechanical, electrical and plumbing (MEP) infrastructure;
- **Changing practice patterns**: Stemming from new therapies, pressures on care givers to perform more efficiently, emphasis on family centered and multidisciplinary care, and new code requirements all affect organization, aggregation of and criteria for space and often the MEP infrastructure;
- **Market incentives**: These affect which programs are funded and their priority, e.g. shifts in reimbursement due to health and health insurance policies or efficacy studies, changes in referral requirements, or recession-driven decreased demand for elective procedures;
- **Increased accountability**: New regulatory requirements and standards to improve public health, safety, and privacy, along with a growing body of knowledge of evidence-based design, require changes in clinical design and MEP infrastructure;
- **Consumerism**: Pressure for healthcare facilities to behave like retail and hospitality industries demand that higher levels of amenities be incorporated into projects;
- **Demographics**: Shifts in demand due to the changing make up and health of the population must be accommodated in both services provided and facility design; and,
- **Pressures to reduce the cost of healthcare**: Rising costs and competition for capital throughout healthcare systems – for information technology, clinical equipment, and facilities – along with a shift toward distributed outpatient care, have reduced capital availability and increased the need for facilities with capacity to adapt to changing requirements.

External forces and demands are unpredictable, uncontrollable and may conflict with each other, so the ability to anticipate and respond quickly and effectively to change is vital to a hospital's mission.

In addition, since hospitals operate 24 hours a day, their operations are extremely vulnerable to disruption from construction activities and the need to access adjacent spaces for MEP changes. Managing real estate change in a healthcare environment is a singular challenge.

Academic Medical Centers are different from other kinds of healthcare facilities

AMCs are a complex subset of healthcare with multifaceted missions, providing multidisciplinary healthcare and face a greater range of facility pressures than non-academic hospitals. AMCs have three-part missions: education, research, and clinical care. Each is a quasi-autonomous enterprise. Balancing the missions is especially difficult due to competition for capital, space, and staff recruiting. AMCs thrive when the teaching, research, and patient care missions have geographic proximity, balanced space allocation, and modern facilities. Physical connections enabling efficient movement between existing and new spaces are crucial for collaboration among the multiple missions of an AMC. Departments often grow, needing larger footprints for integrating operations, communications, coordination of multiple missions and for efficiencies of space and operations. Competition for diminishing real estate assets among the clinical, research and education enterprises affects the physical organization of AMCs and the types of facilities that are built.

AMC facility needs are more complex than stand-alone hospitals. For inpatient care, AMCs typically see patients with higher acuity and multiple medical problems, and a higher percentage of Intensive Care Unit (ICU) patients, resulting in increased intensity of use, whether for staffing, equipment or support. For outpatient care, AMCs' emphasis is on multi-disciplinary approaches to disease management, with increased need to accommodate procedures including anesthesia and recovery in traditional office-exam suites. Since AMCs are early adopters of new technologies and practice patterns stemming from research initiatives, they face the challenge of adapting their facilities earlier and more often than non-AMC healthcare providers.

Despite the urgency of these changing demands, many older AMC facilities cannot easily accommodate new uses due to undersized structural bay spacing, awkward building shape or dimensions, low floor-to-floor heights, and complex connections between buildings (often with floors that do not align) that limit older structures' efficiency. When demands for increased building performance – more air, power, signal capacity, and energy efficiency – cannot be met in existing buildings, AMCs are faced with the choice of reducing the intensity of building use and accepting lower performance and efficiency, or replacing buildings with new construction.

How have MGH facilities responded to pressures over time?

Older buildings at MGH have been remarkably adaptable over their life cycle (see Figure 4.1). They have accommodated new clinical practice patterns, new medical equipment and new code requirements, and have had long lives for their initial use. Several buildings have had extremely long useful lives by accommodating lower intensity uses over time; other buildings have undergone extensive renovation.

Despite variations in building age, structural grids, floor-to-floor heights, and MEP infrastructure, through an aggressive program of capital reinvestment, MGH has maintained state-of-the-art care in several older buildings, including a 75-year-old bed tower and a 32-year-old outpatient clinic. The accommodation of new air flow regulations, state-of-the-art equipment, and continuing changes in practice patterns in existing buildings has been largely driven by the need to maintain ongoing hospital operations in a

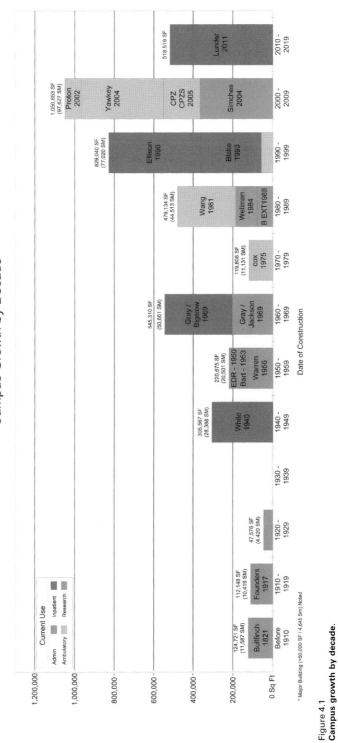

Figure 4.1
Campus growth by decade.

fully occupied facility. As an example of how important it is to avoid disrupting hospital operations, the major circulation/utility corridors in the campus have remained in the same place for over 150 years, and major renovation projects have simply extended the circulation/utility distribution horizontally and vertically.

Inpatient buildings

Comparing inpatient building designs over time, there have been significant changes in room standards, structural grid size, floor-to-floor dimensions, and construction type over MGH's 196-year history. The pace of these changes has accelerated in the past few decades.

Inpatient design changes are driven by code requirements and preference for single rooms, more clinical equipment, evolving nursing practice patterns, more space for families within each patient room, higher information technology requirements, and increased service, information system (IS) and MEP infrastructure and space requirements. As patient acuity and specialized treatment increases, there is a dramatic increase in required support space due to the range of specialized devices, disposables in multiple sizes, and various kinds of equipment. In addition, the need to accommodate more support staff for clinical specialties such as respiratory therapy, dialysis, nutrition, social services, and physical therapy places large demands on space.

From our experience, difficult building shapes such as triangular or cruciform plans, small structural grid dimensions and limited floor-to-floor height have constrained our ability to renovate to meet current room size standards. In addition, small floor plates do not support efficient acute inpatient nursing units (between 30 and 36 beds) given current codes and practices for single patient rooms, and requirements for support space. Current design practice suggests an inpatient unit floor plate of 30,000–36,000 ft^2 (2,788–3,344 m^2) for 30–36 bed units. Earlier inpatient floors were significantly smaller (11,000–16,000 ft^2 [1,021–1,486 m^2]) and housed double or four-patient rooms, or even wards, with minor requirements for bed clearances and support space.

As shown in Table 4.1, three of the current inpatient buildings have substantially smaller floor plates than currently recommended, and therefore support less efficient staffing patterns and have higher operational costs per patient. The new bed tower, the Lunder Building, meets new standards and creates more efficient nursing units.

Despite their limitations, MGH inpatient buildings have successfully accommodated their original use for many years. In addition, the usefulness of many buildings has been extended by adaptation to lower intensity uses. In MGH's oldest remaining inpatient buildings, the intensity of use has decreased to the extent that they are now used for administration, or support a significantly reduced number of beds per floor. The White Building, designed for 40 beds for floor, is now operating at 27 beds per floor. The Gray Bigelow Building, designed for 26 beds, now operates at 18 beds

Table 4.1 Chronology of inpatient building characteristics

Inpatient Building Characteristics		Bulfinch & Additions	Founders	Baker	White	VBK	Gray Bigelow	Ellison	Blake	Lunder
Construction Date		1821/1846/1924	1917	1930	1940	1947	1969	1990	1993	2011
Demolition Date		N/A	N/A	1987	N/A	2007	N/A	N/A	N/A	N/A
Initial Use		Inpatient Administration	Inpatient Administration	Inpatient	Inpatient	Inpatient	Inpatient	Inpatient	Inpatient	Inpatient
Current Use		Inpatient Administration	Inpatient Administration	N/A	Inpatient	N/A	Inpatient	Inpatient	Inpatient	Inpatient
Length of Inpatient Use		147 Years	73 Years	57 Years	62 Years	43 Years	43 Years	27 Years	24 Years	6 Years
Total length of Use		196 Years	100 Years	57 Years	62 Years	70 Years	43 Years	27 Years	24 Years	6 years
Construction Type		Masonry/ Concrete	Reinforced Concrete	Reinforced Concrete	Reinforced Concrete	Reinforced Concrete	Steel	Steel	Steel	Steel
Structural Grid	Ft	Not Original	20 x 20	16 x 18	16 x 20	16 x 20	24 x 25	25 x 34	25 x 30	30 x 36
	M	-	6.1 x 6.1	4.9 x 5.5	4.9 x 6.1	4.9 x 6.1	7.3 x 7.6	7.6 x 10.4	7.6 x 9.1	9.1 x 11
Floor-to-Floor Heights	Ft	Varies	11'	12'	12'	11'	12'	12'	12'	12'
	M	-	3.4	3.7	3.7	3.4	3.7	3.7	3.7	4.3
Average Double Patient Room Size	Ft²	N/A (Ward)	255 sf	175 sf	269 sf	147 sf	260 sf	255 sf	232 sf (ICU)	390 sf (Single ICU)
	M²	-	23.7	16.3	25	13.7	24.2	23.7	21.6	
Average Single Patient Room Size	Ft²	N/A (Ward)	180 sf	112 sf	161 sf	140 sf (ICU)	166 sf	228 sf (ISO)		
	M²	-	16.7	10.4	15	13	15.4	21.2		
Original Beds per Floor		~18	24	36	40	30	26	36	18	32
Current Beds per Floor		N/A	N/A	N/A	27	N/A	18	Same	Same	N/A
Original ft²/Acute Bed/Floor	Ft²	134	393	255	293	236	505	392	719	815
(m²/bed/floor)	M²	12.5	36.5	23.7	27.2	21.9	46.9	36.4	66.8	75.7
Current ft²/acute bed/floor	Ft²	N/A	N/A	N/A	434	N/A	730	Same	Same	Same
(m²/bed/floor)	M²	-	-	-	40.3	-	67.8	-	-	-

Inpatient use of the 1846 Bulfinch Addition continued until 1993.

per floor. A conversion to single patient rooms, if implemented in existing buildings, would further reduce occupancy in current inpatient buildings, with negative effects on revenue generation.

Operating rooms

There have been similar increases in operating room sizes over time – from as small as approximately 200 ft^2 (18.6 m^2) in the White Building built in 1939, to over 600 ft^2 (55.7 m^2) in Blake (1993) and Lunder (2011), which reflect increasing complexity of procedures, more personnel and new equipment. The larger 626 sf (58 m^2) operating rooms (ORs) in Blake reflect their designation as cardiac ORs.

The Lunder Building[1] OR sizes (600–720 sf [55.7–66.9 m^2]) are a new standard for MGH reflecting code changes, the need to accommodate variations in layout, equipment and personnel by specialty, and additional audio/visual and monitoring equipment. In general, image-guided ORs are larger, and are designed around specific equipment, but with the principle that the rooms can be also used for procedures not requiring imaging, which has resulted in higher utilization/revenue. In addition to larger room sizes, MEP infrastructure requirements have resulted in significantly greater floor-to-floor heights to accommodate more air changes/larger ducting.

Outpatient buildings

Comparison of MGH outpatient buildings shows that the size of the structural grid has increased substantially over time. Meanwhile, floor-to-floor heights have fluctuated. From our experience, larger structural grid spacing is more important in accommodating new clinical technologies and increased MEP performance than floor-to-floor height. The campus is

Table 4.2 Chronology of the characteristics of diagnostic, treatment and procedure floors

Diagnostics & Treatment & O. R. Floors		White	Gray Bigelow	Gray Jackson	Blake	Lunder
Construction Date		1939	1969	1969	1993	2011
Length of Use		70 Years	40 Years	40 Years	16 Years	6 Years
Construction Type		Reinforced Concrete	Steel	Steel	Steel	Steel
Structural Grid	Ft	16 x 20	24 x 25	24 x 25	25 x 30	30 x 36
	M	4.9 x 6.1	7.3 x 7.6	7.3 x7.6	7.5 x 9.1	9.1 x 11
Floor-to-Floor Heights	Ft	12'	12'	12'	12'	16'
	M	3.7	3.7	3.7	3.7	4.9
Operating Room Size	Ft	198–483	432–693	415–502	600–626	600–720
	M	18.4–44.9	40.1–64.4	38.6–46.5	55.7–58.2	55.7–66.9
Air Changes/Hour		10	12	12	15	25

mostly at 12 ft (3.7 m) floor-to-floor. It is important to note that MGH has been able to accommodate almost all new clinical technologies through renovations despite these constraints.

Despite similarities in basic building and exam room statistics between Wang and Yawkey,[2] the latter is significantly more efficient in outpatient visit volume, achieving 1.7 visits per square foot per year as opposed to 1.0 visits per square foot per year in Wang. This is a result of operational decisions developed during the Yawkey's programming and design – Yawkey's "Nine Commandments" – as well as improved clinic design.

- Yawkey's "Nine Commandments" were an innovative agreement between administration and departments designed to ensure the building's operational efficiency. Space allocation was determined based on revenue per exam room; efficiency and operational standards were established (e.g. sharing of common spaces such as check-in and phlebotomy, allocation of space based on level scheduling, that is, scheduling appointments for the entire week, rather than allowing them to peak mid-week, and a central scheduling module); and space and occupancy standards were established for both exam room and pod/module size. High throughput, hence improved return-on-investment, resulted from these strategies.
- While elements of the Commandments were developed in collaboration with the design team (room standards and typical clinical layouts), most of them promoted efficient use of space and had not previously been

Table 4.3 Chronology of the characteristics of outpatient buildings

Outpatient Building Characteristics	Clinics	Wang Acc	Yawkey
Construction Date	1903	1981	2004
Demolition Date	2007	N/A	N/A
Initial Use	Outpatient	Outpatient	Outpatient
Current Use	N/A	Outpatient	Outpatient
Length of Use	78 Years	37 Years	14 Years
Total Length of Use	104 Years	37 Years	14 Years
Construction Type	Reinforced Masonry	Steel	Steel
Structural Grid	20''-0'' (max) (6.1 M)	25'-0'' x 30'-0'' (7.6 x9.1 M)	32'-0'' x 36'-0'' (9.6 x 11 M)
Floor-to-Floor Heights	14'-0'' (4.3 M)	12'-0'' (3.7 M)	13'-5'' (4.1 M)
Exam Room Size	70 sf (6.5 M)	100 sf (9.3 M)	115 sf (10.7 M)
Total Exam Room Size Per Floor	246 sf (22.9 sm)	451 sf (41.9 sm)	454 sf (42.2 sm)
Visits Per Sq Foot per Year	Not Available	1	1.7

Table 4.4 Yawkey's Nine Commandments

Yawkey's Nine Commandments

1	Shared Common Spaces \ Areas
2	Level Schedules
3	Standard Office Sizes
4	Office Allocation on a Clinical FTE Requirements
5	Exam Room Allocation based on Utilization Standards
6	Physician and Department Offices not included
7	Standard Hours of Clinical Operation 8am–8pm Monday to Friday
8	Private Physicians included in Department if they conform to Practices Guidelines
9	Designed as Business "Low-Tech" Space

consistently applied by departments. To be considered for occupancy in the Yawkey building, departments were required to adhere to the Commandments.

- Operational flexibility in Yawkey has been enhanced by using a single-loaded public access corridor leading to reception/waiting space, with non-public corridors that provide access to generic exam pods in the back-of-house areas, allowing access from any of the departmental reception/waiting rooms.

Both Wang and Yawkey were designed as "Business" class buildings, rather than "Ambulatory" class (which must meet higher MEP performance and life safety requirements), to reduce initial capital costs.

- In Wang, after 20–25 years in use, as the intensity of use increased to include more ambulatory level patient care, significant upgrading of air-handling and other MEP infrastructure has been required to meet higher levels of building performance. For example, the Wang 2 Breast Center was upgraded with imaging and diagnostics, and Wang 6 Internal Medicine Associates was renovated to increase patient throughput. Procedure space was also incorporated into the building by displacing or densifying functions. Required mechanical system upgrades included introduction of separately ducted air distribution and return (changing from "Business class" ductless plenum air return), and increasing the air flow for exam spaces. This added significantly to mechanical and electrical loads, requiring major infrastructure upgrades or renovations of entire floors and their attendant disruption to normal hospital operations.
- In Yawkey, during the design phase, requests from medical practices for increased medical technology use, anesthesia capability, and procedure rooms led to localized enhancements to infrastructure capacity prior to construction. The revised designs provided additional emergency

power and increased mechanical performance from six to 25 air changes per hour for procedure suites that required MEP infrastructure specific to those units. It is important to note that these local changes to building MEP infrastructure were made not in anticipation of future changes, but to accommodate specific programs of immediate importance, by providing, for example, separate, dedicated air handling units, a stand-alone generator, and critical freezer storage for the In Vitro Fertilization procedure room. Subsequent renovations have similarly addressed the needs of individual departments and uses with no significant difficulty given the building's larger structural grid and higher floor-to-floor heights.

- Reviewing the initial design and assumptions about short- and long-term cost control for each building, it is clear that long-term renovation costs in Wang, which came at higher premiums due to the need to work around existing operations in smaller base building dimensions, have offset the initial perceived savings of building a Class B (Business class) structure. Yawkey's larger base building dimensions and higher initial design standards in certain areas of the building have avoided significant renovation costs, although its lower intensity use areas still somewhat limit extension of clinical uses. Installing MEP infrastructure for high-intensity uses throughout the Yawkey building in its initial construction would have been prohibitively expensive, and likely would have led to underutilized infrastructure and a negative ROI. High-tech uses were programmed and concentrated in the next building, the Lunder Building, with inpatient beds and a procedure platform.

Lessons from MGH facility growth

Length of building use
At the campus level, major campus corridors and connections between buildings for pedestrian, materials, and utility paths have the longest continuous use of any facility element on campus. The major corridors have been in place for 150 years, and sometimes the original corridor structures remain embedded in new buildings. As the campus has grown, corridor systems have extended both horizontally and vertically, but once in place they are rarely changed in order to avoid disruption to existing hospital operations.

At the building level, base building elements, such as structural characteristics, vertical and horizontal functional and building service distribution paths, typically last 60 to over 100 years. With the Bulfinch Building, the hospital's founding building and a National Historic Landmark, the base building has been in continuous use for 196 years. Length of use for MEP infrastructure and equipment is typically 20 to 30 years, and vertical transportation (elevators) can have a life of 50 years with service upgrades.

Reinvestment cycles

Reinvestment cycles vary by use. The lowest intensity use space has the longest useful life before major renovation and the most intense uses have the shortest useful life before major renovation; both receive budgets for planned annual partial upgrades. Office and administrative floors receive major renovation or upgrading investments on an average of a 54-year cycle. Outpatient space undergoes upgrading at a 25-year investment cycle and inpatient space at 26-year cycle. Emergency Services has been renovated four times over 40 years, a ten-year cycle, most recently in 2017. Operating room floors receive major investment on a 22-year cycle, and imaging, diagnostics and treatment spaces have an average of a 37-year cycle; but both benefit from planned annual upgrades.

Full building renovation is rare at MGH because it is too disruptive, requires swing space to temporarily relocate functions, yields limited gains in efficiency since floor plates are relatively small, and is too costly for the increase in return on investment. For improvements to department suites or floors, partial renovation is a quick way of satisfying more constituencies, and easier to fund than major construction projects.

How adaptable are MGH facilities?

MGH has been able to maintain effective use of many of its older buildings despite sub-optimal structural grid sizes, lower floor-to-floor heights and aging MEP infrastructure. Adaptation of older buildings usually does not significantly compromise their original care program or function. Many changes can be adequately accommodated by partial renovation of these older buildings if the proposed program fits in available space.

Not surprisingly, however, the financial investment required to adapt our buildings to respond to new requirements is higher with the older buildings than with newer buildings.

- *Outpatient* renovation costs are about 10% more in our older outpatient buildings than in our newer ones. In both old and newer outpatient buildings, MEP infrastructure improvements increase the cost of projects by about 80% above initial construction costs.
- *Inpatient* renovation costs are about 40% more in older buildings than in newer buildings, and MEP infrastructure replacement increases the cost of projects by about 32% in older buildings, with no premium for newer buildings. Renovations in newer buildings benefit from investment in additional infrastructure distribution capacity if provided in initial design.
- *Diagnostics and treatment/operating room* renovations cost about 20% more in older buildings than in newer buildings, and MEP infrastructure increases the cost of projects by almost 60% in older buildings, again with no premium for newer buildings.

The major constraints in accommodating high-intensity programs (primarily inpatient, diagnostics and imaging, and operating rooms) in existing space given current and evolving building standards are:

- Hard boundaries created by corridors and connections between buildings, which are difficult to relocate due to disruption to existing services and utilities (horizontal distribution above corridor ceilings – frequently fire-rated assemblies) and which often delineate departmental ownership, changes to which often require complex negotiations;
- Older reinforced concrete structures, which are more difficult to renovate for high-intensity use than steel structures due to the relatively small structural grids, difficulty in modifying structure to accommodate point loads, radiation shielding and managing vibration, and difficulty in relocating utilities requiring floor penetrations; and,
- Irregularly shaped and small floor plates in our older buildings, which limit programs that require large rooms or aggregation of rooms with strict operational paths, such as clean corridors.

Accommodating large rooms, greater than 700 sf, for medical technologies such as magnetic resonance imaging (MRIs) and computed tomography (CTs), in existing, or even new buildings, also results in trade-offs in patient throughput. For example, providing two hybrid operating rooms with interoperative imaging requires the same footprint as three conventional operating rooms. The technology can be accommodated, but coming to a programmatic decision requires an extensive negotiation between financial and departmental interests.

All construction is disruptive to the 24-hour hospital and requires extraordinary measures to manage access, noise, demolition, MEP replacement or changes, life safety and infection risks.

When do we stop renovating and choose new construction?

We undertake new construction projects when we need to significantly increase capacity, to consolidate programs and reorganize departments, and to remove obsolete facilities. It is easier to build additional capacity in new buildings than in old. New construction also vacates backfill space for program expansion when targeted users relocate to new buildings. However, the cost of new buildings has increased rapidly and assembling sufficient capital funding for large projects is difficult and time consuming.

Despite this, the pace of new construction has increased over the last 100 years. From 1917 to 1956 the rate of investment in new buildings was an average of one every ten years; from 1969 to 1981 it was one every 8.5 years; and from 1981 to today it has been one every 7.5 years. On average, MGH has invested in new buildings every eight years.

Space within campus boundaries is the primary constraint for any program growth on campus. With many aging buildings and with constant pressure to accommodate new technologies, practice patterns, programs, and changing codes, there is constant pressure for new construction. Acquiring capital for new construction, however, directly competes with capital demands for new equipment and Information Technology development.

Departmental and program competition for new space is fierce, and all proposals for new construction are tested through efficiency of space utilization (e.g. volume of throughput), business plans, and return on investment. Reaching consensus on what to build and how to finance a new project typically takes three years. The actual design through project delivery can take over five years.

What are we doing in our newer buildings to increase capacity for change?

As we plan for new facilities we face significant pent-up demand for program growth space and a need to correct existing space deficiencies. However, the need to achieve a minimum short-term return on investment pushes us to design densely programmed space following immediate priorities. Further, attempts to accommodate the greatest number of departments results in a building that functions like a "Swiss watch" rather than providing for program elements and "soft space" for lower intensity use that can be converted in the future for more intensive use. It is difficult to achieve the right balance between "tight fit" and "loose fit." While it is possible to initially program low intensity spaces for future conversion to higher intensity functions, demand for quick ROI or for higher intensity uses needed in the short term generally takes priority by the time the building is under construction.

Our response has been to expect building designs to provide larger basic building elements. This has been a consistent trend. Larger floor plates, increasing structural grid spacing, higher floor-to-floor heights, increased (and dedicated) horizontal and vertical distribution capacity of mechanical (more air changes) and electrical (plug load) systems and distribution, with room for expansion, and larger room sizes. Specifically, we see these trends:

- *Increasing the size of floor plates.* The trend has been from small floor plate buildings fit into existing small sites, to multi-building demolition programs with more contiguous space, rationalizing connections between buildings to improve materials and pedestrian flow and utilities distribution campus wide.
- *Regularized floor plate shape and increasing floor plate depth.* Earlier clinical buildings (1917–1969) tended toward linear form (long and narrow), with aspect ratios of around 4:1, with building width of 50–80 ft (15.2–24.4 m). Recent construction has aspect ratios of between 1:1 and 3:1, but with widths of 110–220 ft (33.5–67.1 m). Greater width allows more capacity for variable functional layouts, but at the cost of

lost access to natural light. This is a trade-off that recognizes evidence that habitable healthcare spaces should have natural illumination.
- *Increasing typical structural grid spacing.* Regardless of use, there has been a steady trend toward larger grid spacing. Steel construction starting in 1969 allowed the increase in spans. The Lunder Building grid is 32 x 36 ft (9.1 x 11 m to 9.8 x 11 m).
- *Higher floor-to-floor dimensions.* In our newest buildings floor-to-floor heights are 13.5 ft (4.1 m) for ambulatory, 14 ft (4.3 m) for inpatient care, 16 ft (4.9 m) for imaging and procedure. These dimensions correspond to increased structural grid dimensions and offer space for horizontal distribution of air and utilities, though this raises a conflict with physical connections to existing campus buildings, which are typically 12 ft (3.7 m) floor-to-floor.
- *Increased mechanical and electrical capacity.* Building code and MGH standards for air changes in ambulatory buildings have increased. Early 20th century buildings depended on operable windows. Standards have increased from two air changes per hour in 1981 to six air changes in 2004. For inpatient space, there has been a similar trend from operable windows to two air changes from 1939 to 1969; and from four air changes with full HEPA filtration in 1990 to six air changes in 2011 with full HEPA filtration. Operating rooms ranged from ten air changes in 1939 to the current standard of 25 air changes per hour.
- *Room sizes are larger and more repetitive.* The exam, inpatient, and operating rooms have followed national trends by increasing in size.
- *Exam rooms* increased from an average of 98 sf (9.1 m^2) in 1981 to 112 sf (10.4 m^2) in 2004, a 13% increase.
- *Single inpatient rooms* increased from 228 sf (21.4 m^2) in 1990 to 290 sf (26.9 m^2) in 2011, an increase of about 30%.
- *Average operating rooms* ranged from 200 to 625 sf (18.6 to 58.1 m^2) from 1939 to 1990, but both OR and hybrid OR sizes are standard in the 600–700 sf (55.7–65-m^2) range in Lunder.

Standardization of room sizes allows for interchangeability and will presumably reduce future special layout renovation costs, especially when access to electrical and low-voltage wiring, pipes, and ducts is assured for their upgrade. For example, Yawkey adopted a standard of 110 sf (10.2 m^2) for exam, treatment, and offices. Lunder has a procedure room standard of 600 sf (55.7 m^2), rather than customized sizing, to encourage interchangeability of use, and a patient room size of 290 sf (26.9 m^2) for both acute and intensive care.

The Lunder Building: choices and compromises

The Lunder Building at MGH is a 530,000 sf (49,238 m^2) structure completed in 2011 at the center of the MGH campus. It is an expansion of core clinical services and includes 150 inpatient acute and intensive care beds, 28 operating and hybrid procedure-imaging rooms, Radiation Oncology, Emergency Services expansion, sterile processing and new receiving and materials management departments. There are ten floors above grade and four floors below grade, and the new building connects to two buildings, the Ellison and White Buildings, at Basement through Level 3, and by bridge at Level 2 to the Yawkey Center for Outpatient Care.

- *Floor-to-floor height.* Industry standard design and engineering recommendations are for 16 ft (4.9 m) inpatient and 18 ft (5.5 m) procedure and imaging floor-to-floor height standards to accommodate MEP requirements. But most MGH buildings have 12 ft (3.7 m) floor-to-floor heights. On the Lunder Building the decision was made to limit connections to the adjacent buildings to four floors where pedestrian traffic and logistical connections were most critical. The floors that connect to existing core structures are 12 ft (3.7 m) floor-to-floor, yet contain receiving, under-building ambulance discharge, and procedure rooms. The Boston zoning code restricts building height at this site, and a compromise was made for 14 ft (4.3 m) floor-to-floor height for inpatient units and 16 ft (4.9 m) floor-to-floor height for procedural space to allow an additional floor within the zoning envelope. Use of Building Information Modeling (BIM) helped ensure MEP coordination and fit with appropriate access to individual valves, access panels, and equipment.
- *Structural grid size.* A bay spacing of approximately 30 x 36 ft (9.1 x 11 m) was chosen, at the maximum range of structural steel and cost efficiency corresponding to the floor-to-floor dimensions and plenum space for horizontal MEP distribution. This coordinates with an enlarged patient room size (15 ft [4.6 m] wide), and increases the efficiency of useable floor space, eases distribution of services above ceilings, and potentially allows more flexibility on adjacent spaces and lower floors for future change to allow easier changes to MEP services.
- *Mechanical floors.* The rooftop penthouse size was limited to 30% of roof area to increase useable space under city zoning height formulas, and a mid-building, 30 ft (9.1 m) high mechanical floor with stacked air handlers serves both lower and upper portions of the building. Equipment on the mechanical floor is closely packed, resulting in limited access to install, remove, and replace mechanical equipment, which may compromise capacity for future upgrading. To mitigate that risk, the mechanical components themselves are of high quality with basic components of longer than usual life, with the plan to increase performance in the future by exchanging elements, such as more dense coils in the air handling units. The level of infrastructure redundancy and reliability is high with looped or parallel distribution, cross-connected internally, to ensure uninterrupted service for required testing, repair or replacement, and cross-connection of MEP services with adjacent buildings which allows replacement of major systems in those buildings without affecting occupancy and hospital operations.

- *Adaptable infrastructure.* MEP infrastructure equipment has been oversized by 20% over current program requirements, to accommodate future demand, with the anticipation that the major mechanical systems will be replaced within 30 years. Branch distribution has been oversized by 30% in the anticipation that it is more difficult to replace distribution branches because they are embedded in chases and behind fire-rated partitions and less accessible than major mechanical equipment. Floors can be changed to full negative pressure to accommodate contagious epidemics, and ring ducts allow work on parts of floors without shutting down the entire floor.
- *Soft space.* There is very little soft space in the building. While soft space was considered as a strategy for future growth and flexibility, programming and design decisions by clinical services and by the administration focused on maximizing functionality and short-term return on investment.

Conclusions

At MGH, we use our facilities very intensively. We have a 96% inpatient occupancy rate; MRIs are utilized 16 hours a day; the Emergency Department was built for 65,000 visits per year, but is currently approaching 110,000 visits per year. All facility utilization data is at the highest end of the range, and indicates overutilization. There is accommodation capacity in some functions by extending hours (ambulatory, ORs, imaging, Diagnostics and Treatment) but there are operational challenges to doing so.

We use buildings for a long time, and, to avoid excessive disruption, we do not change use often. While we continue to make major investments in upgrading older buildings, we tend to reduce their intensity of use over time. Renewing an intensely built-up campus is challenging and disruptive, but renovations are common. It is desirable to avoid disruption, but there is no significant available swing space to allow construction. Physical connections (i.e. people, material and utility distribution systems and pathways between and through buildings) are important to maintain.

Ideally our facilities would achieve loose fit, long life, low life-cycle cost, and ease of flexibility and adaptability. This would allow us to selectively upgrade intensity of use in response to changing demands. In buildings with sufficient structural capacity, the ability to upgrade MEP equipment at a later date without substantial disruption would be valuable.

Given the financial challenges facing hospitals in the United States, capital investments that maximize a short-term return on investment are prioritized. Investment in possibly higher-cost, long-life buildings is challenging when organizations are driven to short-term return on investment. Separating ROI analysis of a permanent base building from a more mutable fit-out could improve understanding of long-term return, because ROI is largely related to the fit-out rather than the performance of the base building's infrastructure. Small renovations, on the other hand, respond quickly to department-level demands, and can be "good enough."

We would likely reduce costs, avoid disruption, and increase building performance if we built with greater capacity for change. If we made a greater investment in base building infrastructure, our buildings would likely last longer and perform better over time. However, while higher floor-to-floor heights, larger structural grid size, increased floor loading, and supersized infrastructure undoubtedly have value, it is difficult to quantify the value of investment when the building is constructed and even more difficult to obtain funding for an investment that does not quickly increase return.

Our challenge going forward is to begin the quantification of benefits that result from investment in capacity for future flexibility and a higher standard of construction. This accounting would be supported by widespread agreement in the healthcare industry and the A/E community on the identification of specific "flexibility" strategies and their attributes and behavior over time.

Notes

1 Lunder Project: Architects: NBBJ; Structural Engineers: McNamara Salvia; Engineers: Thomson Consultants.
2 Yawkey Center for Outpatient Care: Base Building: Michael Fieldman Architect with Cambridge Seven Associates; Interiors and Clinical Planning (Fit-out): Perkins & Will with Steffian Bradley Architects; Historic Consultant: Ann Beha Architects; Structural Engineers: McNamara Salvia; Engineers: Thomson Consultants.

References

Latimer, S, H Gutknecht, and K Hardesty (2008). Analysis of Hospital Facility Growth: Are We Supersizing Health Care? *Health Environments Research and Design (HERD) Journal*, 1(4), pp. 70–88.

Washburn, FA (1939). *The Massachusetts General Hospital*. Boston: Houghton Mifflin Co.

Chapter 5

Planning for change

Banner Estrella Medical Center, Phoenix, Arizona

John Pangrazio, Ryan Hullinger, Mark Patterson, and Anne Friedrich Bilsbarrow

Introduction

This chapter presents a case study of applied principles of "planning for change" at Banner Estrella Medical Center in Phoenix, Arizona. NBBJ completed the planning and architecture of the first phase in 2005. A second phase was completed by SmithGroup's Phoenix office in 2014.

The medical center of the future: Change by choice, not by chance

Historically, the planning and design of healthcare facilities – like many other building types – have been optimized for first use. On many healthcare campuses in the United States today, one can encounter a collection of buildings, each built for a specific use by a different architecture office, sometimes awkwardly linked to other buildings, and unable to adapt easily to evolving programmatic needs.

Clients of healthcare facilities increasingly recognize that medical centers must be designed to embrace change by planning for it, to facilitate both internal change and growth and to avoid wasteful and ultimately more expensive cycles of demolition and rebuilding. Planning for change should also promote healing, be affordable, be sustainable, and maximize a building's useful life.

Changing by choice, not by chance, requires clients – aided by design service providers – to think through what is likely to change and what is not without attempting to control the future. Care delivery methods, medical technology, best medical care practices and even building codes are constantly advancing and directly impact architecture design and functional layout.

NBBJ's healthcare design teams recognize that what was state-of-the-art and best-practice just a few years ago is likely to become obsolete in the future. It happens every day in healthcare; therefore, space is needed that can support the design or layout of those functions which are highly likely to change during the life of the building. We define such space as "adaptable space."

On the other hand, from a physical planning perspective, some elements of physical layout and design – mechanical, electrical, and plumbing distribution pathways, and major building circulation – are not subject to frequent change, and therefore become the stable infrastructure of planning. We refer to this element of planning the portion of the layout that need not change as "permanent."

Given this understanding of "adaptability" and "permanence," NBBJ developed a planning framework that enables a facility to evolve by establishing a rational system for internal change and facility growth. We organize a building into permanent zones for circulation and infrastructure, and adaptable zones for rapid change with minimal disruption and cost. Conceptually, by keeping permanent infrastructure elements out of the spaces subject to more frequent change, the redevelopment of these areas is significantly less costly and disruptive. This strategy has been evolving over a long period and was applied in the Banner Estrella project discussed here (see Figure 5.1).

The ideal "flexible zone" for departmental or room layouts would be completely free of any impediments such as columns, mechanical shafts, or mechanical systems serving the floor above (see Figure 5.2). Ideally, the volume of space would also be high enough to accommodate any and all potential technologies and medical equipment. However, this dogmatic implementation of such a "flexible zone" would be both cost-prohibitive and, one suspects, unnecessary.

Our practice over many years has taught us that this fully open-ended, "loose-fit" ideal is in fact unnecessary. By studying more closely a range of spaces, from the entire site to the individual room, we have determined there is a practical placement of columns, floor-to-floor heights and placement of mechanical systems that works at all levels; when put together, these become what we call "space fields."

Figure 5.1 Circulation and Infrastructure Systems – the three-dimensional framework which organizes and integrates the structural skeleton, with pathways for the distribution of building systems (heating, cooling, ventilation, plumbing, medical gasses, electrical, communications) and major circulation systems (vertical and horizontal systems of movement of supplies, patients, staff, visitors).

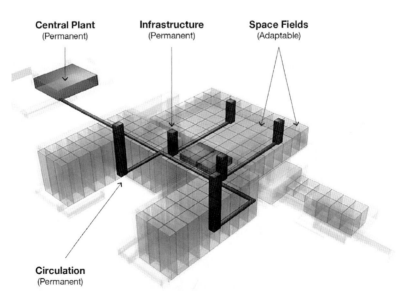

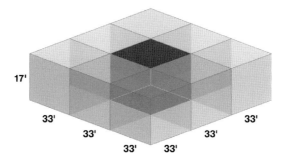

Figure 5.2 The space field (column grid and floor-to-floor heights indicated) accommodates all clinical and procedural services; HVAC systems, mechanical shafts, electrical/IT rooms, elevator cores, and stairs are excluded from the space field zone.

The overall master plan strategy for MEP distribution was based on locating permanent vertical MEP distribution zones on the perimeter of the space field zones. In the Banner Estrella project, the maximum horizontal MEP "reach" would be across three space field modules (approximately 96 ft) in the north/south direction, as the building's future growth would be to the east. After examining various scenarios of functional layouts in the space fields, this "reach" was determined to have the capacity to accommodate any necessary MEP horizontal runs above the (functional space) ceilings and serving the functional space below those ceilings. Some MEP systems (e.g. drainage pipes) serving functions on the floor above were also routed above dropped ceilings, because this design approach is common, has lower first cost than alternatives, and the cycle of expected intervention/change and maintenance of these systems is low.

Planning for change applied to Banner Estrella Medical Center from day one

Banner Estrella Medical Center in Phoenix, Arizona, is an example not only of NBBJ's practice of planning for adaptation and physical change, but also of how those changes are implemented over time, independent of the architecture and engineering teams leading the planning and implementation work. As was the case at Banner Estrella, some members of the client leadership team have changed since the initial building program was implemented.

Banner Estrella Medical Center was designed with future change in mind. A site was chosen to allow for substantial horizontal growth while accepting city urban design regulations. This future growth was graphically simulated to show how the medical center could expand in increments to three times its original size. First, the team planned the campus to full potential build-out and then scaled it back to the Phase I project (about a third of the ultimate build-out). This smaller project was initially built. Key to this strategy was establishing a permanent infrastructure/circulation spine and attached zones of space that would easily accommodate internal change or expansion. Over time the spine could grow and more space could be added to it (see Figure 5.3).

Figure 5.3
Infrastructure – the building is organized along a central spine sized with capacity to furnish all mechanical, electrical, and plumbing needs for patient care and support spaces up to the maximum projected campus build-out.

NBBJ's challenge was to move beyond traditional "first use" master planning principles, which are typically based on the premise that the master plan is a succession of building projects, with each incremental project designed around an initial set of programmatic needs. Yet our own observations of healthcare design suggest programmatic needs change every seven to 12 years, while hospitals have a useful life based on construction of 50 years or more. By planning for the future without requiring the client to commit to building all the infrastructure initially, the design team was able to synchronize these life cycles at minimal cost.

When fully built out, the 50-acre (20.23 ha) Banner Estrella campus would be able to support a 1.2-million-ft^2 (111,483 m^2) hospital with three patient towers and a total of 600 beds. In the planning phase,

NBBJ laid out the "completed" three-tower hospital with all infrastructure in place, including vertical and horizontal circulation routes and major mechanical and electrical equipment and pathways. The team then worked backwards, subtracting elements until arriving at the 450,000-ft^2 (41,800 m^2), single-tower hospital that was constructed as Phase I (see Figure 5.4). This strategy ensured that everything was in place and poised for growth and internal change when needed, without interrupting current operations (see Figures 5.5 and 5.6).

As noted, NBBJ's concept developed an approach based on a simple set of principles: needs that are constantly changing require short-term, flexible planning responses and are accommodated in the aggregate of space fields; and needs that change very little over time are accommodated within zones that serve as a permanent spine.

Growth and expansion programming

The master plan organized services into two function types: (1) inpatient care and (2) diagnostics and treatment (D&T). Each occupies built volumes organized around and attached to the initial build-out of the infrastructure spine. This spine was intended to accommodate major entries and vertical and horizontal circulation, to link to the central utility plant and loading dock for energy distribution and material movement, and to set the "plug in" points for future buildings.

In Phase I, major entrances, user circulation pathways and parking zones were set, not for just the initial phase, but also for the ultimate growth of the campus. As additional program components were added (inpatient care, diagnostics and treatment, ancillary space), the spine would be extended to create new "plug in" points for subsequent new construction. The central

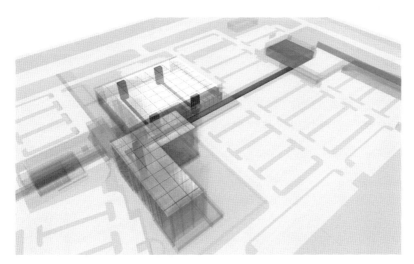

Figure 5.4
Phase I was completed in 2005 and houses one patient tower with 172 beds and one diagnostic and treatment wing.

Figure 5.5
Phase II added a second patient tower, for a total of approximately 400 beds, and was designed by SmithGroup and constructed without disrupting hospital operations.

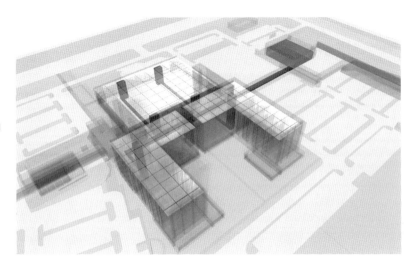

Figure 5.6
Phase III was projected to expand diagnostic and treatment services; the fully expanded hospital would have three patient towers, 600 beds and a total of 1.2 million sf (111,483 m^2).

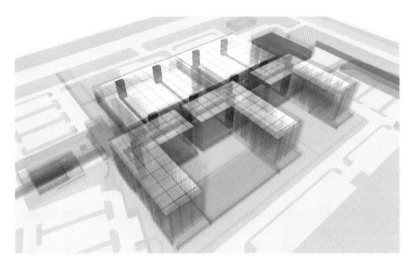

plant and loading dock were strategically located (linked via a sublevel) to accommodate all future growth without needing to be shut down or relocated (see Figure 5.7). The spine creates three distinct user flows: material, public/operations, and staff/inpatients.

The subtractive approach to master planning has many advantages for Phase II and subsequent phases. It is a disciplined process for determining the most efficient use of the site for construction, parking, green space and other uses. In addition, it enables an approach to real estate utilization and business/financial planning by zoning and assigning value to site resources for the optimum sizing and placement of floor plate configurations (beds, D&T, medical office buildings).

Planning for change

Figure 5.7
A sublevel links the utility plant to the main hospital along the central infrastructure spine.

Phase I included the initial program components required for economic viability (see Figure 5.8). Level 1 includes the birthing center and emergency services bundled within two building volumes: inpatient care and D&T. On this level, the spine acts as a public gallery, connecting main lobbies and entries with public circulation to medical services. On Level 2, the spine serves as staff and inpatient circulation between clinical and inpatient care units. On the lower (sub-grade) level, it houses material circulation and building systems distribution between the loading dock/central utility plant and all hospital services.

The design of horizontal and vertical circulation separates certain flows – inpatient and outpatient, and patients and materials, for example. Two unencumbered "expansion faces" (see Figures 5.8 and 5.9) are available for future diagnostics, treatment and ancillary functions. The spine was designed to be extended to accommodate incremental expansions to D&T and inpatient care services.

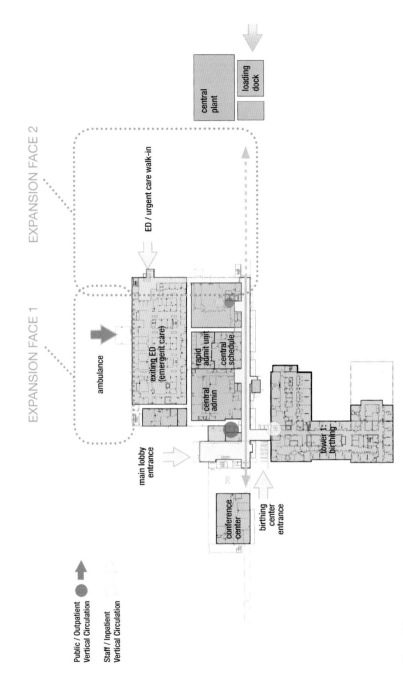

Figure 5.8
Phase I/Built Concept/Floor Level 1.

Full build-out plans could accommodate the ultimate growth of the campus, whether in a single phase (as shown), or in many phases (as has been done). In this plan, the spine has been extended to expand the central plant and loading dock, two additional inpatient care units have been added, the Phase I D&T has expanded along Expansion Face 1 and a second major D&T expansion has occurred along Expansion Face 2.

Growth scenarios may include the expansion of existing services or the addition of totally new buildings (outpatient and inpatient) with autonomous interior and exterior entries. The doubling of program area could be accommodated without changing wayfinding on the site, without requiring new entries and lobbies, or compromising established user circulation pathways. Exterior wall panels could be removed and reused on the new face during construction. Similarly, the design of the spine's plug-and-play circulation and mechanical, electrical, plumbing, and IT infrastructure eliminates disruption of critical user flows and minimizes service interruptions during construction.

How Phase II was planned and built

The success of planning a medical campus to accommodate change depends not only on the appropriateness of the guiding principles but also on the owner's commitment to those principles over time. The guiding principles implemented by NBBJ in Phase I served as the starting point for SmithGroup's Phase II addition of an approximately 170-bed nursing tower and associated renovations.

The SmithGroup team was familiar with the planning principles established for the Estrella campus by NBBJ, but did not interact directly with NBBJ staff in the Phase II work. A few years prior to this, the SmithGroup had been commissioned by Banner Health to develop a system-wide hospital template system that was strongly influenced by NBBJ's "space field" planning model. SmithGroup had previously developed a templated planning system for Kaiser Permanente, a large healthcare system in California, and was familiar with other template programs (Christiansen et al., 2008). SmithGroup had also subsequently implemented the template in the design of Banner Ironwood, a small hospital outside of Phoenix, for the same client. As that project's size was much smaller than the template, it served as an exercise in adapting broad planning principles to varied applications. This experience proved to be useful as the planning team identified points where the initial planning assumptions of the Banner template could be modified.

Changes to underlying planning assumptions

The first issue identified in the Phase II planning was that in the time between the original Banner Estrella master plan (2004) and Phase II (2012), the State of Arizona had changed the version of the Facility

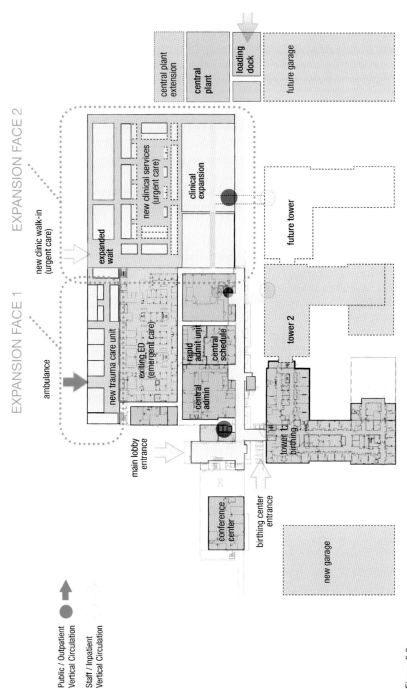

Figure 5.9
Final Phase/Full Build-out Concept (not yet implemented)/Floor Level 1.

Guidelines Institute's Guidelines for Design and Construction of Hospitals and Outpatient Facilities (FGI, 2018) it used to review and approve projects. Specifically, changes to the required clearances at the head and foot of the patient bed dictated that space be added to each room, increasing the overall length of both legs of the nursing tower added in Phase II in comparison to the Phase I nursing tower. The extension of the north/south wing resulted in the tower encroaching within the urban design setback zone established in the original plan. Multiple options were explored to address this, including reducing the number of rooms per floor. Banner felt that maintaining the number of beds per unit was critical for staffing and operational efficiency, and the decision was made to request a zoning variance from the city of Phoenix to allow the longer tower to be built.

More importantly, Banner Health had changed its original vision (shown in Figure 5.6) for the ultimate build-out of the Estrella campus. In its template development work, Banner had assumed that all of its Phoenix-area hospitals would eventually grow to roughly 600 beds, which would have required three towers at Estrella. As new hospitals were built, Banner determined that campuses of about 400 beds, or two towers, were a better model from a staffing and operations perspective.

While the original plan for the Estrella campus assumed that the D&T block would need to double in size when the second patient tower was built, Banner's market studies did not indicate the volume of demand that would support an expansion of that size. The option of a smaller expansion was rejected, as Banner felt that multiple small expansions to the D&T block would be too disruptive. Instead, Banner chose to place a limited set of diagnostic and treatment functions on the second floor of the new patient tower. Departments in the Phase I D&T block that needed to expand would do so into soft space (space with low-intensity use such as office or storage space) that had been built as part of Phase I, and the functions occupying those spaces would be relocated to the basement of the new tower. NBBJ's conceptual framework was adaptable to this major shift in the owner's priorities.

New needs identified

The SmithGroup team initiated the Phase II design process with a detailed analysis of existing conditions, using laser scanning and in-depth programming meetings. While NBBJ's general planning framework was clear to the new team, the specific application of the concept to individual departments required deeper analysis.

The existing Emergency Department was slated to expand in place; the direction of expansion was determined by the location of administrative soft space next to it. However, the original location of the patient walk-in entry did not work well with this expansion plan. Evaluation of the site plan revealed that there was space available for a small addition that would allow the entrance to be relocated, essentially flipping the flow of the department, to better incorporate the expansion area.

Discussions with the Women's and Infants' Services (WIS) department revealed that the NICU (Neonatal Intensive Care Unit) needed to be expanded and upgraded to provide a higher level of service. Again, revisions to the FGI guidelines required substantially more square footage than before. And, while not part of the original master plan, the need for a large observation unit at the Estrella campus had also become clear.

The Phase I exterior building material provides an example of the unexpected challenges that evolving technologies can create for design teams. The increased use of wireless communications had shown that the original exterior copper cladding was an unexpectedly efficient shielding material, requiring that the Phase II exterior cladding material be different.

The decision not to expand the D&T as indicated in the master plan also created the need to reconsider patient flow. The master plan and hospital templates had assumed that the towers would connect to the D&T at an elevator core. Since this core would not be built in Phase II, the connection between the new tower and existing D&T had to be modified from the original master plan, to ensure proper separation of public and patient flows.

Adaptation challenges

The challenge to the SmithGroup team was to modify the master plan and Banner templates to the specific set of circumstances on the Estrella campus. The general outline of the plan proved sound. The central plant location, the utility tunnel connection, and the general form of the new tower could remain as planned. The changes to the master plan are driven by the revised planning assumptions related to the sequencing of expansion – specifically, the decision to add a patient tower without expanding the D&T.

Site adaptation

The SmithGroup team first conducted a series of capacity studies at the campus master planning level to illustrate possible development options (see Figure 5.10).

The alternative that was chosen maintained space for future expansion of the D&T, allowed the helipad to remain in place, complied with the desired ratio of four parking spaces per bed, and placed the 650-space parking garage according to the originally approved site master plan. The selected option did, however, require rezoning to allow the patient tower to extend into the 200-foot setback from the residential neighborhood to the south, which the City of Phoenix approved.

Figure 5.10
Capacity studies of the site considering new development.

Basement renovations

The Phase II basement renovations demonstrated the efficacy of NBBJ's "space field" concepts implemented in Phase I. The kitchen, pharmacy, lab, and central sterile departments all needed to expand in place. The relocation of materials management and environmental services, the downsizing of the health information management department, and the repurposing of the autopsy suite allowed each of these departments to expand with a minimum of disruption.

First floor adaptation for Women's and Infants' Services (WIS)

The WIS expansion grew substantially when the level of need for NICU beds became clear. The original master plan had assumed eight NICU beds, but substantial development around Estrella has increased the population of young families, leading to a need for not just more NICU beds but also a higher acuity level of beds. The original dual tower plan did not provide enough space and did not support the adjacencies and workflow patterns needed for the department to function effectively. The solution was to join the two towers at the first floor, creating an enclosed courtyard for family members and patients. To allow the courtyard to be serviced, an entry was created from the basement so that equipment could be moved without disturbing the nursing unit. Again, NBBJ's overall planning framework was sufficiently robust to support new and enlarged services.

First floor adaptation: Emergency Department

The original master plan had placed the main ED patient entrance and waiting room at the northeast corner of the D&T block so that it would be centrally located when the D&T expanded. The overall master plan strategy was that the ED, with a very likely increase in demand, would expand over time to the east (since there was a limit to the amount of real estate available to the north – see Figure 5.10). It was also assumed that the waiting and reception areas would remain in place, the existing public and staff circulation pathways would remain intact, the ambulance entrance would remain as is, and public vehicular parking, drop-off, and public entrance would expand in place.

During the Phase II expansion, it was decided that, because the Emergency Department would now expand into adjacent "soft" space, the expansion would instead occur at the southwest corner. The planning solution flipped the department, placing a new waiting area on the west side (see Figure 5.11). This did result in a loss of surface parking, but the parking garages that were also part of the Phase II project more than replaced those spaces. The additional spaces available in the garages made it possible to dedicate all of the spaces to the west of the ED entrance to ED parking only, improving wayfinding and access (see Figure 5.12).

The changes to the FGI guidelines also affected the Emergency Department. Originally planned without a seclusion room, the new guidelines required that one be added.

Second floor adaptations

The most striking departure from both the NBBJ master plan and the Banner hospital template occurred at the second floor. Banner's demand studies performed just before initiating Phase II had not shown a need for the Surgery or Emergency departments to expand to the point where the cost of doubling the size of the D&T block would be justified, and Banner didn't wish to expand in smaller increments. Therefore, the second floor of the new nursing/bed tower became the location for departments that were originally to be located in the expanded D&T block. Cath Labs, Endoscopy, and selected imaging functions were located there, along with shared prep and recovery spaces. As the tower footprint had been expanded on the first floor to accommodate the expanded NICU, the second floor could also be made wider than a standard nursing floor. The expanded footprint of the second bed tower provided roof space for the additional mechanical equipment needed by the Cath Labs (see Figure 5.13).

Nursing unit adaptations

The expanded bed clearances in the patient rooms required under the new FGI were the driving factor in the addition to the nursing tower. The original master plan and the Banner templates both assumed that the nursing towers would each connect to the D&T block with an elevator core that extended from the D&T up to the nursing units on each floor. As a cost-saving measure, Banner chose not to build this elevator core, relying instead on an extended elevator core within the nursing tower. To maintain the separation of patient and public traffic, a dedicated patient bridge was provided at the second floor to connect the D&T block to the patient tower (see Figure 5.13).

Utilities and central plant

The central utility plant was expanded in Phase II, as had been expected in the master plan. The utility tunnel had been designed with expansion in mind, with knock-out panels and utility connections in place where the future towers were expected to be located.

Design adaptations

Both cost and function drove the need to change the exterior finishes for the new nursing tower. The shape of the site had driven a master plan that placed most of the patient room windows on the east and west walls of the tower, demanding careful attention to the sun-shading needed in this climatic region. The original NBBJ design created a sawtooth facade

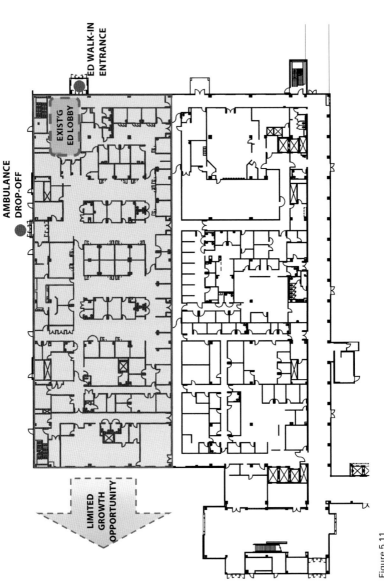

Figure 5.11
The original Emergency Department layout limited the future growth of the department because of site constraints, and created a significant challenge in renovating without disrupting emergency services.

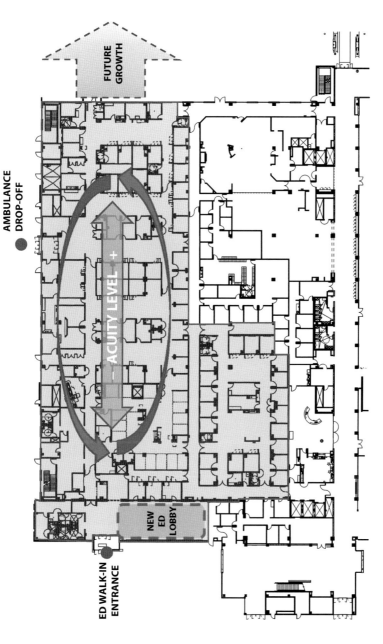

Figure 5.12
Emergency Department renovations included the displacement of unrelated "soft spaces" and a small addition on the west to accommodate a new ED walk-in entrance/lobby. This allowed for the relocation and replacement of ED "front-end" program spaces without disrupting emergency services. Additionally, by moving the walk-in entrance to the west, it allowed for future grown of the department to the east.

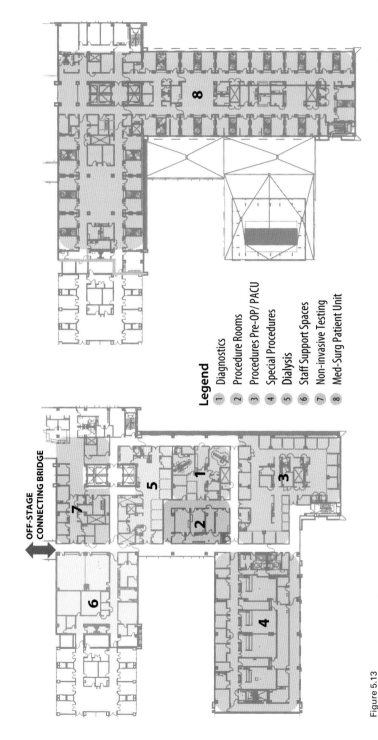

Figure 5.13
The second floor (left image) of the nursing tower was adapted to house expanded diagnostic and treatment (D&T) functions. All remaining upper floors (right image) house acuity-ADA (Americans with Disabilities Act) patient rooms. A bridge was added to provide a dedicated patient/staff connection from the new tower to the existing D&T block.

configuration at the windows, allowing the angled portion of the wall to provide shading. Banner choose not to repeat this in the Phase II expansion because attached exterior sun shading screens were more cost-effective. Extensive shading studies were conducted to ensure that this approach would provide the necessary protection without compromising patient views.

While decisions about exterior materials reduced the amount of copper compared to Phase I, design continuity was maintained by using copper as an accent to highlight entrances. Understanding that the campus would continue to evolve and to limit the amount of investment in walls that will eventually be removed, an inexpensive exterior insulation and finish system was used where the buildings could be expected to expand. Interior design decisions followed the Phase I design, with modifications to conform to newly established Banner finish standards. These were driven by a desire to establish new system-wide cleaning and infection control policies and procedures. The original building had used natural wood accents, but the new tower recreated the wood appearance with more easily cleaned synthetic materials. Rubber flooring had been established as a new standard in place of sheet vinyl and was used throughout the new building. The evolution of the materials palette illustrates the scope of change that must be considered in planning or adding to a healthcare facility. Even in the relatively short time between Phases 1 and 2, new materials that provided better infection control became available.

The importance of natural light in healing environments has long been established. Given this, the design team opened the cafeteria to the central spine, allowing for natural light and views of the healing garden. Sound control panels were installed on the cafeteria walls to address concerns about noise levels.

Lessons learned

With changes in regulations, demographics, costs of construction and medical practices, and the resulting uncertainty, the challenge for healthcare clients and design service providers is to identify those overarching organizational and design concepts that can be held steady under multiple scenarios. In the case of the Banner Estrella master plan, the general development framework – consisting of a primary circulation spine with the D&T block on one side and patient towers on the other, with the central plant and dock at the end – proved sufficiently robust to accommodate substantial changes in the overall campus program.

SmithGroup's philosophy throughout the project was to respect NBBJ's planning concepts while seeking opportunities to improve operational efficiency, enhance the healing environment, and improve operational cost-effectiveness. The modifications at the cafeteria created an improved experience, providing a more open, inviting space. The new finish palette improved the cleanability of patient care spaces. Changes to the Emergency Department reflected both changes to Banner's operational model as well as a reorientation that allows for further expansion.

This illustrates perhaps the most powerful lesson. Planning for change and growth is a continuous exercise involving multiple disciplines, multiple design firms, and changing client leadership. In a constantly changing context, planners must be prepared to continually challenge and re-evaluate both their assumptions and approach.

Conclusions

The planning process established by the NBBJ team working with Banner's hospital system leadership has been tested and proven by SmithGroup's second phase expansion. Despite regulatory and market changes and a change in the design team, the essential planning framework remained sound, providing a clear organizational structure despite a program substantially different than the one originally expected. Estrella served as the prototype for Banner's planning template system-wide, and while the template continues to evolve, the basic principles – the utilities spine connected to the central plant, the D&T buildings separated from the bed towers – continue to guide future projects. Of necessity, the template continues to change as it responds to the real-world conditions of site, market, and other considerations.

Both NBBJ and SmithGroup continue to evaluate, implement, and refine design strategies for change in healthcare facilities across the world, in collaboration with clients and owners and informed by research and science. It should be noted that the current Facility Guidelines Institute guidelines for healthcare facilities in North America support our approach, by suggesting that planning should "allow flexibility in some design to support development of facilities that will be functional over the long term" (Facility Guidelines Institute, 2018). However, the FGI guidelines, while intended to permit flexibility, do not require it – and some authorities having jurisdiction (AHJs) may mistake the absence of explicit requirements for a prohibition against flexibility. In any case, design professionals and healthcare systems' leaders need to advocate for designs that allow for functional change.

Development of the shared knowledge base about planning, design, and construction strategies that address the long-term utility value of healthcare facilities remains the responsibility of everyone who owns, operates, plans, and builds. The work that is being done – in universities, private practices, consultancies and in public research units – needs to be recognized, shared, and supported for the benefit of all.

References

Christiansen, C, S Bruce, and H Chung (2008, February). A Template for Change. *Healthcare Design*, 8(1), pp. 32–36. www.healthcaredesignmagazine.com/architecture/template-change/.

Facility Guidelines Institute (2018). 2018 Edition. www.fgiguidelines.org/guidelines/2018-fgi-guidelines.

Chapter 6

The evolution of a hospital planned for change

Nirit Putievsky Pilosof

Introduction

Healthcare architecture requires a design strategy for future change. A whole life cycle approach to hospital operations must take into account the constant and rapid change of healthcare environments resulting from transformations in medicine, technology, and sociology. The Open Building approach, developed initially for housing and now implemented in the healthcare and educational facilities sectors, recognizes different life spans of building elements and distributed decision-making processes related to built environment transformations, and proposes a design strategy to address the resulting complexity. The approach addresses the conflict between functionality and flexibility and argues that hospitals should be designed to accommodate a variety of functions in order to gain value over time.

The Open Building approach proposes a strategy to design hospitals for flexibility also known as "System Separation" (Kendall, 2005, 2008, 2017) in which a primary system ("base building"), secondary system ("fit-out"), and tertiary system (furnishings, fixtures, and equipment) are distinguished. This method recognizes the different life spans, investment and often distributed (rather than unified) decision-making processes associated with each system level. Since the 1960s, architects have developed theories and methods to anticipate, to the greatest extent possible, where changes are most likely to occur and to design hospitals for optimum flexibility and expansion. While many studies investigate the theories of hospital design for future change, only a few document how hospitals actually have changed over time and if the theories stand in practice. Previous studies have revealed that some hospitals that were designed to be "infinitely" flexible and dynamic, did not fulfill their original vision. They did not expand, and their interior redevelopment was limited in scope (Pilosof, 2005).

This chapter explores the Open Building approach in the context of the Sammy Ofer Heart Building at the Tel Aviv Sourasky Medical Center in Israel, a building, whose initial design process began in 2005, and that was still under construction in 2018. Research documented the evolutionary process of the building from its initial design, and illustrated the changes that were made to the spatial and technical environment resulting from demands for specialized medical units, advances in medical technology, transformation in social healthcare norms, and adaptive health policy standards. The study classified each change by its typology, the level on which the change occurred, the reasons for the change, and the consequences of the change on hospital operations. This information is based on an analysis of architectural documents, hospital data collection, field observation, and expert interviews. The hospital design strategy, following the Open Building or System Separation approach, is analyzed and evaluated to determine whether the design methods were sufficient to support the hospital's need for change. The research demonstrates the importance of the Open Building approach, as it enabled significant changes during all phases of the project (design, construction, and occupancy). The approach also supported the development of different functional programs, and enhanced the design process over a period of time when managers, planners, and consultants changed. The research also points out the conflicts that occur when decision-making in the design of one system level restricts the capacity of the other system levels, requiring constant and time-consuming collaboration between interdisciplinary project teams working in different offices, and which change over time.

Open Building theory

The Open Building approach was developed as a response to the rigidity of mass housing, and represents a departure from the conventional functionalist thinking and architectural management practices in which detailed programs of use (translated into floor plans) are deemed to be necessary to initiate design and produce cost calculations. John Habraken first articulated these principles in his book *Supports: An Alternative to Mass Housing*, first published in Dutch in 1961 (Habraken, 1972). Developed in the context of residential housing, Open Building principles have also been recognized to be the operative design approach to shopping centers and office buildings, and more recently, are being recognized as key to the design of sustainable and adaptable healthcare (and educational) facilities. The term "Open Building" is used to indicate a number of different, but related ideas about the making of environments: (1) The built environment is in constant transformation, and change must be recognized and understood, (2) It is a product of an ongoing, never ending design process, in which environment transforms part by part, (3) Designing is a process of distributed control, with multiple participants including professionals from different fields, and (4) Users may make design decisions as well as professionals (Habraken, 1998).

The Open Building theory distinguishes a hierarchy of levels of intervention in the built environment: higher levels serve as the setting and context in which lower levels can change without disturbing the higher level (e.g. a room (higher level) is a context for furniture (lower level) that can change without disturbing the room, but if the room changes, the furniture will need to change; i.e. the room dominates the furniture) (Habraken, 1998). This approach is often represented by the terminology of "base building" and "fit-out," or "support" and "infill." The recognition that certain "clusters" of building elements have variable life cycle values (and are often controlled by different decision-making parties) led to the definition of three system levels: *Primary level* or the "base building" (structure, envelope, egress systems, and main mechanical and supply pathways); *Secondary level* or "fit-out" (interior spatial organization and service systems specific to uses), and *Tertiary level* or FF&E (furniture, fixtures and equipment). The primary level is expected to last 100 years ± and should be designed to provide capacity for changing functions. The secondary level in expected to be useful for about 20 years, and the tertiary level, for 5–10 years. Because the life expectancy of each level differs, and control over the different levels is distributed over time among different stakeholders and planners, the decision-making process is necessarily sequential rather than an "all-at-once." The terminology of Primary/Secondary/Tertiary comes from the Canton Bern Office of Properties and Buildings System Separation strategy (see Chapter 2).

Case study: the Sammy Ofer Heart Building, Sourasky Tel Aviv Medical Center

The Sammy Ofer Heart Building at Tel Aviv Sourasky Medical Center was designed by a joint venture of Sharon Architects and Ranni Ziss Architects and was designed starting in 2005 and constructed in 2008–2011. The building, located in the center of Tel Aviv, was designed as a monolithic cube clad in glass with prominent red recessed balconies. The building was designed to connect to an adjacent, historical "Bauhaus" hospital building through an atrium with iconic red bridges (Figure 6.1). The 70 m (230 ft) high building consists of 55,000 m^2 (592,000 ft^2) and includes 13 medical floors of 3,100 m^2 (33,300 ft^2) per floor, and four underground parking floors designed with the possibility of conversion to an emergency 650-bed hospital. The 15,000 m^2 (161,400 ft^2) underground "sheltered" floors were innovatively designed to be resistant to chemical and biological warfare.

The building, defined as a cardiac care center, was initially programmed to relocate all the hospital cardiac units, clinics and surgery division onto three main floors, and to include an additional two floors for internal medicine units and outpatient clinics. Seven additional floors were also built, but left open for future programming and fit-out. Accordingly, the building was constructed in five main phases: (1) the underground emergency hospital, (2) core and envelope of floors 1–10 including a mechanical roof floor, (3) interior fit-out of floors 0–3, (4) interior fit-out of floors 4–6, and (5) interior fit-out of floors 7–10, currently still under construction in 2018 (Figure 6.4).

The project was programmed and designed by the architects in collaboration with the hospital CEO, deputy director, head of cardiology units, head nurse, and various internal and external consultants and project managers.

Figure 6.1
Design illustrations of the Sammy Ofer Heart Building, 2006.

Source: Ranni Ziss Architects & Sharon Architects.

Like most hospital facilities, the project was planned under tight budgetary, regulatory and environmental constraints. The design process, which began in 2005, reflected a variety of concepts. The realization of the project depended on finding a solution for an existing (but now obsolete) two-story outpatient building that had been constructed on the site in the 1960s for use as an emergency department. After much discussion, that building was demolished. Because the hospital management was undecided regarding their strategy and program, the design team developed a method of presenting and evaluating diverse design options for the new project.

Most hospital facilities in Israel are "tailor-made" – designed for a highly detailed functional program. The Sammy Ofer Heart Building challenged this traditional practice, because the client wanted to maximize the support of a private donation and to expand the hospital capacity to evolve in the future. The hospital CEO decided to defer the decision on the uses of seven of its 11 floors for later consideration. The need to design a base building as a "container with capacity" that could accommodate unknown functional programs led to the implementation of "the Open Building approach", although this "name" was not used at the time (Figures 6.2 and 6.3). Architect Arad Sharon declared that the building was designed to be flexible and to provide optimal space for future advances in medicine (2012). It is important however to note that the Open Building approach – as a specific set of methods and practices – was not evident to the design team of the project during the design process. Only in retrospect did this case study recognize the similarities between Open Building methods and the strategy used in designing the project. The comparison reveals what was considered at the time to be simply "good practice," and yet what was considered to be too controversial to apply.

The design process from the beginning included capacity studies to analyze if the primary system could accommodate the predicted development of the building in the future as defined by the hospital CEO and medical directors. The preliminary studies included schematic drawings of a typical floor with two inpatient medical units to illustrate the capacity for both: two identical mirrored units vs. one major unit with more ICU rooms and a minor unit with semi-private rooms (Figure 6.2). The architects were also required by the client to prepare a schematic design for the research lab and Neurology units that were expected to be installed in the shell floors of the building. The main purpose of the capacity studies was to analyze if the primary system would support future anticipated programs, the location of heavy equipment, possible connections to MEP infrastructures and efficient configuration of functions. Research for this chapter revealed that the preliminary capacity analysis study drawings were retained and were later used to evaluate the potential of the building for future change and to analyze the interfaces between the different system levels. In this sense, these drawings became a communication tool between the initial design team and the following design teams, their importance unknown at the time of the initial design, to demonstrate the Open Building approach (which at

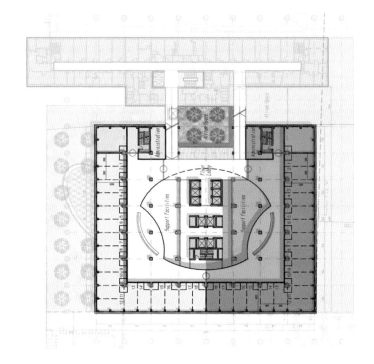
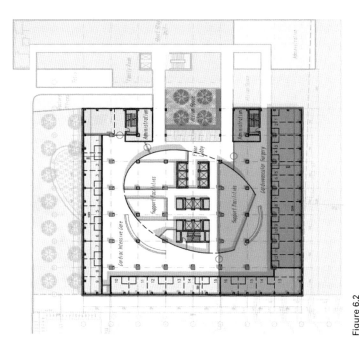

Figure 6.2
Preliminary study of schematic design options of the hospital typical floor, 2005.
Source: Ranni Ziss Architects & Sharon Architects

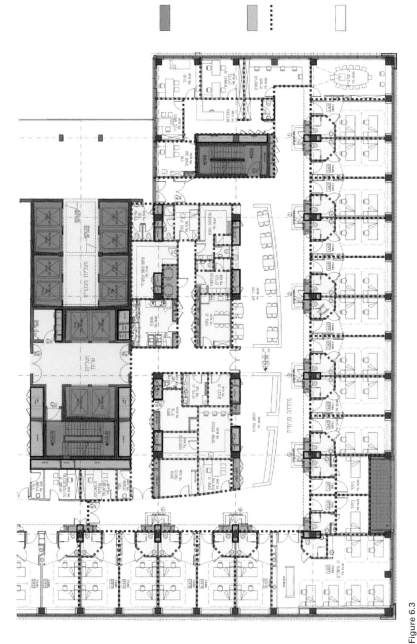

Figure 6.3
Analysis of the design of the hospital medical unit by the three system levels.
Source: Ranni Ziss Architects & Sharon Architects, and the author

that time had no formal name to the design team or client) and to explain the decision-making throughout the design process.

Analysis of the hospital design by the three system levels demonstrate the primary systems' capacity, including design with modularity of rooms, separation of functions and services, and levels (magnitudes) of change (Figure 6.3). The primary system level consists of a 7.6 m x 7.6 m structural grid, central core, distributed MEP shafts, and the building envelope. Secondary system level includes the MEP systems and the interior non-loadbearing walls. Tertiary system level consists of the ward equipment, including medical devices, furniture, and other equipment.

Research method

In order to explore the Open Building approach in the context of the Sammy Ofer Heart Building, the research reported here documented the evolutionary process of the building from its initial design in 2005 through 2018. The research was based on primary data collected from the hospital and the two architecture firms that designed the building, including architectural drawings, programming documents, and reports. The design process was analyzed based on expert interviews including (1) the hospital Deputy Director of Medical Technologies & Infrastructure Development in charge of the project management since the beginning (2005), (2) heads of medical units who were part of the hospital strategy team, (3) head nurses, (4) architects Arad Sharon and Ranni Ziss as well as other leading architects within the two architecture firms, and (5) the project managers from CPM and M. Iuclea that coordinated the design process and construction phases. Survey information was also obtained by site visits and observations of the building's performance-during-use from 2014–2018. It is also important to note that the initiative for this research was the authors' personal experience as the project's design manager, working at the Ranni Ziss Architecture firm in the years 2005–2009.

The research compared the documentation of the hospital's original design and its actual conditions as built. The information gathered is displayed in two documents: a list of the changes during the period 2005–2018 (Table 6.1), and architectural drawings and schemes (Figures 6.4 and 6.5). The building's change over time is analyzed by the changes in building typology, the level at which the change occurred (primary/secondary/tertiary systems), the reasons for the changes, and the consequences of the changes on hospital operations. The changes recorded are also analyzed by their stage in the design process and in relation to the construction phases. The changes that actually occurred in the evolution of the project are later evaluated in comparison to the Open Building approach objectives.

Changes during the project's evolution

The changes examined were classified into seven main categories: Time, Type, Cause, Design stage, Project phase, System level, and Boundary

Table 6.1 Change in practice 2005–2018

Change	Year	Type	Cause	Design Stage	Project Phase	System Level	Boundary Frictions
Shell floors 9–10	2005	Addition	Policy	Bidding	2	Primary	High
Emergency hospital floor 4	2007	Addition	Policy	Construction	1	Primary	Medium
Neurology on floor 4	2012	Completion	Medical	Construction	4	Secondary	Medium
Neurosurgery & Neurology ICU on floor 5	2013	Addition	Medical	Occupancy	4	Secondary	High
Dermatology inpatient & outpatient clinics on floor 6	2015	Addition	Medical	Occupancy	4	Secondary	Medium
Oncology inpatient & outpatient units on floor 7	2018	Relocation	Policy Medical	Occupancy	5	Secondary	High
Oncology clinics on floor 8	2018	Relocation	Policy Medical	Occupancy	5	Secondary	High
Inpatient internal medicine units on floor 9	2018	Addition	Policy Medical	Occupancy	5	Secondary	Low
Research labs on floor 10	2018	Completion	Policy	Occupancy	5	Secondary	High
MRI & CT not in building	2013	Relocation	Policy Medical	Occupancy	4	Primary Secondary	High
Day rooms in inpatient units	2007	Relocation	Policy Social	Preliminary	3	Secondary Tertiary	Low
Doctors' offices & staff wardrobes location	2006	Relocation	Policy Social	Preliminary	3	Secondary Tertiary	Low
Number of ICU rooms	2012	Addition	Medical	Occupancy	3	Secondary	High
Number of single patient rooms vs. semi-private rooms	2013	Addition	Medical Social	Occupancy	4	Secondary Tertiary	Medium
Patient beds in the corridors and day room	2012	Addition	Policy Medical	Occupancy	3	Tertiary	Low
Conference rooms	2015	Addition	Policy	Occupancy	4	Secondary Tertiary	Low
Curtains in the intermediate patient units	2012	Addition	Policy Medical	Occupancy	3	Tertiary	Low
Bathroom in all ICU rooms	2008	Addition	Policy	Bidding	3	Secondary	Medium
Monitoring system	2014	Addition	Technology	Occupancy	4	Tertiary	Medium
Mobile IT equipment	2014	Addition	Technology	Occupancy	4	Tertiary	Medium
Electrical medical equipment in corridors	2012	Relocation	Policy	Occupancy	4	Tertiary	Medium

Friction (Table 6.1). The *Time* refers to the year of design change or the estimated year of actual implementation of the change. The *Type* defines if the change was a *Completion* of construction or fit-out, *Renovation* of already built-out space (including parts of the MEP infrastructure), *Expansion* of a functional unit, *Addition* of function or *Relocation* of function. The *Cause* specifies the driver of change, whether it was a health *Policy* driver influenced by demography, economy or politics, a *Medical* driver forced by advances in science or diseases treatment, a *Technology* driver led by advances of digital systems, equipment or IT, or a *Social* driver forced by change of cultural norms and demographic demands. *Design stage* distinguishes between the *Schematic, Preliminary, Bidding, Construction,* and *Occupancy* stages of the building. *Project phase* relates to the five phases of the building's construction as detailed in Chapter 3 and illustrated in Figure 6.4. The *System level* refers to the *Primary, Secondary, or Tertiary* level of the physical change, and the *Boundary Friction* defines the interfaces between system levels: High, Medium or Low dependency on other system levels.

The main force behind the design and construction of the building was the generous donation of the Sammy Ofer family to the Tel Aviv Sourasky Medical Center in 2005. Since hospital development in Israel relies mostly on private funding, hospital directors attempt to maximize the potential of each donation. In the case of the Tel Aviv Sourasky Medical Center, it was clear from the start that the hospital would construct the largest structure possible even by applying pressure on the municipality planning guideline limitations (Figure 6.4). This strategy led to the design of a base building with five shell floors for future completion, and was even more evident in the "last minute" decision to add two more shell floors to the building just before construction began. This change of the building's height required redesigning the building's primary system including the structure, MEP systems and facades and caused a delay of a few months in the design and construction process. The survey justifies the addition of the two additional floors because all seven shell floors have already been occupied and the hospital is still, in 2018, dealing with lack of space and resources.

The Sammy Ofer Heart Building, defined and designed as a cardiology center, has changed its functional program considerably. The cardiology division in fact occupies less than 30% of the building. The building now contains neurology, dermatology, internal medicine, and oncology units in addition to research labs and outpatient clinics (Figures 6.4 and 6.5). The change of program can be explained by changing needs since cancer became the number one cause of death and statistically surpassed cardiac diseases. The logic of centralizing the oncology units in one location to enhance the hospital efficiency and health services, could have only been accomplished in the new building. The hospital management also decided to relocate other functions to the building since their previous locations required renovation or extension, or because they received funds to reconstruct a specific medical unit. The hospital's dynamic development plan is

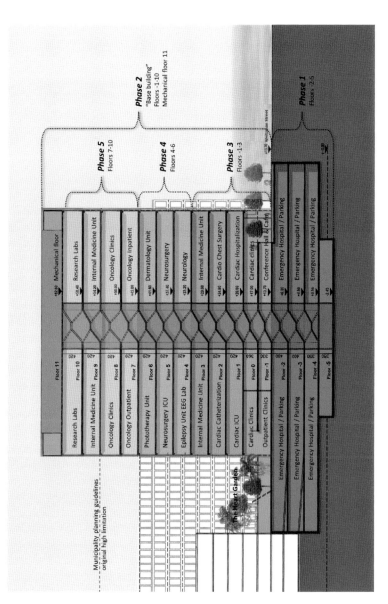

Figure 6.4
Section of the building illustrates the five phases of construction and the hospital's dynamic program.
Source: Ranni Ziss Architects & Sharon Architects, and the author.

driven by forces of economics as well as internal and external organizational politics.

Most of the changes took place after the building was occupied. Although this process of deferred completion of secondary and tertiary systems was planned in advance, it still created a challenge both for the construction and the operation of the running units. The phasing stages, divided by the building's floors, created a process of fit-out from bottom upwards. This strategy might be efficient in order to avoid interruptions of the completion to the operating units, but it limits decision-flexibility during the design process. In many cases the considerations in the fit-out installation phases overruled the importance of locating some medical functions close to other units for process optimization. For example, the inpatient internal medicine units under construction on the 9th floor should have been located on the 4th floor above the existing internal medical units (on the 3rd floor) to centralize the internal medicine division and to enhance staff and equipment flows among the four units. In addition, the hematology units were omitted from the cancer center in the new building. The oncology inpatient and outpatient units were moved to the 7th and 8th floors in order to centralize cancer treatment and care. Unfortunately, this left no space for moving the hematology division because the 6th floor was already occupied by dermatology inpatient and outpatient clinics.

The main limitation to the flexibility of the building was in the Cardiac Intensive Care Unit on the first floor. Following the requirements of the Israel Defense Force, the ICU was designed as a fortified space constructed with concrete envelope, special MEP systems, and protected doors and windows. The specification of this one unit in the middle of the building restricts the potential of the unit to expand or connect to other units, and limits the possibility of changing its function or location. Experts predict that the future hospital will be transformed into an Acute-Care center, and all other functions will be decentralized in the community. This prediction stresses the need to design for ICU units' expansion, and flexibility to change typical patient rooms into ICU patient rooms. In this sense, the need to shelter ICU patients in a "closed" and rigidly fixed protective environment contradicts the Open Building theory. Another limitation on the flexibility of the building is the depth of the floor plates defined by the building's square proportion set by the hospital site. The internal spaces on the floors lack natural light and ventilation since most of the spaces along the perimeter of the building are closed patient rooms, offices or clinics. The prominent recessed red balconies on the west and north facades also constrained the layout of rooms and open spaces in units designed in phases 4–5.

The interfaces between the system levels can be analyzed by the boundary friction of each change documented in the study. A *high* boundary friction refers to a strong dependency between system levels and a *low* boundary friction refers to a limited dependency between system levels. The interfaces demonstrate how a decision made on one level often

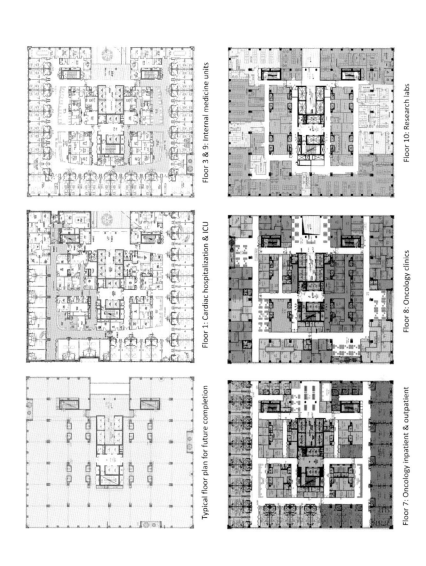

Figure 6.5
Architecture floor plans of the variety of medical programs.
Source: Ranni Ziss Architects & Sharon Architects

restricted the design decisions in other system levels. For example, the location and sizes of the MEP shafts designed as part of the primary system overly constrained (it was subsequently found) the subsequent secondary system decisions on the configuration of the oncology outpatient clinics on floors 7 and 8, and the neurosurgery and neurology ICU on floor 6. Another example is the constraint caused by the position of structural columns and vertical shafts on the design of the research labs on floor 10.

In general, the study found more high dependencies between the primary and secondary levels, and low dependencies between the secondary level and the tertiary level. The main dependencies were defined by the overall layout of the building, the structure, and the location and size of mechanical installation shafts. Other dependencies between the different system levels relate to the modularity size of the rooms (position of separating walls) and the design of the building's envelope (where partitions meet the facade).

Discussion

The development of the project by following the principle of a hierarchy of levels – with higher levels dominating lower levels – differs from the conventional design method of hospital facilities, in which buildings are conceived as a whole with all of their interdependencies, even if construction is realized in phases. The Open Building approach presents many challenges to the designers and clients, primarily in decision-making habits and coordination between the separate firms responsible for each level (Kendall, 2005). Accordingly, the research found that the shift to a serial rather than parallel decision-making process following the realization of the separate levels is not a trivial task. Decisions made in early stages of the design process are necessary even though they might restrict future capacity for change, as each system level has difficult-to-track ripple effects on the other system levels. This calls on the design team to learn new design methods, because the designers (architects and consulting engineers) are trained and expected to take a holistic approach to their design, developing the project from its conceptual scheme to detailed drawings as an interdependent and "integrated" whole. Deferring secondary system design for the future (particularly when that design is the responsibility of another architect) is often perceived, even by the designers themselves, as unprofessional. Furthermore, hospital managers, as all managers, tend to pursue comprehensive, integrated control over their project, wanting to make a significant and current contribution under their name.

Despite these challenges, the Open Building approach implicitly supported the development of the building by phases. It enhanced changes in one system level with minimum impact on other levels. For example, a change of medical unit or change of technological systems could easily be implemented as the structure and MEP shafts were designed separately from the internal walls and envelope following the capacity studies. In fact, most of the changes made were in the completion of the secondary and tertiary levels, while the primary level was changed only before the construction of phase 1 and bidding of phase 2. The dimensional module of patient rooms, defined by the primary level decisions (which is usually the opposite of good Open Building design practice), still enabled change in clinics, offices, and labs in the secondary and tertiary levels. Internal changes in all of the medical units, such as relocation of day rooms, doctors' offices and staff wardrobes, were possible and carried out efficiently because these changes did not require changes in the primary system. The main dependencies were defined by the typology of the building, its structure, and MEP shafts.

The separation of the building into system levels was also useful as a project management and budgeting tool in the design process. The long design process of 13 years, which was still running in 2018, involved many different professionals and decision-makers. Many of the project team members of the hospital were replaced including the CEO of the hospital, heads of medical units and head nurses. Each change of personnel resulted in reconsideration of the design and requests for alternative design options. The design team included a collaboration of two architecture firms, replacement of two project management firms, and consultants who changed over time. The development of the project by phases, using system levels, allowed the architects to divide the workload between the two offices. Each office was responsible for the design of specific floors' secondary systems, with minimal need for consultation and coordination. Design control was shared by the two firms for each level (e.g. the primary, secondary, and tertiary system levels) in order to equalize the scope of work for each firm. The study indicates that capacity study drawings that were developed at a preliminary stage were used as communication tools later, among design teams not even known initially, because they defined the anticipated interfaces between the system levels.

Conclusion

This chapter demonstrates how the client's demand for sustainability, long-term value, assured optimized capacity for change in the face of policy, medical, technology, and social transformation, all impacted the design and the decision-making process, and vice versa. The Open Building or System Separation approach and distributed design management proved to be efficient and productive. Although the approach was not explicitly stated by anyone in the design process, its methods implicitly supported the construction of the project in phases, enabled the design of a variety of changing functional spaces, and enhanced the management and coordination of the design process by different consultants, designers, and contractors. The hospital management's controversial decision to maximize the building potential and build a primary system for future fit-out at a high cost provided the Tel Aviv Sourasky Medical Center with the possibility of promoting a dynamic, strategic plan for the entire campus.

While emphasizing the importance of the building's capacity for physical change (Form), we must recognize that it is only one part of facility change over time. Many changes are made in the operation of the hospital units (Functions) including adjustments of medical procedures or users schedules, without any need to change the physical setting (changes happening only at the tertiary level). Other changes are made by the ability of the users to adjust their behaviors to the given environment (Use). It is also important to acknowledge the evolutionary nature of change: one change may cause a "ripple effect" chain of changes in the Form, Function, or Use of the building. For example, the Sammy Ofer Heart Building, with its separate system levels, can easily support changes of patient room types: from double patient room to triple or single patient rooms, but the physical change is only one aspect to consider. We need to evaluate how such change affects the overall operation and performance of the medical unit. In many cases the greatest limitation for flexibility is not the physical space, but the lack of professional staff or the resistance of the organization culture.

This chapter documents changes over the last 13 years during the design process, construction, and occupancy phases. While this time frame is significant, further work is needed to evaluate healthcare facilities over longer periods of time. In retrospect, a study of the Open Building approach should be conducted over a full life cycle of hospital facilities in order to evaluate the true value of specific implementations of the approach. An economic study of the Sammy Ofer Heart Building should also be conducted to determine whether the strategy of investing in a base building offering capacity for future fit-out was feasible and remains profitable. More studies of healthcare facilities' change over time from different environmental, cultural, and economic contexts, will enhance the knowledge base needed for successful design of sustainable healthcare architecture.

Acknowledgments

This research was supported by the European Research Council grant (FP-7 ADG 340753), and by the Azrieli Foundation. I am grateful to the Tel Aviv Sourasky Medical Center management and staff, and to Ranni Ziss Architects, Sharon Architects, CPM and M. Iuclea project managers for their collaboration.

References

Habraken, NJ (1972). *Supports: An Alternative to Mass Housing* (p. 97). London: Architectural Press.

Habraken, NJ (1998). *The Structure of the Ordinary: Form and Control in the Built Environment*. Cambridge: MIT Press.

Kendall, S (2005). Managing Change: The Application of Open Building in the INO Bern Hospital. Design & Health World Congress, Frankfurt, July 6–10.

Kendall, S (2008). Open Building: Healthcare Architecture on the Time Axis: A New Approach. In R Gunther and G Vittori (Eds.), *Sustainable Healthcare Architecture* (pp. 353–359). New York: Wiley.

Kendall, S (2017). Four Decades of Open Building Implementation: Realizing Individual Agency in Architectural Infrastructures Designed to Last. *Architectural Design*, 87(5), pp. 54–63.

Pilosof, NP (2005, October 19). *Planning for Change: Hospital Design Theories in Practice*. Washington, DC.: Academy Journal, AIA.

Sharon, A (2012). Flexible Building Design Offers Future-Proofing. *IFHE Digest*.

Chapter 7

Finding shared ambitions to design for change
Building the AZ Groeninge hospital

Waldo Galle and Pieter Herthogs (with contributions from Wim Debacker, Anne Paduart, and Niels De Temmerman)

Open Building thinking in Belgium
Over the past two decades, a growing awareness and understanding of the built environment's ecological and societal impacts has steadily increased the number of architectural professionals exploring how design choices affect the long-term value of buildings. Central to that exploration is the search for buildings and building components that stay relevant after the requirements that shaped them have changed.

In Belgium, indications of this slowly shifting mind-set can be seen at various levels. Examples are the recurring demand for integrative life cycle assessments and the rise of performance-based contract models (Debacker and Manshoven, 2016). Another example are so-called *Green Deals*, i.e. declarations of commitment between policy agencies and individual organizations to engage frontrunners in creating lasting, sustainable impact (Circular Flanders, 2017). Little by little, through subsidies, contract models, project briefs, and assessment tools, the idea that a building should have a long-term value is being cemented in place.

This also implies Open Building principles are supported by policy makers and feature in vision documents of governments, administrations, and cities (Flemish Government, 2017). For example, driven by the transition towards an economy of closed material loops, the Public Waste Agency of Flanders OVAM has put the need for "dynamic and flexible construction and renovation" center-stage in its policy program (OVAM, 2013).

At the Flemish policy level, the term *Design for Change* is used instead of Open Building. It has a broader scope, and is defined as such:

> Design for Change (DfC, in Dutch: *veranderingsgericht bouwen*, literally "change-oriented construction") *is an umbrella term for design and construction strategies acknowledging that the needs and requirements of our built environment will always change; the aim*

of Design for Change is to create buildings that support change more efficiently.

(Galle and Herthogs, 2015)

The term was introduced as part of a common language commissioned by the Public Waste Agency of Flanders OVAM to facilitate communication between stakeholders from multiple backgrounds (Debacker et al., 2015; Galle and Herthogs, 2015).

While Design for Change is slowly gaining ground in Belgium, the idea itself is much older. That a building must cope with different uses or is changed from time to time is inherent in the act of building, and pervasive throughout the built environment, but most of the time only implicitly. The explicit goal to create buildings that intend to support change is relatively recent. Hamdi (1991, p. 51) described how *Flexibility* became a widespread design term in the 1960s in response to new demands placed on buildings, particularly on housing (Habraken, 1972), because many things considered to be standard were changing, such as typical family size and composition, or expectations of comfort and efficiency. While change is inherent to the space we continuously create, it was only around this time that the capacity for change "became accepted as a legitimate goal of architecture and planning" (Hamdi, 1991, p. 51).

Contemporary Belgian architecture also had its flexibility frontrunners. The idea echoes for example in the design practice of Lucien Kroll (1927), most known for his iconic participatory development of *La MéMé*, a student housing project for the medical campus of the *Université de Louvain-la-Neuve* in Brussels (1968–1971) (Kroll, 1983). Kroll used the uncertain and divergent needs of students in the seventies as an opportunity to leave behind the conventional programming approach, resulting in a building that could support the needs of both more traditional and more progressive students while demonstrating in the design process the need for a change in role for architects and building users (Strauven, 1976). Similarly, architect Willy Van Der Meeren (1923–2002) identified temporality as a key characteristic of our society and the environment we constructed (Van Der Meeren, 1969). Correspondingly, he designed modular prefabricated student housing units on the new campus of the *Vrije Universiteit Brussel*, founded in 1970. Though remaining unchanged for decades, their generous concrete frames are now being transformed into research facilities such as a Circular Retrofit Lab (Bruzz, 2018). Another well-known point of view is that of Bob Van Reeth, the first Flemish Government Architect, who stressed the importance of generality by understanding a building as a cultural ruin; a building with the same attitude and intentions as all buildings around it, that could have been there for ages, and can stay forever (Van Reeth, 2005).

In Belgium, as in other countries, the initial explorations into Open Building and similar schools of thought of the sixties and seventies remained a niche domain within architecture. In the eighties and nineties, the call for individualism and diverse lifestyles – a key precondition for the field at that time – was replaced by the emergence of contemporary consumerism. This situation started changing from the early 2000s, when the idea that buildings ought to be designed for change rose towards the mainstream once more; this time it was strongly tied to the need to transition to a much more sustainable, less resource-intensive construction sector and built environment.

Over the past two decades, Open Building thinking has re-emerged internationally, both in architectural practice and research. On the one hand, the increased call to design buildings for change is driven by a need for a sustainable built environment, which brings with it a need for policy making, quantification, and research. Here too, current researchers are in part building on the experience of early forerunners. For example, the Design for Change research conducted at the Architectural Engineering department of the Vrije Universiteit Brussel had its roots in the teachings of Willy Van Der Meeren and his colleague Hendrik Hendrickx, both design professors at the department (Galle, 2013). On the other hand, because change is inherent to the act of building, Design for Change principles have always been implicitly interwoven into architectural design, which makes it relatively easy for architects to venture into this topic based on past experiences. Almost anecdotally, Coussée & Goris Architecten's insertion of a removeable steel-and-glass café into the Medieval Great Butchers' Hall of Ghent illustrates an awareness about different paces of change in the built environment (Mattelaer, 2009). Similarly, both renowned and rapidly emerging offices, such as 51N4E, KADERSTUDIO, and BC Architects & Studies, propose general structures as solutions for diverse settings and sites, to open up possibilities rather than to define use. Clearly, contemporary Belgian architectural practice demonstrates it has the potential to implement Design for Change or Open Building principles. Nevertheless, it seems to lack the coherence to respond effectively to the challenge of consistently adding long-term value to its interventions. This is where support from research and policy can play a guiding role.

The design and construction of the AZ Groeninge hospital illustrates this point. A review of the project confirms it is the result of a confluence of design insight, implied principles, and increasing awareness. The hospital was the product of individual experiences and ambitions, not of a sector-wide vision. In this chapter, we examine the design choices made by Baumschlager Eberle Architekten, OSAR Architects, and the larger design team, the corresponding process, and resulting advantages and disadvantages. Lessons learned are offered to complement existing approaches and could form the basis of a design framework that is, at the uptake of a new architectural paradigm, more needed than ever before.

AZ Groeninge, a hospital for the future

The AZ Groeninge hospital was built on the outskirts of the Belgian city of Kortrijk, on a 14-hectare (34.5 acre) unbuilt plot. AZ Groeninge is a general and teaching hospital. It accommodates various facilities and services such as 22 operating theaters, including a robot surgery room, and trains nursing students and clinical fellows in various specialties. On its completion in 2017, AZ Groeninge was the 5th largest hospital organization in Belgium, located on the largest hospital site of the country (Groeninge, 2017). The project emerged through the consolidation of four existing hospitals in Kortrijk. In reaction to the previous fragmentation of hospital activities in the city, the ambition was to realize a centralized "health village," characterized by an increased efficiency that would improve the delivered quality and patient satisfaction (Mattelaer, 2009).

The assignment, a forward-thinking and open design brief

To create the design, the hospital board selected a consortium of offices: Baumschlager Eberle Architekten (Austria) and OSAR Architects (Belgium). The design brief the consortium received, which at the time of writing was about 20 years old, did not ask for an adaptable or Open Building, like some local governments do today (for example, as part of Flanders' Green Deals). Rather the brief asked for a hospital for the future. This was an open question that required many site visits, observations and discussions with the hospital management and employees before shaping the design concept, according to discussions with Hilde Vermolen, partner of the architectural office OSAR Architects in March 2018.

Baumschlager Eberle Architekten (2018) argued that a courtyard layout was the most appropriate solution. The design called for five interconnected blocks, three or four levels high, with interior courtyards of about 20 x 60 m (65 x 197 ft) meant to reduce the building's size to human proportions (Figure 7.1). The central courtyard was surrounded by a medical-technical

Figure 7.1
AZ Groeninge has five interconnected blocks, either three or four levels high; introducing interior courtyards of 20 x 60 m created spaces closer to human scale, despite the large site.

block that houses the hospital's main entrance and served as a circulation hub. The versatile, "use-neutral" design of the four surrounding blocks facilitated a phased realization of the complex and enabled it to accommodate changes or even transformations to other functions. It was believed that the building's uniform facade gave the complex a serene appearance (Corrodi, 2007).

The answer: architects rethinking their way of designing

> Our experience with the hospital sector triggered us to rethink our way of designing; we learned from previous projects that the design program demanded in the brief would never be built. Regulations, financing and the entire hospital landscape are changing constantly.
>
> (Vermolen, 2018)

When merging the city's hospitals, the public sector's organization questioned its role and program. The chance it will again question that role in the future is also likely – history has shown a continuous fluctuation between centralized and decentralized service provision for patients (Vermolen and Ost, 2014). Unable to predict the future, Baumschlager Eberle and OSAR Architects focused on the concept of combining a capacious support with an adaptable infill.

It is important to realize that the design team did not start from a particular theory. Today, the concept Design for Change is part of an emerging discussion in the architectural and urban design discipline. At the start of the project there was indeed a historical background of Habraken's writings and resultant work by architects around the world, but the results of practical implementation were not available to the design team (Vermolen, 2018). Rather, the whole concept was based only on insights created by the design team during previous building projects within the same sector (Vermolen, 2018).

Designing for change, searching for shared ambitions

Acknowledging uncertainty, shaping ambitions and buildings

Compared to commercial real estate or office buildings, hospitals are not transformed as often. "After all, conventionally built health care facilities, and nursing units in particular, postpone necessary refurbishments as the impact of such interventions impedes the hospital's overall operation." (Vermolen, 2018). "By designing and constructing with a change-oriented approach, however, refurbishments can be facilitated, fostering faster, more efficient and effective responses to changing market demands" (ibid.). Although the brief did not necessarily demand such an adaptable building, the hospital board was easily convinced of the concept Baumschlager Eberle Architekten and OSAR Architects proposed. The board's acknowledgment of uncertainty was key, as was the individual experience with construction projects in the healthcare sector of the advisors representing the hospital board (Vermolen, 2018).

To achieve a change-oriented building, many choices must be made, balancing concepts and functional demands with budget, location, and time restrictions.

> This approach is far more interesting for us architects than the increasing administrative burdens. After all, it is a result-oriented process, determining the way the building will and can be used by the client now and in the future.
>
> (Vermolen, 2018)

"[Designing for change] does not require more creativity, but holds other challenges for designers" (ibid.). Those challenges can be rephrased as follows.

First, designing for change is a unique way of thinking and working. It requires designers to question assumptions and previous choices, and to engage in new kinds of dialogue with external experts. In the context of the AZ Groeninge project, an advisory group was established with representatives of the hospital board, as well as others with specific experience in hospital management, healthcare procedures, and medical techniques (Vermolen and Ost, 2014). They did not intervene directly in the design decision-making but were crucial to identify ongoing and emerging trends in the sector. They helped to identify the uncertainties that must be tackled in the design proposals, and the relative importance of those unknowns.

Second, the ability to maintain a design-oriented concept throughout the extensive project period relied on integrated decision-making, according to Vermolen (2018). This implies that all construction disciplines involved in the hospital's design had to be addressed simultaneously, and as early as possible in the project. "This integration is illustrated by the choice for post-tensioned flat floor slabs, avoiding the use of beams and facilitating the horizontal routing and rerouting of technical services" (ibid.). This collaborative approach avoids problems during design, fostering solid and sustainable building concepts, and ideally a future-proof building.

Third, a change-oriented building and its design process currently do not fit conventional procedures or paperwork. How does one go about requesting a building permit for a building with a program of uses that might change? Or how does one request reversible connections in a contractor's tendering procedure? One answer is finding common interests. For this to happen, each partner must look beyond the boundaries of commonly assigned tasks. For example, during the AZ Groeninge project, stakeholders wondered how the project could contribute to the accessibility from the neighborhood, in terms of cycling connections from the city center. In the end, the team actively participated in the redevelopment of the urban infrastructure around the site.

Baumschlager Eberle Architekten stated that:

[t]oday, issues relating to the practical value of a building are largely decided by the quality of the environment it provides or by the extent to which it enables the architecture to achieve lasting added value despite quickly changing use requirements.

(2018)

This points towards the exploration of an interesting tension – and symbiosis – between immediate and long-term value, between generality and adaptability. The resulting design could be simplified to the separation between support and infill, but a closer examination reveals a more elaborate approach and framework, characterized by four challenges: 1) finding the optimal generality for the load-bearing frame (the structural concept); 2) balancing the dependence and independence of spaces (the spatial concept); 3) negotiating the long- and short-term value of a factory-made building skin (the facade concept); and 4) deciding on whether or not to embed technical services into other building elements (the technical concept).

Finding the optimal generality, the structural concept

The load-bearing structure of the hospital wings uses precast facade elements and two longitudinal rows of concrete columns, occasionally alternated with staircases, technical shafts and patios (Figures 7.2 and 7.6). The three resulting longitudinal zones of 8.1, 5.4, and 8.1 m (26.5, 17.1, and 26.5 ft) follow a 0.9-m (3 ft) planning module that shapes the entire hospital complex. For example, a typical patient room is 3.6 m (11.8 ft) wide, and the 4.5-meter-wide single-bed suites (14.7 ft) fit into the same structure (De Troyer et al., 2006).

Figure 7.2 **Precast facade elements and two rows of concrete columns, alternated with staircases, technical shafts, and patios, form the structure of every hospital wing.**

In healthcare, regulations and management strategies will continue to shift, but also society's notion of healing and healthcare itself. Because of the rise of digital technologies, nanotechnical instruments, and renewed insights in health psychology, the design team also projected other functional programs onto the building structure. Minimizing the number of load-bearing elements in the two perimeter (longitudinal) zones of the building ensured ample freedom to develop various room layouts and enables a multipurpose interpretation of the building. In addition, each wing has a finished floor-to-ceiling clear height of 3.61 m (11.8 ft) on every floor (this is the height of the operating theaters), identical staircases and consistent circulation patterns and technical service schemes. As a result, each wing can easily be changed from an outpatient clinic into, for example, a nursing ward with patient rooms, changing and facility rooms, offices and consulting rooms, or even classrooms (Vermolen and Ost, 2014).

During the design phase, changes in the regulations on patient room sizes illustrated the added value of the dimensional module (Vermolen, 2018). Because the triple-bed rooms that were planned had to be replaced by rooms with one and two beds, the infill had to be redrawn. However, the elements of the load-bearing structure, including mechanical system cores and shafts, did not have to be redesigned, and their specifications and related tendering documents did not need to change. Moreover, in 2013, after the completion of the first construction phase, seven 3.6-m rooms (11.8 ft) in the maternity department were transformed into five studio rooms, without inconveniencing the hospital's operation. Thanks to a carefully planned support and infill system, the hospital management could quickly transform a surplus of rooms into a smaller set with increased user comfort and satisfaction.

The convenient, generous framework provided by a coherent building layout and straightforward structural system further encouraged the hospital management to think more systemically, and increased the robustness and resilience of the hospital's working schemes and processes. The generalized organization of different departments, individual nursing wards, and even mobile care stations, combining standard and department-specific elements wisely, resulted in freedom and efficiency when allocating staff and supply (Vermolen and Ost, 2014).

Balancing the dependence and independence of spaces, the spatial concept

AZ Groeninge has a straightforward circulation principle that guarantees that the benefits of the planning module (i.e. the dimensioning grid) and the open load-bearing structure can be exploited in case of adaptations and transformations. As a rule, consulting rooms and laboratories are located on the lowest floors, with the related nursing departments located on the floors above; the result is that most circulation should not cross into other units. Further, a circulation network in the basement provides access to all supporting services. In the future, if there would be less demand for nursing departments, it is possible to change a wing into, for example, a care-related educational function, with its own entrance in the central hall and connection to laboratories and services.

This circulation systems also allowed the hospital to stay open during its multiple construction phases (Figure 7.3). For a hospital, phasing is linked to subsidies. In this case, there is a difference between the financial projects (seven) and the construction phases (two) of the complex's realization. To build a hospital, there are a minimum number of services that need to be provided (to operate as an emergency care hospital, it needs enough specialized departments); hence, the first two financial projects were realized at the same time, in the first construction phase. Afterwards, the financial (subsidy) landscape changed significantly; as a result, the next five financial projects were constructed simultaneously in the second phase.

More demanding medical facilities, such as operating theaters, are clustered in the central block of the hospital and equipped with all necessary technical services, including specialized ventilation, heating, and cooling installations. As the relocation and transformation of these facilities was deemed unlikely for financial reasons, it was decided to group and locate them centrally in the complex. Because of specialized HVAC requirements, the spans in this block differ from the spans in other blocks but are still a multiple of 0.9 m (3 ft). For example, the central block's northern wing has a dimensioning grid of 10.8, 5.4, and 8.1 m (35.4, 17.7, and 26.5 ft).

Whereas the choice to group all medical-technical facilities is a pragmatic way of dealing with the generality of the support, the integration of other quasi-permanent but specific elements within that structure challenges the

Figure 7.3
A well-considered building layout of the hospital wings, implemented in the first construction phase, allowed the first wings to remain operational during the subsequent construction phase.

basic concept of changeability. This includes the thick concrete walls of the radiotherapy department, custom-designed for very specific medical equipment with very specific dimensions. As that equipment evolves as fast as other techniques, it is unclear how these "bunkers" will be able to meet future needs, or if they might jeopardize the structure's inherent transformational potential.

Negotiating between the short- and long-term value of a factory-produced skin, the facade concept

As the facade is part of the load-bearing structure, it belongs to the permanent support. The building's skin is made of prefabricated concrete elements including different types of columns, back beams, parapets, column heads, and floor-column nodes (Figure 7.4). They give the architecture a calm unity. Floor-to-ceiling windows form a curtain wall behind these concrete elements, aligned to the 0.9-m (3 ft) module, giving all rooms ample light. Placing the columns of the facade elements at an angle created permanent sun screens (Figure 7.5).

According to Febelarch (2018), the national organization for manufacturers of elements in architectural concrete, prefabrication saved several hundred thousand euros. The load-bearing facade helped optimize the construction cost, shifting more budget to other design features, such as the post-tensioned concrete floor slabs avoiding beams, or the production of window frames following a 1.8-m (6 ft) grid. A general and adaptable building concept can have higher initial costs. Separating the structural facade and the curtain wall, installing a modular heating system and decentralized ventilation all require more initial material and work, but these

Figure 7.4
The prefabrication and on-site assembly of the facade reduced construction costs and enabled the designers to allocate more of the budget towards other aspects to improve the building's generality.

Figure 7.5
The columns of the facade elements are angled, serving as permanent sun blinds while providing the building its serene appearance.

investments are expected to deliver a return on investment throughout the life span of the building.

However, the load-bearing facade elements impede large changes to the facade. Hence, some of the elements, i.e. those that would need to be removed in subsequent construction phases, were made demountable. In addition, the reinforcement in the floors where these demountable elements were located was sized accordingly. Despite taking all the necessary precautions, the demountable facade elements were not reused during the second construction phase. Their disassembly would have impacted the functioning of the existing parts of the hospital, both in terms of general nuisance and perimeter security. Aside from their removal, reinstalling the elements would have been difficult: despite their near identical appearance, some elements are still unique (their rainwater drainage is different, fully embedded); and the (labor) costs required to carefully disassemble, move, and replace a facade element would exceed the production price of a new one.

Whether or not to embed services: the technical concept

The hospital design features a clear difference between support and infill, as we know it from Habraken (Hoogstraten et al., 2000). But as shown above, in this case the goal of separation does not necessarily result in a strict separation between load-bearing structure and skin, or between structure and technical services; the in-situ cast concrete floor slabs have a series of ducts embedded in them (Figure 7.6). For vertical services, the floors feature

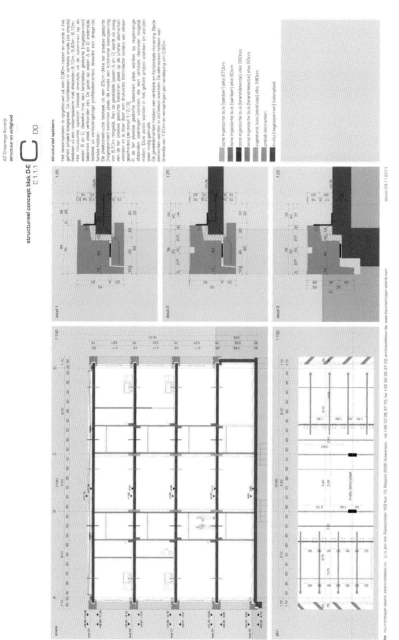

Figure 7.6
This typical section shows how a series of ducts has been integrated in the concrete structure: by providing placeholder ducts at regular intervals in the structure, the framework for technical services adds generality to the support.

cast openings (450 by 350 mm – 1.48 by 1.15 ft), through which wastewater pipes can be placed every 2.7 m (8.8 ft) in alignment with the columns and every 0.9 m (3 ft) at a 1.8-m (6 ft) offset from those columns. Tubes to hold wiring are embedded every 3.6 m (11.8 ft) aligned to the columns or every 0.9 m (3 ft) aligned to the facade. The post-tensioned slabs have embedded horizontal ventilation ducts with a nominal diameter of 100 mm (4 inches) every 1.8 m (6 ft) distributing fresh air from the corridor zone to the perimeter of the building. Although the technical services in a building have a high replacement rate, these distribution ducts and pipes cannot be altered; however, the mechanical equipment can be replaced. Yet the idea of providing a large number of potential connections and aligning them to the building's modular grid adds generality to structure and reduces or avoids entanglement of services.

As all floor openings are strategically positioned and cast-in-place, the whole drainage system is adapted to them. All drains run in the 1 m (3.2 ft) plenum space above the lowered ceiling in the corridors, directed towards one of the vertical shafts in the central zone of each wing. The central vertical shafts are sufficiently large to support a hospital program, assuring that they have sufficient capacity for any other future building function. Larger technical equipment has been housed in technical rooms on top of the building. The roof above these rooms features a special zone where a steel plate covering can be removed after the roof tiling has been cut away; this is a potential entry point to remove and replace large technical equipment.

Unfortunately, the grid-based placement of embedded ducts and pipes was not implemented in each wing of the project. Because of budget cuts in the outpatient department, the sanitary cells of these rooms do not have showers, and thus no pipe sleeve every 0.9 m (3 ft). This reduces the future utility of that floor and increases the refurbishment costs. When the early transformations in the maternity department took place in 2013, it clearly demonstrated the added value of the general pipe and duct sleeve layout in the concrete structure, and the decision not to implement the system in every wing was regretted. The designers and the client refrained from these short-term budget cuts during the second construction phase (Vermolen, 2018).

Conclusion

The design of the AZ Groeninge hospital brought together a client with an open-ended request for a hospital for the future and an architectural consortium with experience in the healthcare sector. Their acknowledgement of uncertainty resulted in the ambition to create a change-oriented building and enabled an effective collaboration. Their common understanding of the long-term impacts of initial choices helped to form a vision for a general infrastructure that has the capacity to support not only its users, but also the neighborhood, city, and region.

The decision to design for change has also proven to be an effective paradigm in use, supporting the ambitions of the client even in the short term: changes in room size regulations could be implemented at the infill level, without impacting the support level, and the rooms of the maternity department were successfully transformed into suites while the hospital was in use.

One of the core challenges of an architect is deciding on the buildings' appearance, how it should be shaped, and which components it should be constructed with. This is far from straightforward when designing for permanence and change. It forces designers to think beyond a conventional architectural program, and include time, space, and budget as interdependent parameters rather than prescribed boundary conditions.

In this case, both the client's program and the site were two influential parameters. A hospital is a very particular, location-based building, and needs to be more adaptable per definition, because of its uniqueness – in case of something as ubiquitous as a house, people can adapt simply by moving. Less straightforward is to what extent the design for change of AZ Groeninge is related to its location on a large greenfield site. According to Vermolen (2018), the empty site was not a necessary precondition to create an Open Building. Nevertheless, the freedom of an open plot made it easy to make technical and spatial choices that might not be possible within an existing building or urban fabric, and which have for example helped create flexibility in allocating the budget.

Despite the success of this particular project, the research for this chapter has demonstrated that there is not a system in place to facilitate learning from this example. In case of a building designed to last for a long time, a loss of knowledge could jeopardize its long-term value. This was also noted by the design team, who wondered who would be responsible for all the information on the project's technical possibilities, 20 or 30 years in the future. The development of a formal knowledge transfer system between building design and management seems necessary for future success. Information is available in the tendering and as-built documents, but it is difficult to interpret and thus may be difficult to use during future interventions.

This suggests that there is no single formula to produce buildings with long-term value. AZ Groeninge also demonstrates that such a formula is not indispensable to create added value; in this case, the knowledge, skills, and insight needed to create a building that supports change relied on the individual experiences of those involved. However, architectural practice cannot depend on singular experiences alone if it desires to contribute to a sustainable built environment. With the understanding that the long-term value of buildings is increasingly important, developing a formal (and practical) framework to support the transfer of that knowledge, skills, and insight might be a way forward – for the education of construction professionals, fostered in practice, established by regional governments, and shared through learning networks of architect and advisors. This new paradigm could be an opportunity to give a new meaning to the architectural profession at a time when it is questioned, and increase the understanding of the built environment's ecological and societal impacts.

Facts and figures of the program
Location President Kennedylaan 48,500 Kortrijk, Belgium (50°48'6"N 3°15'53"E).

Client AZ Groeninge, a non-profit public-private partnership between the city of Kortrijk and the Boards of the former Christian hospitals; general manager during the project was Jan Deleu.

Architect Baumschlager Eberle Architekten (Vaduz) and OSAR Architects (Antwerp) **Management** Christian Tabernigg (BE), Hilde Vermolen (OSAR), Louis Lateur (BE), Bert Van Boxelaere (OSAR) **Consultants** Topokor (infrastructure), Atelier GRAS (landscaping), Jan Van Aelst (stability), Ingenium, Sorane SIA and Lenum (services), Scala (acoustics) **Art** Dan Graham, Bernd Lohaus, Richard Venlet, Koenraad Dedobbeleer, Müller & Wehberg, Ian Kiair **Contractors** Cordeel (structural work phase 1), THV Jan De Nul & CEI De Meyer (structural work phase 2), Prefadim (facade), Albitum (green roofs), Vanhout (finishing), Electro Entreprise (electrical services), Van Maele (sanitary services), Chauffage Declercq (heating and ventilation services), Heyer (medical gases), Coopman (elevators), Aercom (pneumatic post), Honeywell (security).

Project Cost 82 million euro ($99.6 million) (phase 1), 202 million euro ($245.4 million) (phase 2)

Schedule
2000 Start of design
2005 Start of first construction phase
2010 Completion of first phase
2012 Start of second construction phase
2017 Completion of second phase

Land area 144,000 m^2
Building footprint 31,460 m^2
Volume 489,485 m^3
Usable area 105,280 m^2
Capacity 1,054 beds (in 2017)
Hospitalizations 35,022 patients (in 2016)
Admission 248,575 days (in 2016)

Acknowledgement

This analysis strongly relies on an interview with two collaborators of the architectural office OSAR (partner Hilde Vermolen and project architect Tim Ost) by Wim Debacker and Anne Paduart on April 11, 2014, and a second interview with Hilde Vermolen by Waldo Galle, on March 6, 2018; additional technical information was kindly provided by the architectural offices and the AZ Groeninge hospital.

References

Baumschlager Eberle Architekten (2018). Krankenhaus AZ Groeninge Kortrijk, Belgien. (Project webpage) www.baumschlager-eberle.com/werk/projekte/projekt/krankenhaus-az-groeninge.

Bruzz (2018). Wetenschap kaapt iconische studentenkoten Van Der Meeren. Bruzz Online 06/2/2018. www.bruzz.be/onderwijs/wetenschap-kaapt-iconische-studentenkoten-van-der-meeren-2018-02-06.

Circular Flanders (2017). Green Deal Circulair Aankopen. (Project webpage) http://vlaanderen-circulair.be/nl/onze-projecten/detail/green-deal-circulair-aankopen.

Corrodi, M (2007). 1.000-Betten-Krankenhaus, A.Z. Groeninge Kortrijk, Belgien. In W Nerdinger (Ed.), *Baumschlager Eberle 2002–2007* (pp. 66–71). Vienna: Springer.

Debacker, W, W Galle, M Vandenbroucke, L Wijnants, W Lam, A Paduart, P Herthogs, N De Temmerman, D Trigaux and Y De Weerdt (2015). *Veranderings-gericht bouwen: ontwikkeling van een beleids-en transitiekader (Final Report)*. Mechelen: Openbare Vlaamse Afvalstoffen Maatschappij OVAM.

Debacker, W and S Manshoven (2016). *Key Barriers and Opportunities for Materials Passports and Reversible Building Design in the Current System (Buildings as Material Banks Synthesis of the State-of-the-Art)*. Brussels: European Union's Horizon 2020 Research and Innovation Programme.

De Troyer, F, R Kenis, and J Van Dessel (2006). *Industrieel, Flexibel en demontabel bouwen, toekomstgericht ontwerpen*. Brussels: BBRI in collaboration with FEBE, KU Leuven.

Febelarch (2018). AZ Groeninge. (Project webpage) www.febelarch.be/prefadim-belgium-nv.

Flemish Government (2017). Vlaanderen Circulair, een stuwende kracht naar een circulaire economie in vlaanderen. (Starting note for the policy priority "transition circular economy") www.vlaanderen.be/nl/vlaamse-regering/transitie-circulaire-economie.

Galle, W (2013). Transform. In *7x5. 35 jaar opleiding ingenieur-architect aan de Vrije Universiteit Brussel (1979–2014)*. Brussels: Department of Architectural Engineering, Vrije Universiteit Brussel.

Galle, W and P Herthogs (2015). *Een Gemeenschappelijke taal* (A Common Language). Mechelen: Openbare Vlaamse Afvalstoffen Maatschappij OVAM.

Groeninge, AZ (2017). Jaarverslag 2016. (Online annual report) www.azgroeninge.be/Pub/start/PDF/Jaarverslag-2016.pdf.

Habraken, N (1972). *Supports: An Alternative to Mass Housing*. London: Architecture Press.

Hamdi, N (1991). *Housing without Houses: Participation, Flexibility, Enablement*. New York: Van Nostrand Reinhold.

Hoogstraten, DV, M Vos and J Habraken (2000). *Housing for the Millions: John Habraken and the SAR (1960–2000)*. K Bosma (Ed.). Rotterdam: NAI Publishers.

Kroll, L (1983). *Composants-faut-il industrialiser l'architecture?* Brussels: editions SOCOREMA.

Kroll, L (1983) *Composants-faut-il industrialiser l'architecture?* Brussels: Editions Socorema.

Mattelaer, J (2009). *Van Hospitaal tot AZ Groeninge: de geschiedenis van de ziekenzorg in Kortrijk.* Kortrijk: PANA in collaboration with Uitgeverij Groeninghe.

OVAM (2013). Materiaalbewust bouwen in kringlopen. Preventieprogramma duurzaam materialenbeheer in de bouwsector 2014–2020. Technical Report D/2013/5024/31, OVAM, Mechelen.

Strauven, F (1976). De anarchitectuur Van Lucien Kroll. *Wonen-TA|BK*, 12, pp. 5–14.

Van Der Meeren, W. (1969). Rol van de ontwerper in het ontwikkelingsproces van een statische naar een dynamische beschaving (From Static to Dynamic Environment). In *Serca Revue*. October 1969..

Van Reeth, B (2005). Cultural Durability. In B Leupen, R Heijne and J Van Zwol (Eds.), *Time-Based Architecture: Architecture Able to Withstand Changes through Time* (pp. 110–115). Rotterdam: 010 Publishers.

Vermolen, H (2018). Interview by W Galle. With Partner of the Architectural Office OSAR Architects Hilde Vermolen on March 6, 2018. Translation by the Authors.

Vermolen, H and T Ost (2014). Interview by W Debacker and A Paduart. With Partner of the Architectural Office OSAR Architects Hilde Vermolen and Collaborator Tim Ost on April 11, 2014. Translation by the Authors.

Chapter 8

Transformation of an existing hospital building to a hospice

Open Building as strategy for process and product

Karel Dekker

Introduction
This case study describes a five-year search for and construction of a new facility for a hospice in Voorburg, the Netherlands. The project involved the transformation planning, design and construction of part of an existing polyclinic hospital into a hospice of 1,200 m^2 (13,000 ft^2). The Open Building approach was used as the strategy for design decision-making, financing, and construction. Applying the Open Building principles resulted in the client renting a building for 30 years with a low rent and investing in renovating it with an expected use period of 30–40 years, and acting as owner for the newly built interior of the base building.

A competitive tendering (bidding) process was used for choosing a contractor to work closely as part of the design team. A distinction in tendering was also made, corresponding to a technical separation between a more permanent Base Building and more changeable Fit-Out, in which all mechanical installation technology and other interior construction belongs to the Fit-Out. To increase the capacity of the Base Building for future changes, buffer spaces were created for future expansion of the hospice functions. The need for flexible wire management called for specifying Gyproc's *CableStud* as part of the Fit-Out. Decentralized HVAC systems with controlled CO2 measurement were used, offering maximum flexibility and low energy use in future transformation of spaces.

History of the hospice
The hospice Het Vliethuys (see Figure 8.1) offers palliative care and support to people with limited life expectancy, in a warm and loving environment that feels as much as possible like staying at home. Since 2001, the hospice was part of a nursing home. Because the rental contract was set to expire in 2012, a search for a new location began in 2009. The objective was to establish a new

Figure 8.1
Original and new location of the Hospice as part of the total Hospital facility. A Heath Centre adjacent to the new Hospice was created in a building previously housing another function.

facility that would offer circumstances for the hospice organization and especially for the temporary inhabitants, cared for in the last period of their lives.

One of the options in 2009 was to rent 1,000 m^2 (10,763 ft^2) of empty floor space in a newly built nursing home and to act as owner of the new interior Fit-Out of that building. Because of environmental circumstances, the project was delayed, forcing the hospice to examine other solutions, resulting finally in transforming an empty building on a polyclinic hospital campus (see Figure 8.2).

Capacity analysis of the existing building for the hospice

An analysis of the empty building's capacity on the hospital campus to accommodate the hospice program was carried out by a capacity analysis tool developed previously by ARO and KD Consultants (ARO). The method employs a rectangular grid (raster) of 0.6 x 0.6 m^2 (2 x 2 ft^2) overlaid on a floor plan of the existing building.

In the capacity study, the functions and areas needed for each were given different colors, each associated with a functional code (e.g. patient rooms, staff offices, etc.) Quantities of functional areas possible in the empty building were automatically calculated and compared with the needed areas of the program. This process was repeated several times until agreement was reached about a good layout. One such iteration is given in Figure 8.3. Using the capacity analysis tool, the raster drawing can be automatically colored to show the functional codes to assist in discussions between the client, caregivers, and the architect. This method can be used effectively for capacity analysis of any existing building planned for transformation. The conclusions of this feasibility phase (capacity analysis phase) were clear: the polyclinic building could accommodate a hospice with the capacity of nine beds.

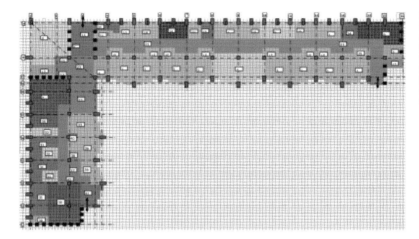

Figure 8.2
One of several iterations of the capacity analysis process using the raster method.

Negotiations with the hospital board

The next step was to start negotiations with the board of the hospital organization. The first problem was the impossibility for the hospital to sell the existing polyclinic building. The second problem was that the hospital organization had no funding for refurbishment of the empty building. We (the author) proposed that the Open Building approach could be a solution for these problems.

Explaining the Open Building principals

First of all, the Open Building principals were explained to the board of the hospital organization. Open Building proposes that a strict partitioning should be made between parts (and spaces) in a building that can be expected to have long-term use-value (i.e. the *Base Building*), and the parts (and spaces) that are bound to change more frequently (i.e. the *Fit-Out*). These two "levels" are distinguished to disentangle yet coordinate decision-making control based on long-term and short-term interests. In a technical sense, these levels relate to each other in such a way that the parts that change can do so without causing change of the long-lasting parts. A third "level" is often defined as the furnishings, fixtures, and equipment (i.e. the *FF&E*), which can change without disturbing the Fit-Out or room layout. Because this "partitioning" is both legal and technical, it is possible that decision-control (administrative and financial) of these levels can be distributed – one party controlling the long-lasting parts and another the more mutable parts.

The proposition was that the levels distinction could solve the first problem by dividing the legal and economic ownership of the property. The legal ownership for the total facility would belong to the hospital organization and the hospice organization could have the economical ownership for the Fit-Out. The economical ownership for the Fit-Out in this case includes all installation (mechanical and electrical) systems and equipment.

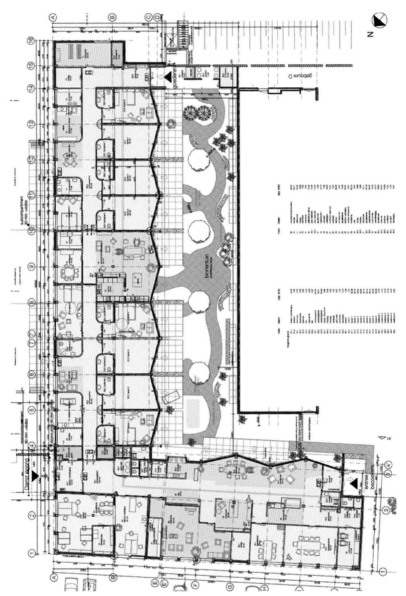

Figure 8.3
The definitive layout of the hospice.

The second problem – financing – could be solved by the following proposal:
All investments for the Fit-Out would be paid by the hospice organization, equaling about two-thirds of the total cost of refurbishing the emptied building.

1. The rent level for the land use and the emptied Base Building before refurbishment would be agreed at a low level. The difference between this low rent level and the market-oriented level after renovation could be calculated as the Present Value and could be available for financing the refurbishment of the Base Building (structure, facades, and roof).
2. The maintenance of both Base Building and Fit-Out should be the responsibility of the hospice organization during the contract period of 30 years.
3. An agreement was reached following the above proposal's conditions for a 30 year contract, with an extension of ten years. After this 40 year period, both Base Building and Fit-Out of the facility will be returned to the portfolio of the hospital organization. The hospice organization would maintain ownership of the furnishings and movable equipment.

Organizing committees of the project

During the design, tendering, construction, and commissioning phases, the management of the project consisted of a number of committees:

1. Overall design committee: (seven meetings) (Responsible for the total design and planning including the Fit-Out, furnishings and movable equipment for the hospice)
2. Building committee (17 meetings)
3. Board of the hospice (14 meetings) (Final decisions about budgets, design and planning of the hospice facility; decisions were always prepared by the architect of the hospice)
4. Participation committee: (seven meetings) (Virtual reality sessions in the early design phase for the Fit-Out and movable equipment and for preparing decision-making about layout and user aspects of the hospice facility)

Design principles and methods

Capacity analysis

As mentioned, the first capacity analysis and design of the layout was made with a capacity analysis tool. The first layout of the hospice indicated that a part of the empty building could be used for the hospice and another part for a health center. After extended negotiations with the General Practice Centre (a national organization of local health centers of which this is one), the decision was made to separate this health center from the hospice building and to extend the layout of the hospice into the whole building.

The General Practice Health Centre would be established in a nearby building on the hospital site (Figure 8.2).

3D building model of the empty building

The design for the transformation of the existing building started with a 3D building model of the empty building, without the Fit-Out. Virtual reality walk-throughs showed the potential of the empty Base Building. After the capacity analyses mentioned above, the functional areas (Fit-Out), as defined in the feasibility study, were filled in to the 3D model. This model was completed with examples of wall and floor finishes, furniture and equipment. A series of virtual reality sessions between the architect, future users and staff were organized to improve the layout and movable equipment and to prepare choices for the decisions by the Hospice Board. A full size physical mock-up was made by the co-architect to explain the design to the Board and interested participants.

After discussions with future users, the Board of the hospice and the construction company, the definitive design was presented with the corresponding budgets. A building permit was then given by the local authorities on the final design. The finalized layout of the hospice is shown in Figure 8.4.

Budgeting process

Feasibility phase

The first budget analysis was done with a quick scan method for refurbishment costs[1] enabling the design team to calculate the building costs of refurbishment. The method calculates the building cost per square meter depending on the intensity level of the refurbishment ("Standard Renovation Profile" – 1–10 shown in Figure 8.5) related to a new reference building. The user of the quick scan is able to change parameter settings according to local circumstances. These parameters give building costs for building elements in both the Base Building and the Fit-Out. The movable equipment is not included in this cost model. The estimated refurbishment costs in this case are €1,591 per m^2 ($217.00 per ft^2), so for 1,200 m^2 (12,900 ft^2) the project was budgeted at approximately 1.9 million euro including VAT ($2.34 million). In the case shown in Figure 8.5, the intensity level is chosen at "5."

Tendering principles

Tender for establishing a building team

The Hospice Board wanted a competitive tendering process for the choice of a contractor. Traditionally, this would be organized by designing the complete facility including the detailed specifications of the construction method. This

Quick Scan Refurb Costs for HOSPICE

Decreasing factors	Primary Systema, included primary installations					Secondary system	Explanation
	Foundation	Skeleton	Envelope	HVAC	Electric insta	Elevator		
New construction	0,940	0,950	0,950	0,960	0,960	0,960	0,960	<- factors related to quantities and relative costs for new construction
Demolishing	0,920	0,930	0,920	0,950	0,950	0,950	0,950	<- factors related to quantities and relative costs for demolishing elements
Refurbishing costs	0,937	0,947	0,947	0,959	0,959	0,959	0,959	<- factors related to quantities and relative costs for refurbishing

| Partial building costs | 10% | 15% | 20% | 15% | 10% | | 30% | <- division of building cost for refence building |

5	Profile refurbishment	10%	75%	100%	100%		100%	<- choosen level of refurbishment, in this case level 5
	New Building Costs per sqm2	30,00	300,00	300,00	200,00		600,00	<- reference new building cost per building part
	Prize level related to new building	120%	110%	110%	110%	110%	110%	<- price level of refurbishment related to a new reference building
	Costs not corrected with decreasing factors	36,00	330,00	330,00	220,00		660,00	<- calculated refurb cost per sqm2 by 100% replacement
	Corrected by decreasing factors	43,19	337,50	330,00	220,00		660,00	<- calculated refurb cost by partial replacement
	Factor corrected costs	1,20	1,02	1,00	1,00		1,00	<- factors correction related to partial replacements

| Costs New building per square m2 | €2.000 | reference new building | | | | <- costs per sqm2 for reference new buildings |
| Refurbishment costs per square m2 | €1.591 | related to chosen profile | | | | <- calculated costs per sqm2 for refurbishment by choosen level 5 |

Standaardrenovatieprofielen	Primary Systema, included primary installations					Secondary system	
	Foundation	Skeleton	Envelope	HVAC	Electric insta	Elevator	
1	Very light building adaptation							30%
2	Adaptation 60% infill + 20% base installations				20%	20%		60%
3	New infill + 30% installiions				30%	30%	50%	100%
4	ditto + 50% renovation envelope			50%	50%	50%	50%	100%
5	ditto + 75% renovation envelope	10%	10%	75%	100%	100%	100%	100%	<- for this case the choosen level of intensity for refurbishment
6	remaining 90% foundatation and skeleton	10%	10%	100%	100%	100%	100%	100%
7	remaining 70% foundatation and skeleton	30%	30%	100%	100%	100%	100%	100%
8	remaining 50% foundatation and skeleton	50%	50%	100%	100%	100%	100%	100%
9	only remaining 70% foundation	30%	100%	100%	100%	100%	100%	100%
10	Total demolishment and new building	100%	100%	100%	100%	100%	100%	100%

Figure 8.4
Quick Scan Refurb costs, used for defining first budgets for Base Building and Fit-out.

Figure 8.5
Comparing selection results for the short-list of 7 contractors. The white bar is for the Hospice building and the light grey bar for the Health Centre. The dark grey bar shows the cumulative result of this selection phase.

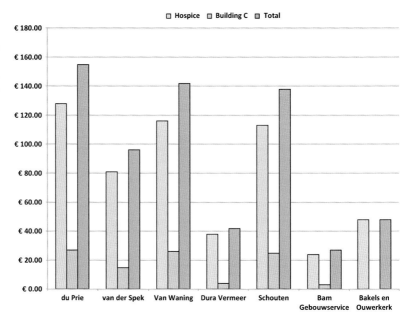

would be followed by a competitive public or restricted tendering and comparing offers at the lowest price. In the case of the hospice, an innovative tendering system was used to select a construction company to join the building team at an early stage. The construction company selected needed to be responsible for the detailed specifications and fulfilling the requirements for planning and budget. From the beginning the budgets were separated for the Base Building, Fit-Out, and FF&E.

Procedure for selecting a contractor

The selection of a contractor for the design team was organized in two phases.

The first phase involved the selection of 20 potential contractors proposed by the participating partners, for both the hospice and renovation of the Care Center.

From this first group of candidate firms, seven contractors were selected to offer competitive bids based on the preliminary design, giving relevant data for the definitive design and construction phase. The criteria for selecting the seven companies included:

- Availability
- Motivation
- Experience with Open Building implementation
- Experience with healthcare building construction

- Experience in building teams
- Experience in refurbishment
- Experience in implementing sustainability measures
- Fast Track processes
- Capacity of their organization
- Regional employment
- Knowledge of general construction, HVAC, and electrical work
- Certification

The selection method for the second phase was more detailed. The information from the selected seven contractors were compared with the budget estimates. The information needed in this second phase is depicted below. The first three aspects reflect on the quality of the contractor. The other aspects are economical and could be compared with the corresponding aspects in the calculations for the separated budgets.

Requested information from the seven companies
View on the project and planning process
Quality assurance system
Quality of participating staff

Financial analysis
Cost of the building organization in %
Cost of the building organization in Euro
Cost per person-hour
Cost of coordinating the subcontractors
General management costs
Profit and risk as % of building costs
Design costs, working in the building team

Comparing the answers and data provided by these seven companies with the data of the reference hospice project resulted in the choice of one contractor as partner in the definitive design and construction phase. The data for both the reference project and the definitive design were divided into Base Building and Fit-Out.

Contractor 1 (see Figure 8.6) was chosen, based on their offer of a lower budget of about €33.872 for the Base Building and €62.750 lower for the Fit-Out. This compared with the calculated budgets calculated for the reference building.

Open Building calculations

All further calculations and budgets were divided in costs for the Base Building and the Fit-Out and also for the equipment costs. After the selection of the du Prie construction company to join the design team, all further estimates were carried out by the contractor and discussed in

Figure 8.6
Hospice "Het Vliethuis".

detail with the architect and co-architect. Finally, separated building contracts were written for the hospice and for renovation of the health center.

Design phase

In the design phase, the budget calculations were based on the 3D model and the total quantities extracted from the model. A definitive budget was made combining the total building element costs. The construction company calculated a building cost which could be compared with earlier budget constraints. The negotiations between the architect and the contractor resulted in a definitive proposal to be presented to the Hospice Board. This budget fulfilled the requirements of the program, but discussions between the Hospice Board and the Board of the Association of the "Friends of the Hospice," – which has been responsible for fundraising – resulted in the decision that there should be a 15% reduction of the budget. The architect did not consider saving money by lowering the quality of the hospice building.

Based on the architect's experience with Open Building in practice (Nicolai and Dekker, 1990), he proposed not to lower the quality of the hospice but to design a buffer space instead of completing the Fit-Out in the part of the project given to more public functions, thus offering space for future occupancy and change of use.

This resulted in the desired cutback of 15% of the budget. In a few years after the building was initially occupied, this part was completed according the wishes of the users of the hospice, but not following the original layout plan. This outcome also accords with one of the flexibility strategies in *Healthcare Facility Design for Flexibility* (Kendall et al., 2012).

Construction principles

Base Building
Refurbishment for the Base Building consisted of renewing all exterior window frames and glass panels with high performance materials. A new main entrance and a new installation service entrance were added. Also, the roofing and thermal isolation were renewed.

Fit-Out
The Fit-Out and all mechanical installation technology is new. The existing interior construction was totally removed, including all installations. As a second step, a subfloor system was installed including a hydronic floor heating system for 60% of the building on the south-facing side that receives direct sunlight. On the north and west sides an innovative decentralized HVAC system was installed.

Flexibility

Separation walls
Gyproc CableStud (www.infillsystems.nl) was used in the interior non-load-bearing separation walls. These metal stud and gypsum board walls offer a maximum flexibility in combination with very good noise and fire insulation (see Figures 8.7, 8.8, and 8.9).

The walls between the rooms are required to achieve a high fire resistance and also a very good acoustical isolation. For fire resistance, a solution was found by separating the lightweight concrete subfloor. The position of these separation walls between the tenant rooms are fixed as a result (rather than flexible as the other CableStud walls).

Electrical system
The electrical cabling and terminations are also flexible. With the use of Wieland technology (www.wieland-electric.com/en/products/building-installation-systems) it was possible to postpone decisions about the location of power plugs and ICT cable technology to a very late stage (after the gypsum board walls were installed and finished). This product also offers the opportunity to add new power connections and plugs during occupancy quickly and at much reduced cost compared to conventional wiring

Figures 8.7, 8.8, and 8.9 **CableStud installation in metal stud interior non-load-bearing walls, ready for electrical and data wiring installation; Wieland's "Gesis" quick-connect cabling system (www.wieland-electric.com/en/products/building-installation-systems).**

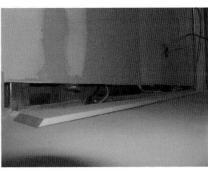

solutions. After building commissioning and in the first year in use, several changes in the electrical system were made quickly and inexpensively.

HVAC system

For the individual hospice rooms, basic hydronic floor heating provides a constant temperature. The need for a higher temperature in winter or lower in summer is provided by the decentralized flexible HVAC system. For all

Figures 8.10, 8.11, and 8.12 **The garden and interior semi-public areas.**

other rooms, decentralized HVAC technology was installed with a combination of hydronic radiators and CO_2-measured heat recovery ventilation and cooling systems. This system is highly flexible and allows future changing of functions.

Conclusions and recommendations

After four years in use it was possible to evaluate the process and product innovations used in this project.

- The end users, both organizational, caregivers, volunteers, and temporary tenants of the hospice are very satisfied with the building and the facilities.
- The Open Building approach provided a very user-oriented and clear decision-making process.
- Separating the economical ownership between the Base Building and the Fit-Out was helpful and the only way to solve juridical and financial problems.
- Financing of the whole project was possible by fundraising within the population of Voorburg and Rijswijk.
- The use of a buffer zone has been proven in practice to offer decision-flexibility; since occupancy, this zone has been fully used for new functions.
- The built-in flexibility provided by CableStud walls and Wieland electrical systems has been proven many times when changes of installations were needed.
- Decentralized HVAC systems are giving the users individualized influence of their indoor climate and are very flexible when functions have to be changed.
- Based on this and other experiences in applying the Open Building approach in building transformation projects (Dekker, 1998), a number of general observations and recommendations are possible:
- First, transformations of existing real estate to new functions is a reality in most countries in recent years and will be of increasing importance in the coming decades (Bijdendijk, 2015). Using the Open Building approach makes decision-making much clearer and efficient and gives the needed decision-flexibility for future change.
- Second, using capacity analysis in early feasibility studies should be normal in preparing the functional program, budgeting, and project planning.
- Third, including end-users in the design of the Fit-Out and movable equipment is feasible and effective, when a clear demarcation is made about the scope of this work.
- Fourth, 3D virtual reality technology is an effective tool to use in informing end-users and decision-makers about alternatives and how to evaluate them.
- Fifth, separating Base Building, Fit-Out, and FF&E in design, construction, and overall decision-making streamlines decision-making, but requires careful project management of separated contracts.

- Sixth, it is highly recommended not to tender at the lowest price after detailed specifications. After a fair and transparent competition, include the selected construction company in the design, planning, and specification phases.

Note

1 ARO (Office for Architecture and Town Planning, 1973–1986), and later KD/Consultants developed a method for spatial planning (raster technology). This was the basis for the development in KD/Consultants for spatial planning in buildings (2005–2015).

References

Bijdendijk, F (2015). The Future of Open Building Resides in the Existing Building Stock. *Proceedings: The Future of Open Building*, ETH Zurich, September 9, 2015. www.openbuilding2015.arch.ethz.ch/program.html.

Dekker, K (1998). Research Information: Open Building Systems – A Case Study. *Building Research & Information*, 26(5), pp. 311–318.

Kendall, S, T Kurmel and K Dekker (2012). *Healthcare Facility Design for Flexibility*. Delft: KD/Consultants, Center for People and Buildings.

Nicolai, R and KH Dekker (1990). *Flexibility in Hospital Building – A Strategy for the Design and Building Process*. Utrecht: On behalf of the National Hospital Institute. (In Dutch).

Chapter 9

Simulation

Tools for planning for change

William Fawcett

Basic propositions

Healthcare infrastructure is durable, but healthcare activities are changeable. Over time, increasing divergence can be expected between the ways that healthcare buildings were used when first built and the ways they come to be used. Knowing that new or evolved uses will occur, two questions arise about performance over the service life:

- How easy is it to adapt healthcare buildings for new or evolved uses?
- How well do healthcare buildings meet the requirements of new or evolved uses?

If adaptation is difficult or impossible, new uses may have to put up with substandard conditions, and if the mismatch between buildings and use crosses a threshold of acceptability, the buildings are obsolete and are demolished or drop out of healthcare use.

The design of healthcare buildings for a long and useful service life has to make provision for new or evolved uses. Many proposals that aim to do this have been put forward since 1960 or earlier, and many of the proposals have been built. Rather than putting forward new proposals, this chapter addresses the question of evaluation: how do we distinguish between strategies that are more or less effective, to guide the designers and decision-makers in current and future healthcare projects? The objective is to make appropriate provision for new or evolved uses that occur in the future, so it is necessary to take a view about future activities. This chapter argues that this can be done by simulating a range of possible future scenarios, and using these scenarios to evaluate proposed design strategies.

A note on terminology. Design strategies that provide for new or evolved uses have been given many labels, including (in alphabetical order): adaptability, duffle coat design, flexibility, indeterminate architecture, long-life loose-fit, multi-strategy buildings, open building, open systems, robust design, supports, system separation. Sometimes the same strategy has more than one label and sometimes the same label is used for more than one strategy. This chapter will refer to strategies for adaptation, which is meant to cover the full range of proposals, however labelled by their originators.

Methods of evaluation

There are two ways of evaluating strategies for adaptation that are put forward for healthcare buildings:

- retrospective: evaluate the strategy during or at the end of the buildings' service life
- prospective: evaluate the strategy before or at the start of the buildings' service life.

Retrospective evaluation

At first sight retrospective evaluation seems definitive – when a healthcare facility with adaptable features is built it becomes a full-scale, real-time experiment with tangible outcomes, and one might expect an unambiguous verdict on the success or failure of the adaptability features. However, when existing healthcare buildings are studied some complicating factors are encountered.

Retrospective evaluation can make use of three tests:

i) *Survival test.* The first test is whether a healthcare building survives or becomes obsolete. Most healthcare buildings last a long time regardless of whether or not they were designed for adaptation, and unsatisfactory buildings often remain in use for lack of alternatives; so survival does not in itself provide strong evidence for the success of strategies for adaptation. Equally, healthcare buildings may become obsolete, and be demolished or taken out of healthcare use, after a shortened service life for reasons other than the failure of strategies for adaptation. Greenwich Hospital in south London is a striking instance of early demolition: built in the 1960s, it was a complex and expensive design with intermediate service floors to maximize flexibility (AJ, 1969; Green and Moss, 1971). Plans for upgrading were developed in the early 1990s but not carried out (Stow, 2008, pp. 38–39), and the hospital was vacated after only 30 years and demolished. Two factors unrelated to adaptation contributed to this outcome: health service reorganization that made the hospital redundant, and the high cost of asbestos decontamination (Rabeneck, 2016). Evidently, a building's survival or obsolescence is a blunt instrument for evaluating its strategies for adaptation.

ii) *Life history test.* It is possible to study the life histories of long-lasting healthcare buildings and record the adaptations that actually took place. But it is difficult to evaluate strategies for adaptation using this data. If it is found that a building had many adaptations, it might be because the building was easy to adapt, or because the activities changed frequently and adaptations had to be made regardless of whether they were easy or hard; equally, if a building had few adaptations it might be because the building was hard to adapt, or because the activities were stable and the opportunities provided by an excellent strategy for adaptation were not needed. The observed adaptations are specific to the particular activities and events of the life history that actually occurred, but many other possible life histories with different outcomes might have occurred, and data for a single life history provides an imperfect basis for evaluation.

iii) *First-hand experience test.* The people who have been responsible for maintaining and adapting healthcare buildings can give first-hand reports, but it tends to reflect their personal experience and may be anecdotal. If their experience is limited to a few specific adaptations, the finding that they were straightforward or difficult may overstate or understate the building's overall adaptation potential. First-hand experience provides valuable insights but it may be an incomplete test of a building's adaptation strategy.

The retrospective approach was taken in a comparative study of five UK hospitals that had been designed with strategies for adaptation, called *How do we lengthen the useful life of hospital buildings* (Smyth, 2004). The study was carried out when the hospitals had been in use for between 20 and 30 years. The external and internal changes that had taken place were logged; the number and type of changes varied widely between the five hospitals. The report concluded, "The visits to the hospitals have provided overwhelming evidence of how unpredictable the needs for growth and change are on any particular site" (p. 51). Building attributes like floor-to-floor height, column spacing and building depth were recorded in a comparative chart, but preferred values were not identified. The report's finding with greatest relevance for new designs was that increases in building depth could limit future adaptation, noting:

> there is an urgent need to develop ward plans which reflect the new models of care within a building width (approximately 15–16 m or 49–53 ft) which makes it possible to give windows to all rooms occupied for a material proportion of the working day.
>
> (p. 51)

At site scale, there were several instances of poorly placed extensions blocking the hospitals' expansion potential: instances of a strategy for adaptation being undermined during the service life.

Although studies of the life history of healthcare facilities are always fascinating, retrospective evaluation has limitations as a way of evaluating strategies for adaptation.

Prospective evaluation
When design for adaptation is an objective for a new healthcare building, designers have to select strategies using prospective evaluation – by definition, retrospective evaluation is not available. However, the new or evolved uses

that will occur during the building's service life are uncertain. Designers often sidestep this problem by focusing on design features that favor adaptation: the greater the potential for adaptation, the more highly rated the design. An example of a hospital with highly ambitious strategies for adaptation is the McMaster University Health Sciences Centre (MHSC) in Hamilton, Canada, which opened in 1972 (Figure 9.1; Fawcett, 2017). It has intermediate service floors, a grid of 21 m^2 (69 ft^2) square column-free bays capable of extension in any direction, and cladding that can be demounted and modified. It was a complex, expensive, and impressive design; but retrospective evaluation using the life history test shows that the provision for adaptation was far in excess of what was used by the new or evolved activities that actually occurred (Pilosof, 2005). This observation is not unusual: when the life history test is applied to buildings designed with ambitious strategies for adaptation, the actual use of the strategies is often disappointingly small.

The MHSC example shows that maximizing the potential for adaptation is inadequate as a design objective. Elaborate design for adaptation risks overinvestment – that is, expending current resources for future benefits that never materialize. Equally, the omission of strategies for adaptation risks underinvestment – that is, saving current costs but incurring high future costs when adaptations are required.

To minimize the risk of overinvestment or underinvestment in strategies for adaptation, designers should not ask, "Does Design A provide greater adaptation potential than Design B?" (if so, Design A risks overinvestment);

Figure 9.1 The McMaster University Health Sciences Centre (MHSC) at Hamilton, Canada, by Eberhard Zeidler of Craig Zeidler & Strong was opened in 1972. It incorporates elaborate and expensive strategies for adaptation.

(Photo: Ian Elllingham, 2016)

nor, "Is Design A cheaper than Design B?" (if so, Design A risks under-investment); but rather, "Does Design A make more appropriate provision for adaptation than Design B for the anticipated new and evolved uses?"

Defining the anticipated new and evolved uses is problematic when the future is uncertain, but it cannot be avoided. Uncertainty was put forward as the justification for the complex and expensive MHSC design with: universal "plug-in" space that could accommodate any function, ranging from factory use, living, or hospital spaces, to complex uses such as nuclear research. Each use had to be interchangeable, as nobody could predict where each should be located or what size it should be five or ten years from now (Zeidler, 1973). But far from regarding the future as uncertain, the MHSC design implied a definite belief about the future, namely that there would be extensive and radical changes in the use of the building; otherwise the high level of investment in strategies for adaptation would not have made sense. Like MHSC, every other design strategy for adaptation has an implied belief about the future – that new and evolving uses will make use of the adaptation features being provided.

The beliefs about the future should be explicitly stated. Any attempt to predict precisely what will happen is doomed, but it is usually feasible to make reasonable estimates about the bounds of what can be envisaged during the building's service life, based on research and expert judgment. This relies on client-side input but experienced healthcare architects can contribute their knowledge of cyclic and disruptive change in healthcare buildings.

When the defined bounds of new and evolved uses have been established it is possible to generate numerous feasible scenarios using simulation techniques, where a scenario's particular values are picked randomly from the range of possibilities within the bounds. Each scenario has precise values for the building's life history, but every scenario has different values; collectively a large number of simulated scenarios sets out the range of life histories that should be allowed for by a strategy for adaptation. The scenarios can be used for prospective evaluation of design strategies – examples are given below. This is only one potential use of simulation in the healthcare sector, where there are many applications for operational issues as well as infrastructure design (Barlow and Bayer, 2011; Virtue et al., 2012; another infrastructure example is given in Fawcett, 2017).

Case study of retrospective and prospective evaluation: Northwick Park Hospital

Northwick Park Hospital (NPH) in north London was designed with a well-defined strategy for adaptation. It has survived up to the present so can be subject to retrospective evaluation. Also, unusually, it was analyzed in a pioneering exercise in prospective evaluation.

NPH was a new district general hospital, built in 1965–1972 (Weeks, 1999); it is still in use (Figure 9.2). The lead architect was John Weeks (1921–2005) who believed that architectural design should be driven by functional

Figure 9.2 Northwick Park Hospital by John Weeks of Llewelyn-Davies Weeks was built in 1965–1972. It incorporated Weeks's loose-fit and indeterminacy strategies for adaptation. The corrugated panels indicate an "open end" for extension that was never used.

(Author's photo, 2018)

considerations (Harwood, 2005). From the 1950s he specialized in hospital buildings and advocated design for growth and change, proposing a loose-fit or "duffle coat" strategy (Abramson, 2016, pp. 88–92; Hughes, 2000; Weeks, 1960). Although the duffle coat argument has logical flaws (Fawcett, 2011), the emphasis on flexibility is cogent. Weeks also put forward the adaptation strategies of indeterminate architecture and multi-strategy buildings (Weeks, 1964, 1969). When Weeks's practice (Llewelyn-Davies Weeks, later Llewelyn-Davies Weeks Forestier-Walker & Bor) was commissioned to design Northwick Park Hospital, the theories were put into practice.

Strategy for adaptation at Northwick Park Hospital

NPH is the clearest expression of Weeks's thinking on how to plan for growth and change in response to the "unequal life span of building structure and human function" (Weeks, 1973). He advocated *loose-fit* buildings (not function-specific) in an *indeterminate* organization (capable of alteration in unpredictable ways), proposing that there should be:

> disintegration rather than integration between structure and services, between services and equipment, between equipment and furniture, between furniture and walls. Buildings are therefore most likely to be useful when the 'hard' parts are reduced to a neutral supporting shell, when partitions enclose a rather banal set of rooms and when equipment can easily be plugged in to one room or another in order that the function of the room can be easily changed. No function should be built in. ... All the solutions have one thing in common and that is their designers do not see the resulting buildings in terms of a finite built element but as part of an evolving structure.
>
> (Weeks, 1973)

An early description of NPH shows how these ideas were applied (Figures 9.2 and 9.3):

> The design of the hospital is based on the ideal of staged building expansion and the continuing opportunity of replacing obsolete parts without interfering with the life of the organization. The buildings are planned around an internal "street" system which is extendible ... to give access to additional buildings. The buildings themselves are, in most cases, open-ended. ... A repetitive structural system ... is based on a coffered reinforced concrete slab on a constant grid, an internal column system with some flexibility and a precast external walling system of beams and structural mullions. ... All buildings incorporate large vertical main rising shafts connecting with horizontal distribution voids above false ceilings.
>
> (AR, 1965, p. 455)

Retrospective evaluation of Northwick Park Hospital

i) *Survival test.* Northwick Park Hospital remains in use nearly 50 years after it was built (Figure 9.3). Plans for phased replacement were put forward in the early 2000s, about 30 years into the service life, but not carried out: "It would appear that this proposal reflects both the rather forbidding appearance of the buildings and the inflexibility of the overall organisation" (Smyth, 2004, p. 71). The hospital strategy published in 2014 says: "As there is no current opportunity for a major rebuild, NPH will require phased renewal/development over the coming years to upgrade the woeful accommodation to acceptable NHS standards" (LNWH, 2014, p. 21). The hospital is not seen to be performing well for current uses: "The layout is out of date and not up to current space and functional standards for clinical delivery. ... with wards generally failing to support good clinical care. The site is congested with mixed flows evident across the site" (p. 16).

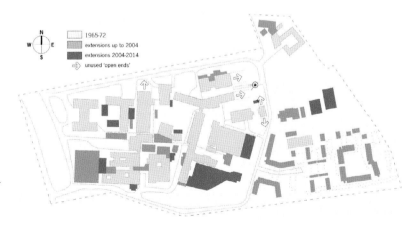

Figure 9.3 Northwick Park Hospital site plan, showing the original construction of 1965–1972, the extensions added up to 2004 (including the replacement of the residential accommodation at the southeast of the site), and extensions added between 2004 and 2014. The "open ends" for extensions that have been left unused are shown with arrows. The viewpoint of the photo in Figure 9.2 is marked with an asterisk.

(Sources: AR, 1965; LNWH, 2014; Smyth, 2004)

Although NPH passes the survival test, the current situation does not provide strong endorsement for its strategy for adaptation.

ii) *Life history test.* In 2004 it was noted:

> Although the hospital has been open for more than thirty years a surprisingly small amount of growth has occurred over the period. ... Several of the blocks thought likely to grow were specifically planned with open ends for expansion ... [but] none of the relevant departments has been extended.

And: "We understand that the various internal adaptations which have taken place over the life of the hospital have been carried out without any serious difficulty" (Smyth, 2004, p. 71). At this time it appeared that the hospital had adapted well for the new or evolved uses that had occurred. Ten years later in 2014 it was noted: "Since the hospital opened there have been many additions, extensions and conversions. However, the overall layout of the hospital generally remains consistent with the original design" (LNWH, 2014, p. 16); "The internal layout of the majority of the buildings is as originally designed, with only minor alterations following localised department refurbishment or upgrade" (p. 28); and: "Much of the original mechanical and electrical (M&E) services in use today are original, had reached the end of their design life long ago and are no longer suitable for use" (p. 29). Regarding adaptation of the Weeks buildings:

> The combination of the use of piers and load bearing ducts, not columns, which are often set out in a herring bone fashion, and the load bearing nature of the external [mullions] places very considerable constraints on conversion and clinical re-planning. The structural grid is similar to many others of this period (6.9 m or 22.6 ft) which does not readily convert to the 7.8/8.1 m (25.6/26.6 ft) dimensions that are currently required for inpatient accommodation or theatre floors. ... The floor to floor heights are again typical of their period (3.55 m or 11.6 ft) and are significantly less than current practice (3.9–4.8 m or 12.8–15.7 ft). ... Blocks which provide the bulk of the inpatient accommodation (+/ – 350 beds) were designed to provide 1 ward per floor within each building and are 780 m^2 (8400 ft^2) in area. This cannot accommodate 24 beds at current standards which is the minimum number that can be efficiently nursed on a ward. Therefore these buildings have no future as inpatient accommodation.
>
> (LNWH, 2014, p. 27)

Current thinking is that the original buildings are obsolescent, and remain in use because replacement is not possible. The study of 2004 and report of 2014 indicate very different assessments of NPH's success in adapting to new or evolved uses. There are a number of possible explanations, including one or more of the following:

- changes in use between 2004 and 2014 went beyond the adaptation capacity of the original buildings, causing deterioration of performance
- between 2004 and 2014 standards of acceptable performance rose beyond what could be provided by the original buildings
- between 2004 and 2014 wear and tear and deterioration of the building fabric and services caused their performance to fall below acceptable standards
- the adaptation and upgrade potential of the buildings was not exploited.

iii) *First-hand experience test.* The apparent deterioration in performance between 2004 and 2014 may be due to different people making the assessments, with different experiences and expectations. Although the 2014 report makes it clear that the hospital now requires substantial upgrading, it does not provide a definitive evaluation of Weeks's 1960s strategy for adaptation.

Prospective evaluation of Northwick Park Hospital

A pioneering exercise in prospective evaluation was carried out in 1973 to compare the performance of NPH and other contemporary hospital designs (Llewelyn-Davies Weeks Forestier-Walker & Bor, 1973, Note 1). It was an experimental study carried out after NPH had been designed and built.

The study focused on the structural system for hospital building and compared seven design alternatives that were being used or proposed in the 1970s:

Hospital A: interstitial, wide-span structure (Greenwich Hospital)
Hospital B: two-module structure
Hospital C: three-module structure
Hospital D: grid structure
Hospital E: U-duct structure (NPH; see Figure 9.4)
Hospital F: grid and twin-beam structure (see Figure 9.5)
Hospital G: twin-beam structure.

For each design alternative, the costs of initial construction and adaptation were estimated (Table 9.1). To evaluate the design alternatives, four service life scenarios were defined with 20, 40, 60, or 80 adaptations. The cumulative costs of construction and adaptation were calculated for each design alternative for all four scenarios (Table 9.2). The cost rankings can be plotted as a graph (Figure 9.6).

The graph shows a trade-off between construction cost (short term) and cumulative cost (long term). Alternatives A and G with high construction cost had the lowest cumulative cost for 80 adaptations; and alternatives D and B/C with low construction cost had the highest cumulative cost for 60 or 80 adaptations. Alternative E, based on NPH, ranked midway for both construction and cumulative costs. Alternative F showed the most striking

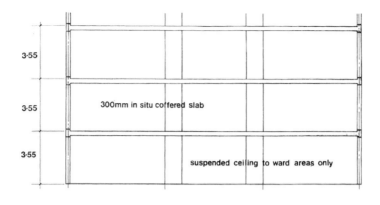
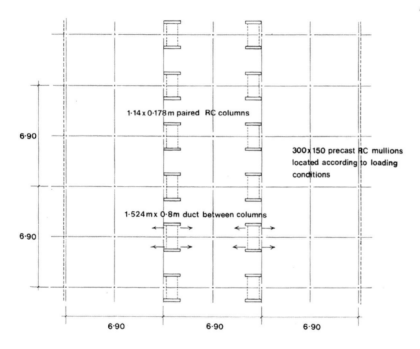

Figure 9.4
The structural system for Northwick Park as shown in the 1973 prospective evaluation exercise (identified as Hospital E).

(Source: Llewelyn-Davies Weeks Forestier-Walker & Bor, 1973, p. 33)

results: it had lowest construction cost, the lowest cumulative cost for 20, 40, or 60 adaptations, and the third lowest cumulative cost for 80 adaptations. Unless a decision-maker was sure that there would be in excess of 60 adaptations, the evaluation places alternative F as the preferred strategy.

In this study no alternative performed best across all future scenarios: decision-makers would have to take a view on which scenario or scenarios to rely on when selecting their preferred solution – matching the solution to the decision-makers' belief about the future.

The experimental study was never developed as a practical decision-making tool, but it shows how simulation modeling can be used in

William Fawcett

Figure 9.5
The structural system for best performing strategy in the 1973 prospective evaluation exercise (identified as Hospital F).

(Source: Llewelyn-Davies Weeks Forestier-Walker & Bor, 1973, p. 34)

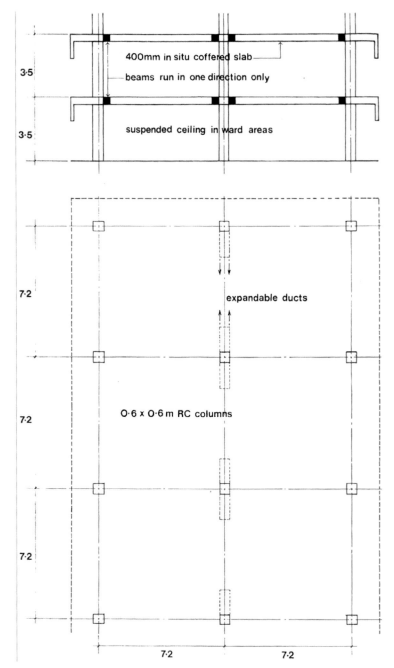

Table 9.1 Indexed cost data for the 1973 prospective evaluation of seven alternative hospital structures (with the lowest costs set to 100), showing the construction cost and the cost of adaptation for changes of use. Blank entries indicate that the hospital did not have the relevant departments. Alternative A is Greenwich Hospital and alternative E is Northwick Park Hospital. The range of adaptation costs is much narrower than the range of construction costs

Hospital	Construction	Admin to Library	Outpatient to Wards	Dining to Outpatients	Laboratory to Wards	Laboratory to Intensive Therapy
A	193	158	113	100	113	100
B	104	164	125	112	126	108
C	105	164	125	112	126	108
D	103				124	
E	122	159		105		
F	100	159	117	105	123	102
G	152	159		103		101

(Source: Llewelyn-Davies Weeks Forestier-Walker & Bor, 1973)

Table 9.2 Indexed cost data for the 1973 prospective evaluation of seven alternative hospital structures, showing the cumulative cost of construction and adaptations for 20, 40, 60, and 80 changes of use. The range of values for cumulative costs is narrow

Hospital	Construction cost	Scenario: number of adaptations				
		20	40	60	80
A	193	1,220	2,240	3,270	4,300
B	104	1,190	2,280	3,360	4,450
C	105	1,190	2,280	3,360	4,450
D	103	1,170	2,230	3,290	4,360
E	122	1,180	2,240	3,280	4,340
F	100	1,150	2,210	3,260	4,320
G	152	1,190	2,230	3,270	4,310

(Source: Llewelyn-Davies Weeks Forestier-Walker & Bor, 1973)

prospective evaluation. Today the approach can be taken much further with computer-based simulation, as discussed below (Prospective evaluation using simulation).

Conclusions from Northwick Park Hospital case study

The story of NPH's ambitious design ethos and its 50 years of use is a fascinating one, but retrospective evaluation does not provide entirely clear lessons. Were the loose-fit buildings and indeterminate site plan a success

William Fawcett

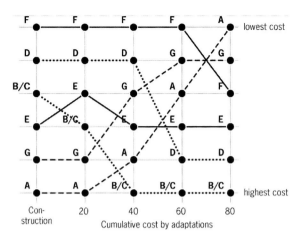

Figure 9.6 Results from the 1973 prospective evaluation of seven alternative hospital structures, showing the rankings for construction and cumulative costs (data from Table 9.2). The rankings vary with the number of adaptations. Hospitals A and G with high construction cost and low adaptation cost are shown with broken lines; Hospitals D and B/C with lower construction cost and higher adaptation cost are shown with dotted lines. Hospital E represents Northwick Park Hospital; Hospital F performed best in this exercise.

or a failure? How might John Weeks update his theories of adaptability with feedback from the 50-year experiment at NPH?

At the site scale, the current program of piecemeal upgrading and replacement of individual buildings is arguably in accordance with Weeks's concept of indeterminate architecture, in which the organization (or organism) is perpetually adapting.

At the building scale, how much change can loose-fit buildings reasonably be expected to accommodate? They cannot hope to satisfy all functional requirements for an indefinite period. It would not be reasonable to argue that the designers of the 1960s should have specified an 8.1 m (26.5 ft.) structural grid rather than a 6.9 m (22.6 ft.) grid, because 8.1 m (26.5 ft.) would be required 50 years later; nor that the 780 m^2 (8,396 ft^2) wards should have been larger because they are undersized 50 years later. The extra cost of a higher specification could never have been justified by savings made 50 years later – and any savings were highly uncertain when viewed from the 1960s. Weeks recalled that the client: "insisted on rigorous monitoring of costs and the design teams were warned that flexibility was not to be secured by building redundant space" (Weeks, 1999).

In 1997 I wrote to John Weeks, observing that little seemed to have changed at NPH and that surely this was contrary to expectations. He replied: "In fact there have been many small and two large extensions of the original chassis, and countless alterations within it. ... The interesting thing is that many departments are just as they were planned in 1965 (!)" (Weeks, 1997). The "(!)" seems to indicate that Weeks was surprised at the durability of what he expected to be changeable layouts within the buildings.

Loose-fit buildings do not attempt to satisfy changing functional requirements, but to facilitate future adaptations as and when they are needed. There were fewer adaptations at NPH than Weeks intended or expected, perhaps because the adaptation potential was forgotten by changing managerial staff over the years. NPH may have suffered from the failure to adapt; for example, many of the buildings suffer environmental discomfort and excessive heat losses from the original 1960s single-glazed curtain walling, which should surely have been replaced many years ago.

In addition to functional performance, an important factor in determining whether buildings are retained or demolished is whether people like them, and visual appearance is a significant factor in subjective esteem. NPH is generally regarded as an ugly group of buildings (Figure 9.2); the following terms were used in 1970: "... the monster of Northwick Park ... an uncomfortable inchoate mass ... a disturbing lack of clarity or directness in the principal routes ... disappoints at the detailed level too ..." (AR, 1970, p. 324 and 335). John Weeks's modern movement principles rejected aesthetic motives in design, believing that good functional and technical solutions would have an inherent beauty, but NPH suggests that this belief was mistaken. The perceived ugliness of the NPH buildings is likely to shorten their useful life.

Prospective evaluation using simulation: a worked example

Introduction
The approach to prospective evaluation used in the 1973 experiment can now be applied much more effectively with computer simulation, as demonstrated in a worked example. It models the growth, shrinkage, or reconfiguration of departments during the service life of a hypothetical new hospital. As in 1973, it is a cost-based study and in the ranking of design strategies lower costs are preferred.

The worked example is a simplified hospital with five departments. The departments' floor area requirements are known at the time of design and provided for in the new hospital building, but future departmental growth or shrinkage is uncertain. During the service life the departments' floor area demands grow or shrink by small percentage each year, causing a mismatch between the demand and actual floor area. Some mismatch can be tolerated, but if it is greater than 10% a department either requires additional floor space or is able relinquish surplus floor space. If one department is growing while another is shrinking, floor area can be exchanged between the two departments, incurring a cost of adaptation. If no floor area is available for a growing department it has to add new floor space, but this is more expensive than adaptation.

The computer model simulates the growth or shrinkage of all five departments over 50 years and records the exchanges of floor area between departments (adaptations), as well as the additions of new floor area.

Alternative design strategies for the hypothetical hospital are defined in cost terms, by varying the costs for initial construction and subsequent adaptations. The strategies for adaptation that are evaluated have higher initial costs in exchange for lower adaptation costs, but other strategies that reduce adaptation costs without increasing initial costs could also be modeled. The design features of the strategies are not defined, just their costs. In effect, the study compares performance specifications. It would be straightforward to rerun the study with cost data for real design proposals taking account of clear spans, floor-to-floor heights, floor loading capacities, reconfigurability of components and servicing systems, and so on.

Data for hypothetical hospital

The five departments of the hypothetical hospital are described in Table 9.3.

The study evaluates five design strategies, a "reference" case (H) and four variants. Cost data for initial construction costs, running costs and the costs of adaptations are given for the reference case in Tables 9.4 and 9.5. The four alternative design strategies are defined by adjusting the costs compared to the reference case, as shown in Table 9.6. Three of the design alternatives (J, K, L) are adaptive strategies with increased initial costs and reduced costs of adaptation, and one (M) reduces initial costs with increased adaptation costs. Other alternatives could be defined in the same way, for example strategies that reduce adaptation costs without increasing

Table 9.3 The five departments in the hypothetical hospital

Department:	D1	D2	D3	D4	D5
Initial size (m^2)	5,000	7,000	10,000	8,000	12,000
Grade	General	Ward	Treatment	Ward	Genera

Table 9.4 The construction and running costs for the three space grades in the hypothetical hospital, for the reference case (£/m^2)

Grade:	General	Ward	Treatment
Construction cost (£/m^2)	2,000	3,000	4,000
Running costs (£/m^2 yr)	50	75	100

Table 9.5 The adaptation cost when floor space is exchanged between departments in the hypothetical hospital, for the reference case (£/m^2)

from (below) to (right)	General	Ward	Treatment
General	500	1,500	2,500
Ward	750	750	1,500
Treatment	1,000	1,200	1,200

Simulation

Table 9.6 The five alternative design specifications for the hypothetical hospital, defined by cost adjustments compared to the reference case (H)

	H (reference)	J (pro rata)	K (adaptive)	L (strong adaptive)	M (low first cost)
Adjustment in construction costs	0	+20%	+10%	+15%	−10%
Adjustment in adaptation costs	0	−20%	−40%	−60%	+50%

initial costs: the simulation model can be run with any input data, whether or not a corresponding design is feasible in practice.

The rate of growth or shrinkage in each year can take three possible values. With a low rate of growth or shrinkage there are few adaptations over the 50 year service life, and with higher rates there are more adaptations:

- low rate: average of 5.6 adaptations over 50 years (approximately one per department)
- medium rate: average of 20 adaptations over 50 years (approximately four per department)
- high rate: average of 39 adaptations over 50 years (approximately eight per department).

In the simulation model the rate is controlled by the parameter σ (Greek *sigma*); mathematically, it is the standard deviation of a normal distribution with a mean of zero that describes the probability of growth (positive value) or shrinkage (negative value) in a department in one year. The three values used for the parameter are 0.04, 0.08, and 0.16.

When floor area is exchanged between departments it is always done in modules of 1,000 m^2 (10,750 ft^2). If a growing department has to build new floor space it is added in modules of 1,000 m^2.

Monte Carlo simulation

To run a simulation of the hypothetical hospital, the value of σ and the design strategy are specified as input data. The model then simulates the five departments' growth and shrinkage over 50 years, using ratios for the annual change that are chosen randomly in accordance with the specified value of σ. Because the growth or shrinkage ratios are chosen randomly, each run of the simulation model generates a new life history for the hospital; two contrasting life histories for the same input data are shown in Figure 9.7. The occurrence of adaptations (exchanges of floor area between departments) and additions of new floor area are recorded in each simulation run; an example of a department's floor area growth and shrinkage is shown in Figure 9.8.

Figure 9.7 Graphs showing departmental growth and shrinkage over the service life of the hypothetical hospital in two contrasting "life history" scenarios, for the medium rate of growth and change.

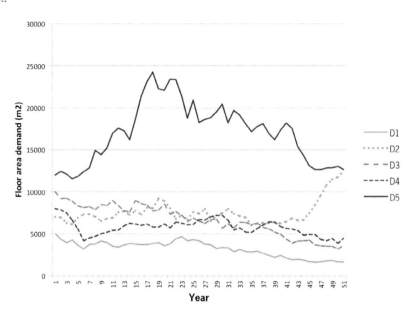

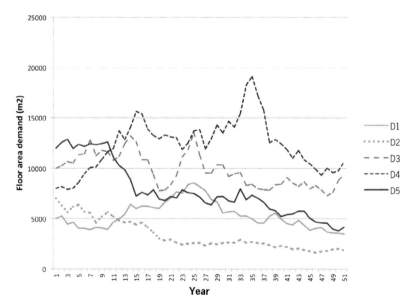

The simulation model does not predict exactly what will happen in the service life, but instead it generates a large number of scenarios that collectively show the range of possible outcomes: this is the method of Monte Carlo simulation. It relies on computer power to generate many scenarios and contrasts with the 1973 study which had just four scenarios.

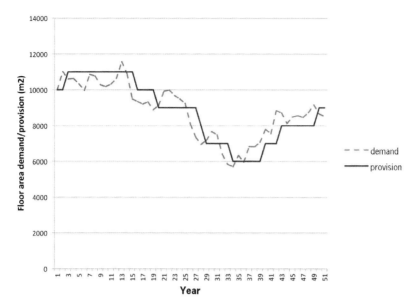

Figure 9.8 Graph of growth and shrinkage over the service life in Department D3 in the hypothetical hospital, for one "life history" scenario for the medium rate of growth and change, showing the year-to-year variation in: (i) the floor area demand (broken line), and (ii) the floor area provision where adaptations in 1,000 m² increments respond to changes in demand (solid line).

The simulation model was run 1,000 times for each of 15 sets of input data, corresponding to the three values of σ and the five design alternatives. It takes about 60 seconds for 1,000 runs, but the software has not been optimized for speed.

Results

Each simulated scenario begins with the initial construction followed by a sequence of adaptations and extensions at various times in the 50 year service life. The costs of initial construction and all the adaptations and extensions are recorded, and can be added together to give the cumulative cost for the scenario. Although there is considerable variation in the cumulative costs in the 1,000 scenarios for a given set of input data (Figure 9.9), the simplest statistic is the average cumulative cost. This is shown for the 15 sets of input data at the top of Table 9.7, labelled "no discounting."

A decision-maker using the simulation results for prospective evaluation may wish to take account of two additional factors, time preference and risk aversion. Time preference reflects the fact that most decision-makers prefer to invest when benefits arise in the near future rather than the distant future. The impact of time preference is captured by discounting future costs by a small percentage each year; so a benefit from reduced adaptation costs that arises far in the future is more heavily discounted than the same benefit occurring sooner, and is therefore given less weight in the decision-maker's evaluation. Risk aversion reflects the fact that most decision-makers prefer to invest with certain

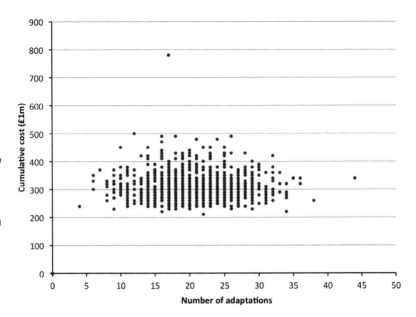

Figure 9.9 Scattergram of results for 1,000 simulated "life history" scenarios for hospital H (reference), medium rate of growth and change and no discounting. The average cumulative cost over 50 years is £315 m (including £119 m initial construction cost) and the average number of adaptations is 20, but there is wide variation between scenarios; and there are a few extreme outliers.

rather than uncertain benefits, and attach less weight to uncertain benefits. In the simulated scenarios the uncertainty increases in each successive year, so the discounting of future benefits is also consistent with risk aversion.

The strength of time preference and risk aversion varies in different situations. Stronger time preference and risk aversion is represented by higher percentage discount rates. This study uses two discount rates: 3.5% which is the discount rate recommended by the UK Treasury for public sector investment (Treasury, 2003), and 7% which might be used by a commercial investor; in some situations higher discount rates might apply. With discounting, the total of the discounted costs over the service life is called the present value, which is always lower than the cumulative (undiscounted) cost, not because the costs of future adaptations are reduced but because the future costs are given less weight by today's decision-makers. The results of the evaluation with the two discount rates are shown in the lower part of Table 9.7.

To apply discounting it is necessary to know the timing of future adaptations, as is the case with the simulated life history scenarios. In the 1973 study the four scenarios specified the number of adaptations but not their time of occurrence, so it was impossible to apply discounting; the evaluation could only use undiscounted cumulative costs with no allowance for time preference or risk aversion.

Taking the average of cumulative costs or present values is the simplest way of analyzing the results from Monte Carlo simulation runs, but further analysis of the spread of results is also possible and would give additional understanding and insight.

Table 9.7 Average life cycle costs for the hypothetical hospital (initial construction plus 50-year service life, in £m) for 1,000 simulated "life history" scenarios, for five alternative design specifications (H-M) and three rates of growth and change (σ), with no discounting (top), 3.5% discount rate (centre) and 7% discount rate (bottom). In each line the lowest cost alternative is boxed and the higher cost alternatives are toned

discount rate	rate of growth and range (σ)	H reference	J pro rata	K adaptive	L strong adaptive	M low first cost
no discounting	low σ	286	311	295	301	277
	medium σ	313	337	314	316	314
	high σ	390	392	347	339	419
3.5% discount rate	low σ	197	222	209	214	186
	medium σ	212	236	219	223	205
	high σ	245	259	238	236	255
7% discount rate	low σ	165	190	177	182	153
	medium σ	174	198	184	189	165
	high σ	194	215	197	197	194

average life cycle costs for 1,000 Monte Carlo runs, in £m

Discussion

The primary objective of the worked example is to demonstrate the use of simulation in prospective evaluation. The methodology is more important than the data for the hypothetical hospital, which could easily be replaced with new data.

The following observations can be made from the results of the worked example:

- There is no universally best solution: the preferred design alternative varies depending on the rate of growth or shrinkage (the value of σ) and the discount rate. These are not design attributes but reflect the hospital managers' belief about the future and their strength of time preference and risk aversion.
- Adaptive strategies that increase initial construction costs in exchange for cost savings in future adaptations are only cost effective if there are many future adaptations, that is, if a high rate of growth and shrinkage is anticipated. These strategies perform badly if there are few future adaptations.
- Strategies for adaptation that increase initial construction costs need leverage that gives a proportionally greater reduction in future adaptation costs. Design Alternative J ("pro rata") that increases construction costs by 20% in exchange for 20% reduction in adaptation costs performs worst in almost all comparisons. The lack of leverage in the strategies that were compared in the 1973 study (Table 9.1) should raise alarm bells.

- Strategies for adaptation that increase initial construction costs perform worse if discounting is applied, increasingly so with higher discount rates.
- If few future adaptations are anticipated, and especially if there is discounting, the strategy of minimizing the initial construction cost (Design Alternative M, "low first cost") is cost effective, despite the increased adaptation costs.

These general trends would probably apply to other situations, but the quantified results are specific to the input data for the hypothetical hospital and cannot be transferred to other situations. However, it is straightforward to rerun the simulation model for other situations by changing any of the input data values and generating new quantified results. The simulation approach is flexible and the model can be customized or elaborated for new situations.

Some limitations of the present study can be identified. Many could be addressed by revising the input data or adapting the simulation model.

- The hypothetical hospital is very small: this is appropriate for a worked example, but the simulation model can be run with input data for a larger hospital, although it would take longer to run.
- The worked example only considers departmental size and ignores other requirements that might trigger adaptations, for example, the need for changes to the spatial subdivision within the departments or the mechanical/electrical servicing systems: if the processes that generate other needs for adaptation can be defined they can be included in an elaborated simulation model.
- The worked example only considers cost as the basis for evaluation: other performance criteria could be used in an elaborated model if they can be defined quantitatively, such as access to circulation systems, connectivity/separation of functional elements, availability of daylight, capacity for large/heavy medical equipment, etc. It is also possible for decision-makers to use the quantified results of the simulation model alongside other qualitative criteria, such as appearance, speed of construction, suitability for phased development, etc.
- The worked example only considers incremental change to a fixed set of departments and does not allow for new departments to be started or existing ones closed: if the incidence of changes to the departmental structure in a hospital could be defined probabilistically, it could be included in an elaborated simulation model.
- In the worked example, floor space can be exchanged between any two departments if one is growing while the other is shrinking, but in practice spatial layout could restrict feasible exchanges to, for example, adjacent departments or departments on the same floor level. For this reason the number of adaptations in the worked example may be inflated: the simulation model could be elaborated to take account of spatial layout constraints on feasible exchanges.

- In the worked example, the same adaptations (based on growth or shrinkage of departmental floor area demands) take place for all design strategies, but in practice the ease or cost of adaptation would influence whether or not they are carried out: the model could be elaborated to set adaptation thresholds that are sensitive to adaptation cost or difficulty.
- In the results for the worked example the variation between the results for different design alternatives is sometimes very small (Table 9.7): the simulation model relies on many estimated values, so marginal differences between alternatives cannot be regarded as significant – in such cases, the alternatives should be regarded as performing equally well in the simulation. Interpretation of the results should prioritize broad trends and big differences.

There are many opportunities for elaborating the simulation model to make it more realistic. However, a word of caution is appropriate: over complexity can defeat the objective of a simulation model, which should be quick to run, easy to rerun with updated input data, and show a clear linkage between changes in the input data and results. Elaborations that defeat these objectives, or that lead to only marginal differences in the results, are probably counterproductive.

Conclusions

The benefits of adaptable healthcare infrastructure are self-evident, and creative thinking by designers in devising imaginative strategies for adaptation is highly desirable, but to maximize the benefits in practice the author argues that proposed strategies should be evaluated before making infrastructure decisions. Evaluation has been the subject of this chapter, examining retrospective evaluation and prospective evaluation.

Retrospective evaluation of healthcare buildings in use produces fascinating data and adds greatly to the experience and judgment of designers and decision-makers, but it is often ambiguous. It rarely produces findings that are directly applicable to new healthcare infrastructure, due to the lack of comparability between facilities built in different eras and countries or regions, and for different functional programs. One lesson that might be drawn from retrospective studies is that less adaptation often takes place than anticipated by designers, as at the McMaster University Health Sciences Centre and Northwick Park Hospital where adaptable features were left unused. This signals the risk that overestimation of the amount of future adaptation could lead to overinvestment in new healthcare infrastructure projects.

Prospective evaluation carried out at the time of design should reduce the risks of overinvesting or underinvesting in the provision for future adaptation in new healthcare infrastructure projects, but it immediately hits the problem of future uncertainty. How is it possible to design the right provision for adaptation when the future demand for adaptation cannot be predicted? It is impossible to avoid this linkage between the provision for adaptation and the anticipated level of demand for adaptation. Even when the linkage is not made explicit, the anticipated level of demand for adaptation is implicit in the level of provision for adaptation in a chosen infrastructure design.

Simulation modeling offers a way out of the impasse. Without attempting to make precise predictions about the future, multiple life history scenarios can be simulated that are consistent with the anticipated rate of growth and change. The life history scenarios provide a test set for evaluating design alternatives that offer different strategies for adaptation. Effective simulation models should be straightforward to run so that they can be rerun many times by designers or decision-makers with incremental adjustments to the input data, until there is confidence that they have arrived at an infrastructure strategy with a satisfactory balance between the need for and the provision for adaptation.

Although prospective evaluation using simulation modeling is unlikely to be the sole basis for decision-making for healthcare infrastructure, the contribution of quantified data from simulation alongside other factors that may be harder to quantify should improve the rigor and effectiveness of healthcare infrastructure decision-making.

Acknowledgements

Valuable information and comments about Northwick Park Hospital were provided by Christopher Shaw of the practice Medical Architecture and Chair of the Architects for Health organization; and by John Cooper of the architectural practice JCA, who contributed to the 2014 review of Northwick Park Hospital (LNWH, 2014) and designed the new Accident & Emergency Unit at the hospital. The simulation model was programmed by Danny Rigby of Modux Ltd.

Note

1 John Weeks gave the author a copy of the unpublished report *Long-Life Loose-Fit: A Comparative Study of Change in Hospital Buildings* (Llewelyn-Davies Weeks Forestier-Walker & Bor, 1973) at a seminar in Cambridge University Department of Architecture in November 1973. The study was led by Gordon Best. Weeks also prepared a three-page note for the seminar (Weeks, 1973).

References

Abramson, DM (2016). *Obsolescence: An Architectural History*. Chicago: University of Chicago Press.

AJ (Architects' Journal) (1969). Greenwich District Hospital. *Architects' Journal*, November 26, pp. 1369–1386.

AR (Architectural Review) (1965). Northwick Park Hospital. *Architectural Review (Special Issue on Health and Hospitals)*, June, pp. 454–455.

AR (Architectural Review) (1970). Northwick Park Hospital. *Architectural Review (Special Issue on Health and Welfare)*, May, pp. 330, 334–335.

Barlow, J and S Bayer (2011). Raising the Profile of Simulation and Modelling in Health Services Planning and Implementation. *Journal of Health Services Research and Policy*, 16(3) July, pp. 129.

Fawcett, W (2011). The Sustainable Schedule of Hospital Spaces: Investigating the 'Duffle Coat' Theory of Flexibility. In S Th Rassia and PM Pardalos (Eds.), *Sustainable Environmental Design in Architecture: Impacts on Health*. New York: Springer.

Fawcett, W (2017). The Measurement and Efficiency of Adaptive Design Strategies. In WFE Preiser, AE Hardy and JJ Wilhelm (Eds.), *Adaptive Architecture: Changing Parameters and Practice*. London: Routledge.

Green, D and R Moss (1971). *Hospital Research and Briefing Problems*. London: King Edward's Hospital Fund for London.

Harwood, E (2005). Proponent of Flexible Hospital Design [Obituary of John Weeks]. *The Independent* (London), June 30.

Hughes, J (2000). The Indeterminate Building. In J Hughes and S Sadler (Eds.), *Non-Plan: Essays on Freedom, Participation and Change in Modern Architecture and Urbanism*. Oxford: Architectural Press.

Llewelyn-Davies Weeks Forestier-Walker & Bor (1973). *Long-Life Loose-Fit: A Comparative Study of Change in Hospital Buildings*. Unpublished report – see Note 1.

LNWH (London North West Healthcare NHS Trust) (2014). *Estates Strategy*. London: LNWH NHS Trust.

Pilosof, N (2005). Planning for Change: Hospital Design Theories in Practice. *AIA Academy of Healthcare Journal*, 8th edition, pp. 13–20.

Rabeneck, A (2016). Flexibility in Practice. In W Fawcett (Ed.), *Activity-Space Research: Built Space in the Digital World*. CreateSpace Publishing.

Smyth, P (2004). *How Do We Lengthen the Useful Life of Hospital Buildings: A Study of the Design of Hospitals to Improve Their Adaptability to Change*. Report by ESHA Architects for NHS Estates, unpublished.

Stow, D (2008). Transformation in Healthcare Architecture: From the Hospital to a Healthcare Organism. In S Prasad (Ed.), *Changing Hospital Architecture*. London: RIBA Publications.

Treasury (2003). *The Green Book: Appraisal and Evaluation in Central Government*. London: UK Treasury.

Virtue, A, T Chaussalet, and J Kelly (2012). Healthcare Planning – The Simulation Perspective. In: Proceedings of the Operational Research Society Simulation Workshop (SSW12).

Weeks, J (1960). Planning for Growth and Change. *Architects' Journal*, July 7, pp. 20–22.

Weeks, J (1964). Indeterminate Architecture. *Transactions of the Bartlett Society*, 2, pp. 83–107.

Weeks, J (1969). Multi-Strategy Buildings. *Architectural Design*, June, pp. 536–540.

Weeks, J (1973). Seminar Notes, Cambridge University Department of Architecture, November 1973. (Unpublished – see Note 1).

Weeks, J (1997). Letter to W Fawcett, 18 March 1997, unpublished.

Weeks, J (1999). Changing Spaces [Review of Northwick Park Hospital]. *Hospital Development*, 30(7) July, pp. 18–19.

Zeidler, E (1973). Designing for the Unknown Future. *Business Quarterly*, 37(3), p. 28.

Chapter 10

The growth and change of hospital buildings

Kazuhiko Okamoto

Background
This chapter aims to find how the concept of growth and change in hospitals has been introduced and developed in Japan, through a literature review and interviews. It is based on a research project "Study Report on the Growth and Change of Hospital Architecture" (Takemiya et al., 2016). A literature review was implemented; 245 papers concerning hospital design published between 1874 and 2007 were collected and analyzed. Interviews were carried out with Professor Emeritus Makoto Yanagisawa at Nagoya University, and Professor Emeritus Yasushi Nagasawa at the University of Tokyo. The 245 papers are arranged in chronological order and results are described for each historical period.

Present hospital situation in Japan
Japanese medical law defines a hospital as a medical facility with more than 19 beds. In 2016, 8,442 hospitals existed for a population of 127 million. Modern Japanese hospitals have been criticized for their large patient capacity and their long inpatient stays. As a result, the number of beds and hospitals has gradually decreased.

As Table 10.1 shows, 81.2% of them are run by the private sector, however they accommodate only 70.3% of beds (Table 10.2) because the public sector has relatively big sites inherited from old army camps or arsenals originating from Shoguns' castles or houses in the middle ages. Statistics show that the construction budgets of public hospitals are larger than budgets for private hospitals.

Before the end of WWII (1945)
The oldest paper we found is the Japanese translation of "Hygiene theory in the Navy and Army" (Tsuboi,1874) written by a professor at the Naval Medical University of the Netherlands in 1866, in which, surprisingly, vacant space for hospital expansion has already been mentioned. Hospitals – which means military hospitals in this paper – are classified into Class 1

Table 10.1 Number of hospitals according to hospital administration

	Type of Hospital Administration	No. of Hospitals	Percentage (N=8,442)	3	4	5	6	7	8	Average No. of Applied Methodologies
Public Sector	National Sector	327	3.9%	1	1	0	0	2	0	26.78
	Official Sector	1,213	14.4%	15	12	4	3	0	1	13.26
	Insurance Sector	53	0.6%	0	0	0	0	0	0	26.51
Private Sector	Healthcare Corporation	5,754	68.2%	1	1	0	0	0	0	288.12
	Others	1,095	13.0%	5	6	2	0	0	0	24.88

Table 10.2 Number of beds according to hospital administration

	Type of Hospital Administration	No. of Beds (N=1,561,005)	Percentage	3	4	5	6	7	8	Average No. of Applied Methodologies
Public Sector	National Sector	1,29,185	8.3%	1	1	0	0	2	0	9938.94
	Official Sector	3,17,827	20.4%	15	12	4	3	0	1	3117.32
	Insurance Sector	16,006	1.0%	0	0	0	0	0	0	8003.01
Private Sector	Healthcare Corporation	8,63,183	55.3%	1	1	0	0	0	0	43159.56
	Others	2,34,806	15.0%	5	6	2	0	0	0	5105.55

(temporary hospitals at the front line), Class 2 (main hospitals at headquarters), and Class 3 (true main hospitals at the rear). The paper says that Class 3 hospitals must have vacant space in the hospital site because patients are transferred from Class 1 and 2 hospitals. This paper is the first example of growth and change theory introduced to Japan from overseas.

The first article in the first issue of the journal of the Architectural Institute of Japan in 1887 concerns design methods for hospital architecture beginning with "Hospital architecture design is one of the most sensitive and difficult ones" (Watanabe, 1887). The paper explains that hospital architecture is the building type with a short history, emerging in the 18th century and maturing in 1854 with the Lariboisière Hospital in Paris. Thereafter, it pointed out the importance of the hospital site, which enables patients to recover if the site has good views and fresh air. In addition, the dimension of patient rooms for infection prevention (1,500–2,000 ft^2 for fresh air or 8 ft of space between beds) are almost identical to *Notes on Hospitals* by Florence Nightingale in 1859 (Nightingale, 1859). This information must have been imported from Europe and translated into Japanese.

The first non-translated growth and change publication by a Japanese author is *New Hygiene: Second Edition* published in 1899 by Ogai (Rintaro) Mori, a medical doctor dispatched to Europe to learn Western medicine, who later became a famous novelist (Mori and Koike, 1899). He found, while visiting Denmark, that the Oresunder Hospital in Copenhagen required 320 m^2 of site area (3,444 ft^2) per bed for future buildings. He reports of unhealthy hospitals in the United Kingdom caused by the mistakes during extension or refurbishment, meaning that some hospitals there failed to grow or change at that time.

The most influential Japanese hospital architect in this era was Masao Takamatsu, who studied hospital architecture in the United States and theorized growth and change. He mentioned several findings in the United States: that "flexible" floor plans were necessary in patient wards; future extensions must be expected in clinical departments at large hospitals; therefore future development must be considered in hospital site design. He also imported the terms "open ended" and "close ended" corridors (Takamatsu, 1923).

After WWII and the reconstruction period (1945–1959)

"Design and Construction of General Hospitals," serialized in *Architectural Record* in the United States from August 1945 to August 1946 by Marshall Shaffer, a senior engineer at the US Public Health Service, was first translated into Japanese in 1949 (Kenchiku Bunka Editorial Office, 1949). In this serial translation, minimized function and composition, separation of operation department and ER, and expandable administration departments are illustrated as the most typical for general hospitals with 40 beds tending to expand to 50 to 60 beds. He insisted that extra site area as big as 100% of the existing site should be prepared for future expansion. This recommendation of "100%" site capacity lasted for a long time because Professor Yasumi Yoshitake at the University of Tokyo and Takehiko Ogawa at National Institute of Public Health in Japan repeatedly translated this article.

Yanagi Osuga's design method is notable for the reconstruction period (Osuga, 1951). While a reinforced concrete structure was required for hospital architecture because of fire and earthquake resistance, the economic situation did not allow this method to be realized. Therefore, he proposed a "divided building method" in which minimum requirements are satisfied within the limited budget as the first step (including circulation and piping interfaces) followed by a connecting second step building which will be constructed later in unified architectural design.

A model hospital plan by Professor Yasumi Yoshitake was published in 1950 and was successively cited not only in architectural but also medical magazines (Medical Affairs Office of the Ministry of Health and Welfare, 1950). He then reported on an architectural research conference in London and introduced architect Richard Llewelyn-Davies, a colleague of John Weeks, recommending that hospital architecture change along with medical and social development.

Rapid economic growth period (1960–1979)

A book on design methods (Architectural Institute of Japan, 1960) and another on design theory (Yoshitake et al., 1962), both on hospital architecture, were edited by Professor Yasumi Yoshitake in the early 1960s. These sister books addressed mechanical equipment issues as well as Richard Llewelyn-Davies. John Weeks and the words "growth and change" do not yet appear.

John Weeks was first introduced to Japan by Professor Makoto Ito at Chiba University in 1965 (Ito, 1965). In his paper, John Weeks defined hospitals, university research centers, and airports as "Indeterminate Architecture" and a methodology implicitly aligned with growth and change is explained, while the words "growth and change" were not yet used.

The words "growth and change" were first presented in a paper by Professor Makoto Yanagisawa at Nagoya University in 1969, who later visited John Weeks in the UK, and the McMaster Hospital in Hamilton, Canada, which John Weeks recommended him to see as a good example of "growth and change" (Yanagisawa, 1969). After these papers, Weeks's "growth and change" concept spread and was accepted throughout Japan through textbooks and drawings, and its application in the Chiba Cancer Center. Questions have been raised by some researchers including Professor Ito and Professor Yanagisawa over the following: 1) difficulty of moving LGS (light-gauge steel) walls; 2) unreasonably small rooms between long span structure; 3) challenging expansion at center of the site; 4) too many windowless rooms; and 5) conflict of "rational systems" and humane spaces.

Bubble economy period and later (1980–2004)

Professor Makoto Ito, who first introduced John Weeks to Japan, raised questions in 1987 on his representative project, Northwick Park Hospital completed in 1970. Ito thought that preparedness for future extension requires an excessive budget and forces staff to walk longer distances.

The concept of growth and change was evaluated in a post-occupancy study by John Weeks himself in 2000 and found unsuccessful in the case of the Northwick Park Hospital (Weeks and Nagasawa (Translator), 2000). Only one extension was carried out at an expected open ended corridor while others are executed on the rooftop or in vacant lots connected with awkward corridors. The vice president of the National Health Service (NHS) questioned the concept, stating "it was symbolic, but not realistic" (Yamashita, 2003).

Typology of growth and change in Japanese language literature

Literature survey

This section aims to clarify the characteristics of the methodology of preparing for growth and change described in the Japanese language architecture literature. The following popular journals and reports on hospital architecture were selected for the literature survey: *The Journal of Japan Institute of Healthcare Architecture* No.1–184; Japan Institute of Healthcare Architecture, 1968–2014; *BYOIN* 54(1)–74(12); *Igaku-Shoin*, 1995–2015; *Overseas Study Tour Report* No.1–29, Japan Institute of Healthcare Architecture, 1979–2013.

Comments on growth and change are extracted from those sources except in the following cases: unrealized projects, healthcare facilities without hospital beds, and projects without comment on methodology. Finally, 183 domestic and 56 overseas hospitals were selected for analysis (Table 10.3).

Results

The methodologies mentioned in the literature are classified into 17 types as Table 10.4 shows. Figures 10.1 and 10.2 illustrate each methodology and Table 10.5 explains domestic hospitals' administration according to the classification by the Japanese Ministry of Health, Labor and Welfare.

Analysis was carried out within the scope of the following topics.

Popular methodologies within overall hospitals

Among four large categories, Building Layout (74.3%) was most often mentioned followed by Floor Plan (69.4%), Structure (36.1%), and Mechanical equipment (32.2%) in 183 domestic hospitals (Table 10.6). In each category, Extra Site Space (51.9%), Vacant Floor Space (24.0%), Long Span Structure (21.9%), and Interstitial Floor/Mechanical Trench (14.8%) were the most common design strategies.

Overseas methodologies were quite similar to the domestic methods in terms of these four large categories; however Block Plan and External Pipe Shaft were

Table 10.3 Hospital site at each era

	Country	No. of Hospitals
Domestic	Japan	183
Overseas	United States	21
	United Kingdom	8
	Germany	5
	Finland	5
	Canada	3
	Denmark	3
	Switzerland	2
	Sweden	2
	France	2
	Italy	1
	Iraq	1
	Austria	1
	Greece	1
	Belgium	1
Overseas Subtotal		56
Total		239

Table 10.4 Types of methodologies

LargeCategory	Methodology
BuildingLayout	01 Extra Site Space
	02 Finger-type Plan
	03 Independent Energy Center
	04 Ise Grand Shrine Reconstruction System
	05 Block Plan
FloorPlan	06 Vacant Floor Space
	07 LGS (Light-gauge Steel) Partition
	08 Open Ended Corridor
	09 Spinal Street
Structure	10 Long Span Structure
	11 Connection for Vertical Extension
	12 Enough Floor Height
	13 Enough Load Allowance
MechanicalEquipment	14 Interstitial Space/Mechanical Trench
	15 External Pipe Shaft
	16 Raised Floor
	17 Concentrated Pipe Shaft

not mentioned. The reason why Connection for Vertical Extension and Enough Load Allowance were more popular in overseas hospitals is that many of them might be free from risk of earthquake which is a major issue in Japan.

Popular methodologies classified according to the type of administration

Among domestic Public hospitals, more than two-thirds of hospital projects used the Building Layout and Floor Plan methodologies of the four large categories; all the national hospitals in Japan introduced both (Table 10.7). It became clear that these two categories are the main methodologies. Within Building Layout category, over 40% of all hospital administrators prepared Extra Site Space.

In terms of the Mechanical Equipment category, Official hospitals often used methodologies in this category and over 30% of national hospitals use an Interstitial Space/Mechanical Trench strategy. As mentioned earlier, national hospitals seem to have enough budget to install Interstitial Space/ Mechanical Trench.

Popular methodologies classified according to number of beds

Hospitals are sorted into six sizes according to the number of beds (Table 10.8). Among four large categories, Building Layout is influential as

Table 10.5 Types of hospital administrations

Public Sector (N=117)	National Sector (N=13)	Ministry of Health, Labor and Welfare
		National Hospital Organization
		National University Corporation
		Japan Labor Health and Welfare Organization
		National Centers and Other National Organizations
	Official Sector (N=102)	Prefectural Government
		Municipality
		Incorporated Administrative Agency
		Japanese Red Cross Society
		Social Welfare Organization SAISEIKAI Imperial Gift Foundation, Inc
		HOKKAIDO SHAKAIJIGYO Community Service Association
		Japan Agricultural Cooperatives
		National Health Insurance Organization
		Association of National Social Insurance Society
		Japan Community Healthcare Organization
	Insurance Sector (N=2)	Mariners Insurance Organization
		National Federation of Health Insurance Societies
		Mutual Aid Associations for National and Municipal Personnel
		National Health Insurance Society
Private Sector (N=66)	Healthcare Corporation (N=20)	Healthcare Corporation
	Others (N=46)	Public-interest Corporation
		Private School
		Social Welfare Corporation
		Health Co-operative Association
		Private Company and Others

more than half of all hospitals, especially over 85% of hospitals with 200 beds or less, adopted it. Within Building Layout, over 45% of hospitals have Extra Site Space.

The category Floor Plan method is also essential, as more than half of hospitals, especially almost all the hospitals with 300 beds or less, adopted it. Regarding Structure and Mechanical Equipment, hospitals with over 501 beds attempted to use as many methodologies in this category as possible.

Number of growth and change methodologies per hospital

Table 10.9 shows that almost all the domestic hospitals adopted four or fewer of the above methodologies (the average number is 2.12), while overseas hospitals applied two or fewer methodologies (average: 1.54).

The growth and change of hospital buildings

01 Extra Site Space

To prepare extra space in the hospital site for future extension or rebuilding.

02 Finger-type Plan

To layout buildings like fingers to make every function extends.

03 Independent Energy Center

To stand energy center alone to make mechanical equipment easy to replace.

Figure 10.1
Illustrations of types of methodologies.

04 Ise Grand Shrine Reconstruction System

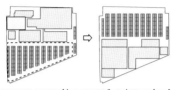

To prepare extra space as big as present footprint to make whole new building to be built at once like Ise Grand Shrine's periodical reconstruction.

05 Block Plan

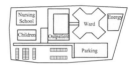

To allocate different functions in separate buildings regarding different functional duration.

06 Vacant Floor Space

To prepare vacant floor space for future use.

07 LGS (Light-gauge Steel) Partition

To use LGS partition to make room layout easy to change.

08 Open Ended Corridor

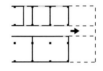

Not to make room at the end of corridor to prepare for future expansion.

Number of methodologies classified according to administration type

The average number of these methodologies used per domestic hospital was 2.12, which differs by administration category (Table 10.10). The highest average is in national hospitals (2.69) followed by official hospitals (2.20), because they have larger floor areas and budgets as mentioned before.

Number of methodologies classified according to number of beds

Large domestic hospitals with 501 beds or more tend to adopt more of these methodologies (average: 2.71) compared to all hospitals (average: 2.12), however some small hospitals installed more methodologies (up to eight) (Table 10.11).

Number of methodologies classified according to construction era

As Table 10.12 shows that most of the hospitals were constructed from the 1960s to 2010s both in Japan and overseas, we discount the rest of them in

Kazuhiko Okamoto

Figure 10.2
Illustrations of types of methodologies.

09 Spinal Street

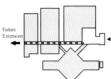

To lay main street connecting to every building expecting large future extension.

10 Long Span Structure

To have long span structure to make room layout easy to change.

11 Connection for Vertical Extension

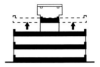

To prepare structural and mechanical end ready to be connected to future vertical extension.

12 Enough Floor Height

To have floor height enough to make mechanical equipment in the ceiling easy to maintain or replace.

13 Enough Load Allowance

To have strong structure enough to have extra load of future vertical extension.

14 Interstitial Space/Mechanical Trench

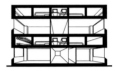

To have interstitial space or trench to make mechanical equipment easy to maintain or replace.

15 External Pipe Shaft

To install pipe shaft outside not to disturb insidewhen maintainance or replacement.

16 Raised Floor

To have raised floor to install or replace medical equipment in the future.

17 Concentrated Pipe Shaft

To concentrate pipe shaft to make mechanical equipment easy to maintain or replace.

this section. Not only in Japan but also overseas, more methodologies are applied in the 1970s (Japanese average: 2.59, overseas average: 2.56) than in other eras (Tables 10.13 and 10.14). This result may corroborate John Weeks's influence described above.

Among domestic hospitals, no specific methodology was applied in a particular era (Table 10.15). Extra Site Space and Vacant Floor Space are employed in all eras. Finger-type Plan, LGS Partition, Spinal Street, Long Span Structure, Interstitial Space/Mechanical Trench, Raised Floor appeared in 1970s and are always active methodologies. The Finger-type Plan, LGS Partition, Spinal Street, and Interstitial Space/Mechanical Trench were introduced to Japan due to John Weeks's influence.

Until the end of 1980s, Extra Site Space was used frequently, but its use sharply decreased in 1990s as was the trend of Block Plan, which disappeared in the 2010s. It could be possible that land acquisition became more difficult after the economic bubble era. Use of the Open Ended Corridor also decreased consistently; the reason is that it might have become too common to be mentioned. On the other hand, Long Span Structure gradually increased perhaps because technical developments lowered its construction cost.

The growth and change of hospital buildings

Table 10.6 Applied methodologies in domestic/overseas hospitals

Large Category	Methodology	Domestic Hospital (N=183) No. of Mention	Percentage	Overseas Hospital (N=56) No. of Mention	Percentage
Building Layout	01 Extra Site Space	95	51.9%	24	42.9%
	02 Finger-type Plan	18	9.8%	2	3.6%
	03 Independent Energy Center	13	7.1%	3	5.4%
	04 Ise Grand Shrine Reconstruction System	6	3.3%	1	1.8%
	05 Block Plan	4	2.2%	0	0.0%
	Total	136	74.3%	30	53.6%
Floor Plan	06 Vacant Floor Space	44	24.0%	10	17.9%
	07 LGS (Light Gauge Steel) Partition	33	18.0%	5	8.9%
	08 Open Ended Corridor	28	15.3%	4	7.1%
	09 Spinal Street	22	12.0%	4	7.1%
	Total	127	69.4%	23	41.1%
Structure	10 Long Span Structure	40	21.9%	5	8.9%
	11 Connection for Vertical Extension	12	6.6%	7	12.5%
	12 Enough Floor Height	10	5.5%	4	7.1%
	13 Enough Load Allowance	4	2.2%	5	8.9%
	Total	66	36.1%	21	37.5%
Mechanical Equipment	14 Interstitial Space/Mechanical Trench	27	14.8%	9	16.1%
	15 External Pipe Shaft	12	6.6%	0	0.0%
	16 Raised Floor	11	6.0%	2	3.6%
	17 Concentrated Pipe Shaft	9	4.9%	1	1.8%
	Total	59	32.2%	12	21.4%

Though it is not clear how John Weeks influenced overseas hospitals, a similar trend was observed in Table 10.16. The only difference from Japanese hospitals is that Structure and Mechanical Equipment are not mentioned after the 2000s.

Typology of growth and change through drawings

Drawings survey

While methodologies are analyzed above by searching text documents, here we present and discuss architectural drawings as a means to understand the actual growth and change process in Japan.

173

Table 10.7 Applied methodologies according to domestic hospital administration

Large Category	Methodology	Public Sector - National Sector (N=13) No. of Mention	Percentage	Official Sector (N=102) No. of Mention	Percentage	Private Sector - Insurance Sector (N=2) No. of Mention	Percentage	Healthcare Corporation (N=20) No. of Mention	Percentage	Others (N=46) No. of Mention	Percentage
Building Layout	01 Extra Site Space	7	53.8%	59	57.8%	1	50.0%	8	40.0%	20	43.5%
	02 Finger-type Plan	3	23.1%	14	13.7%	0	0.0%	0	0.0%	1	2.2%
	03 Independent Energy Center	2	15.4%	7	6.9%	0	0.0%	1	5.0%	3	6.5%
	04 Ise Grand Shrine Reconstruction System	1	7.7%	4	3.9%	0	0.0%	0	0.0%	1	2.2%
	05 Block Plan	0	0.0%	2	2.0%	0	0.0%	0	0.0%	2	4.3%
	Total	13	100.0%	86	84.3%	1	50.0%	9	45.0%	27	58.7%
FloorPlan	06 Vacant Floor Space	3	23.1%	19	18.6%	0	0.0%	8	40.0%	14	30.4%
	07 LGS (Light Gauge Steel) Partition	5	38.5%	19	18.6%	0	0.0%	2	10.0%	7	15.2%
	08 Open Ended Corridor	2	15.4%	19	18.6%	1	50.0%	2	10.0%	4	8.7%
	09 Spinal Street	3	23.1%	11	10.8%	0	0.0%	1	5.0%	7	15.2%

	Total	13	100.0%	68	66.7%	1	50.0%	13	65.0%	32	69.6%
	10 Long Span Structure	2	15.4%	24	23.5%	0	0.0%	3	15.0%	11	23.9%
	11 Connection for Vertical Extension	1	7.7%	5	4.9%	0	0.0%	0	0.0%	6	13.0%
Structure	12 Enough Floor Height	1	7.7%	4	3.9%	0	0.0%	1	5.0%	4	8.7%
	13 Enough Load Allowance	0	0.0%	1	1.0%	0	0.0%	0	0.0%	3	6.5%
	Total	4	30.8%	34	33.3%	0	0.0%	4	20.0%	24	52.2%
	14 Interstitial Space/Mechanical Trench	4	30.8%	19	18.6%	0	0.0%	0	0.0%	4	8.7%
	15 External Pipe Shaft	1	7.7%	7	6.9%	0	0.0%	1	5.0%	3	6.5%
Mechanical Equipment	16 Raised Floor	0	0.0%	6	5.9%	1	50.0%	1	5.0%	3	6.5%
	17 Concentrated Pipe Shaft	0	0.0%	4	3.9%	0	0.0%	1	5.0%	4	8.7%
	Total	5	38.5%	36	35.3%	1	50.0%	3	15.0%	14	30.4%

Table 10.8 Number of methodologies according to hospital size

Large Category	Methodology	20–100 Beds (N=15) No. of Mention	20–100 Beds Percentage	101–200 Beds (N=32) No. of Mention	101–200 Beds Percentage	201–300 Beds (N=23) No. of Mention	201–300 Beds Percentage	301–400 Beds (N=38) No. of Mention	301–400 Beds Percentage	401–500 Beds (N=20) No. of Mention	401–500 Beds Percentage	501- Beds (N=48) No. of Mention	501- Beds Percentage	No. of Beds Unknown (N=7) No. of Mention	No. of Beds Unknown Percentage
Building Layout	01 Extra Site Space	10	66.7%	17	53.1%	13	56.5%	19	50.0%	9	45.0%	23	47.9%	4	57.1%
	02 Finger-type Plan	3	20.0%	5	15.6%	2	8.7%	3	7.9%	2	10.0%	3	6.3%	0	0.0%
	03 Independent Energy Center	0	0.0%	5	15.6%	1	4.3%	2	5.3%	0	0.0%	5	10.4%	0	0.0%
	04 Ise Grand Shrine Reconstruction System	0	0.0%	1	3.1%	0	0.0%	2	5.3%	1	5.0%	2	4.2%	0	0.0%
	05 Block Plan	0	0.0%	0	0.0%	0	0.0%	0	0.0%	3	15.0%	1	2.1%	0	0.0%
	Total	13	86.7%	28	87.5%	16	69.6%	26	68.4%	15	75.0%	34	70.8%	4	57.1%
Floor Plan	06 Vacant Floor Space	7	46.7%	5	15.6%	7	30.4%	8	21.1%	5	25.0%	10	20.8%	2	28.6%
	07 LGS (Light Gauge Steel) Partition	0	0.0%	4	12.5%	5	21.7%	4	10.5%	3	15.0%	17	35.4%	0	0.0%
	08 Open Ended Corridor	4	26.7%	4	12.5%	6	26.1%	3	7.9%	4	20.0%	7	14.6%	0	0.0%
	09 Spinal Street	1	6.7%	5	15.6%	4	17.4%	5	13.2%	0	0.0%	7	14.6%	0	0.0%
	Total	12	80.0%	18	56.3%	22	95.7%	20	52.6%	12	60.0%	41	85.4%	2	28.6%
Structure	10 Long Span Structure	0	0.0%	7	21.9%	3	13.0%	7	18.4%	4	20.0%	17	35.4%	2	28.6%
	11 Connection for Vertical Extension	2	13.3%	3	9.4%	1	4.3%	2	5.3%	1	5.0%	3	6.3%	0	0.0%
		0	0.0%	3	9.4%	1	4.3%	1	2.6%	0	0.0%	4	8.3%	1	14.3%

	12 Enough Floor Height	0	0.0%	0	0.0%	1	2.6%	0	0.0%	3	6.3%	0	0.0%
	13 Enough Load Allowance	2	13.3%	13	40.6%	11	28.9%	5	25.0%	27	56.3%	3	42.9%
	14 Interstitial Space/Mechanical Trench	0	0.0%	5	15.6%	4	10.5%	4	20.0%	12	25.0%	1	14.3%
	15 External Pipe Shaft	1	6.7%	0	0.0%	0	0.0%	0	0.0%	11	22.9%	0	0.0%
Mechanical Equipment	16 Raised Floor	0	0.0%	1	3.1%	1	2.6%	4	20.0%	4	8.3%	0	0.0%
	17 Concentrated Pipe Shaft	2	13.3%	1	3.1%	2	5.3%	1	5.0%	1	2.1%	0	0.0%
	Total	3	20.0%	7	21.9%	7	18.4%	9	45.0%	28	58.3%	1	14.3%

Table 10.9 Number of applied methodologies in domestic/overseas hospitals

Domestic/Overseas Hospital	No. of Applied Methodologies								Average No. Application
	1	2	3	4	5	6	7	8	
Domestic Hospital (N=183)	86	43	22	20	6	3	2	1	2.12
Overseas Hospital (N=56)	36	13	5	1	1	0	0	0	1.54

Table 10.10 Number of applied methodologies according to hospital administration

Type of Hospital Administration	No. of Mentioned Methodologies								Average No. of Applied Methodologies
	1	2	3	4	5	6	7	8	
National Sector (N=13)	4	5	1	1	0	0	2	0	2.69
Official Sector (N=102)	49	18	15	12	4	3	0	1	2.20
Insurance Sector (N=2)	1	1	0	0	0	0	0	0	1.50
Healthcare Corporation (N=20)	14	4	1	1	0	0	0	0	1.45
Others (N=46)	18	15	5	6	2	0	0	0	2.11

Table 10.11 Number of applied methodologies according to hospital size

Hospital Size	No. of Applied Methodologies								Average No. of Applied Methodologies
	1	2	3	4	5	6	7	8	
20–100 Beds (N=15)	6	5	2	2	0	0	0	0	2.00
101–200 Beds (N=32)	19	6	2	2	0	1	1	1	2.06
201–300 Beds (N=23)	12	5	2	2	1	1	0	0	2.04
301–400 Beds (N=38)	22	11	1	3	1	0	0	0	1.68
401–500 Beds (N=20)	9	5	3	2	1	0	0	0	2.05
501+ Beds (N=48)	13	10	11	9	3	1	1	0	2.71
No. of Beds Unknown (N=7)	5	1	1	0	0	0	0	0	1.43

The following popular journals and reports among hospital architects are selected for the survey of drawings: 1) Japan Hospital Architecture Association & Association of Japan Hospital Equipment; *Hospitals in Japan*, Rikoh Tosho, 1960; 2) Japan Hospital Architecture Association; *Hospitals in Japan*, Shokokusha, 1965; 3) Japan Institute of Hospital Architecture; *Modern Hospital Design in Japan*, Kajima Publishing, 1986; 4) *The Journal of Japan Institute of Healthcare Architecture* No.1–184, Japan Institute of Healthcare

Table 10.12 Number of hospitals in year of completion

Domestic/Overseas hospital	1930s	1940s	1950s	1960s	1970s	1980s	1990s	2000s	2010s	Unknown
Domestic Hospital (N=183)	0	0	0	3	37	41	40	40	22	0
Overseas Hospital (N=56)	1	2	0	3	9	12	8	6	1	14

Table 10.13 Number of domestic hospitals according to completion year and methodologies applied

No. of Applied Methodologies	1960s (N=3)	1970s (N=37)	1980s (N=41)	1990s (N=40)	2000s (N=40)	2010s (N=22)	Total (N=183)
1	2	16	24	18	14	12	86
2	1	7	8	7	15	5	43
3	0	3	4	9	5	1	22
4	0	6	4	4	4	2	20
5	0	1	1	2	1	1	6
6	0	1	0	0	1	1	3
7	0	2	0	0	0	0	2
8	0	1	0	0	0	0	1
Total No. of Applied Methodologies	4	96	73	85	86	44	388
Average No. of Applied Methodologies	1.33	2.59	1.78	2.13	2.15	2.00	2.12

Table 10.14 Number of overseas hospitals according to completion year and methodologies applied

No. of Applied Methodologies	1960s (N=3)	1970s (N=9)	1980s (N=12)	1990s (N=8)	2000s (N=6)	2010s (N=1)	Total (N=39)
1	3	2	8	5	5	1	24
2	0	3	4	3	1	0	11
3	0	2	0	0	0	0	2
4	0	1	0	0	0	0	1
5	0	1	0	0	0	0	1
Total No. of Applied Methodologies	3	23	16	11	7	1	61
Average No. of Applied Methodologies	1.00	2.56	1.33	1.38	1.17	1.00	1.56

Table 10.15 Number of domestic hospitals according to completion year and methodologies applied

Large Category	Methodology	1960s	1970s	1980s	1990s	2000s	2010s	Tot
Building Layout	01 Extra Site Space	2	26	29	13	14	11	95
	02 Finger-type Plan	0	5	1	3	1	3	13
	03 Independent Energy Center	0	0	0	3	2	1	6
	04 Ise Grand Shrine Reconstruction System	0	0	1	2	0	1	4
	05 Block Plan	0	8	5	4	1	0	18
	Total	2	39	36	25	18	16	136
Floor Plan	06 Vacant Floor Space	1	5	5	7	21	5	44
	07 LGS (Light Gauge Steel) Partition	0	10	5	8	6	4	33
	08 Open Ended Corridor	1	9	10	5	3	0	28
	09 Spinal Street	0	3	4	5	9	1	22
	Total	2	27	24	25	39	10	127
Structure	10 Long Span Structure	0	7	2	12	11	8	40
	11 Connection for Vertical Extension	0	8	3	0	1	0	12
	12 Enough Floor Height	0	3	0	2	4	1	10
	13 Enough Load Allowance	0	0	1	1	2	0	4
	Total	0	18	6	15	18	9	66
Mechanical Equipment	14 Interstitial Space/Mechanical Trench	0	5	5	8	6	3	27
	15 External Pipe Shaft	0	4	1	3	0	3	11
	16 Raised Floor	0	1	1	6	2	2	12
	17 Concentrated Pipe Shaft	0	2	0	3	3	1	9
	Total	0	12	7	20	11	9	59

Architecture, 1968–2014; 5) *Data File of Healthcare Architecture*, Japan Institute of Healthcare Architecture, 1996–2014.

We defined literature 1, 2, and 3 as "old drawings," and 4 and 5 as "new drawings" with a total of 78 hospitals. We eliminated hospitals which moved away from their old site or whose building layout is not available, resulting in 25 hospitals to be analyzed.

Definition of growth and change types

We classified growth and change types from the viewpoint of "old building" and "new building site." In terms of old building, we found two cases: demolishing all old buildings (Type A) and retaining some old buildings (Type B). Relating to new building site, we also found two

Table 10.16 Number of overseas hospitals according to completion year and methodologies applied

Large Category	Methodology	1960s	1970s	1980s	1990s	2000s	2010s	Total
Building Layout	01 Extra Site Space	0	2	3	5	4	1	15
	02 Finger-type Plan	2	0	0	0	0	0	2
	03 Independent Energy Center	0	0	1	0	0	0	1
	04 Ise Grand Shrine Reconstruction System	0	0	0	0	0	0	0
	05 Block Plan	0	1	1	0	0	0	2
	Total	2	3	5	5	4	1	20
Floor Plan	06 Vacant Floor Space	1	3	2	1	3	0	10
	07 LGS (Light Gauge Steel) Partition	0	2	0	1	0	0	3
	08 Open Ended Corridor	0	1	0	1	0	0	2
	09 Spinal Street	0	1	1	0	0	0	2
	Total	1	7	3	3	3	0	17
Structure	10 Long Span Structure	0	3	0	0	0	0	3
	11 Connection for Vertical Extension	0	2	4	0	0	0	6
	12 Enough Floor Height	0	1	0	1	0	0	2
	13 Enough Load Allowance	0	3	0	0	0	0	3
	Total	0	9	4	1	0	0	14
Mechanical Equipment	14 Interstitial Space/Mechanical Trench	0	3	3	1	0	0	7
	15 External Pipe Shaft	0	1	1	0	0	0	2
	16 Raised Floor	0	0	0	0	0	0	0
	17 Concentrated Pipe Shaft	0	4	0	1	0	0	5
	Total	0	8	4	2	0	0	14

cases: constructing new buildings on an existing vacant site (Type 1) and new construction on the sites of demolished old buildings (Type 2). We combined them and defined four growth and change types (Table 10.17):

A1: All of the old buildings were demolished after their functions were transferred to new buildings constructed on existing vacant sites

A2: All of the old buildings were demolished because their site was necessary for constructing new buildings

B1: All or some of the old buildings were retained after new buildings are completed on an existing vacant site

B2: Some of the old buildings were demolished because their site was necessary for constructing new buildings

Table 10.17 Type of hospital building and site

Hospital Name (Gray: Public Sector)	No. of Beds	Type of Building	Type of Site	Type of Growth and Change
Aichi Cancer Center	500	A	1	A1
Japanese Red Cross Medical Center	708	A	1	A1
Nihonmatsu Hospital	160	A	1	A1
Spinal Injury Center	150	A	1	A1
Tottori Prefectural Kousei Hospital	304	A	1	A1
Kyoto Medical Center	600	A	2	A2
NTT Medical Center Tokyo	665	A	2	A2
Osaka Red Cross Hospital	1,021	A	2	A2
Otemae Hospital	400	A	2	A2
St. Luke's International Hospital	520	A	2	A2
Yokote Municipal Hospital	229	A	2	A2
Aichi Medical University Hospital	1,014	B	1	B1
Asahi Rosai Hospital	250	B	1	B1
Chiba Emergency Medical Center	100	B	1	B1
Juntendo University Urayasu Hospital	653	B	1	B1
Osaka International Cancer Institute	500	B	1	B1
Takarazuka City Hospital	446	B	1	B1
Toho University Omori Medical Center	948	B	1	B1
Tokyo Medical University Hachioji Medical Center	610	B	1	B1
Kurashiki Central Hospital	1,166	B	2	B2
Musashino Red Cross Hospital	611	B	2	B2
NTT East Izu Hospital	196	B	2	B2
Osaka National Hospital	694	B	2	B2
Tokyo Metropolitan Bokutoh Hospital	772	B	2	B2
Yokohama Municipal Citizen's Hospital	650	B	2	B2

We grouped the 25 selected hospitals among the four types above, and found no difference among the total number of hospitals of each type, as Tables 10.18, 10.19, and 10.20 show. We examined the reason why each hospital chose the type in detail from the aspect of site location, age of building, and construction era.

Discussion on site location

We examined 25 hospitals in terms of site location after distributing them into two categories: city area hospitals and those in "local" areas (rural areas or small towns) (Table 10.21).

The growth and change of hospital buildings

Table 10.18 Results of type of building

Type of Building	Explanation	No. of Hospitals
	All of the old buildings were demolished	11
	All or some of the old buildings were retained	14

Table 10.19 Results of type of site

Type of Site	Explanation	No. of Hospitals
	New buildings were constructed on an existing vacant site	13
	New buildings were constructed on the sites of demolished old buildings	12

Table 10.20 Results of type of growth and change

Type of Growth and Change	Construction Step	No. of Hospitals
A1	1: Construct a new building, 2: Transfer all functions, 3: Demolish all the old buildings	5
A2	1: Construct a part of the new buildings, 2: Transfer some functions, 3: Demolish the vacant old buildings, 4: Construct the rest of new building on demolished old building's site	6
B1	1: New building is extended to existing vacant site, 2: All or some of the old building is retained	8
B2	1: Demolish some old buildings, 2: New building is extended to newly born vacant site	6

In terms of site, eight cases out of 13 city area hospitals are Type 2 which seemingly had to demolish old building in order to generate building sites. Other cases (Type 1) are as follows: Japanese Red Cross Medical Center and Osaka International Cancer Institute constructed high-rise building; Toho University Omori Medical Center obtained an adjacent site prior to rebuilding; Aichi Cancer Center originally had a big site; Chiba Emergency Medical Center added a small building as their number of beds was small. This result suggests that 11 hospitals out of 13 struggled to secure sufficient floor area in limited site size.

On the other hand, eight cases out of 12 local area hospitals are Type 1 which means they had large extra sites available. However, the following four Type 2 cases show that even hospitals in local areas cannot respond to growth and change; Yokote Municipal Hospital and Musashino Red Cross Hospital did not have enough space beyond the end of the main corridor;

183

Table 10.21 Hospital type in city/local area

Hospital Name (Gray: Public Sector)	No. of Beds	Type of Building	Type of Site	Type of Growth and Change	Hospital Location
Aichi Cancer Center	500	A	1	A1	City
Japanese Red Cross Medical Center	708	A	1	A1	City
Kyoto Medical Center	600	A	2	A2	City
NTT Medical Center Tokyo	665	A	2	A2	City
Osaka Red Cross Hospital	1,021	A	2	A2	City
Otemae Hospital	400	A	2	A2	City
St. Luke's International Hospital	520	A	2	A2	City
Chiba Emergency Medical Center	100	B	1	B1	City
Osaka International Cancer Institute	500	B	1	B1	City
Toho University Omori Medical Center	948	B	1	B1	City
Osaka National Hospital	694	B	2	B2	City
Tokyo Metropolitan Bokutoh Hospital	772	B	2	B2	City
Yokohama Municipal Citizen's Hospital	650	B	2	B2	City
Nihonmatsu Hospital	160	A	1	A1	Local
Spinal Injury Center	150	A	1	A1	Local
Tottori Prefectural Kousei Hospital	304	A	1	A1	Local
Yokote Municipal Hospital	229	A	2	A2	Local
Aichi Medical University Hospital	1,014	B	1	B1	Local
Asahi Rosai Hospital	250	B	1	B1	Local
Juntendo University Urayasu Hospital	653	B	1	B1	Local
Takarazuka City Hospital	446	B	1	B1	Local
Tokyo Medical University Hachioji Medical Center	610	B	1	B1	Local
Kurashiki Central Hospital	1,166	B	2	B2	Local
Musashino Red Cross Hospital	611	B	2	B2	Local
NTT East Izu Hospital	196	B	2	B2	Local

Kurashiki Central Hospital and NTT East Izu Hospital had less space as they repeatedly constructed new buildings over the years. With respect to architecture, eight cases out of 12 hospitals are Type B. The other four cases demolished old buildings; Nihonmatsu Hospital, Tottori Prefectural Kousei Hospital, and Yokote Municipal Hospital could not use old buildings as they were too small (less than 40 m^2 per bed); Spinal Injury Centers' old buildings were not able to accommodate the latest equipment required for the special treatment. This result means that hospitals tend to use old buildings even after new buildings have sufficient floor space. In addition, as eight out of local 12 hospitals are public hospitals, old buildings have to be kept until their depreciation period expires. Japan's taxation system stipulates the legal durable years of RC (reinforced concrete) hospital building is 39 years.

The growth and change of hospital buildings

Discussion on buildings' age difference

We sorted 25 hospitals in order of the age difference of old and new buildings (Table 10.22). Eight cases were less than 30 years and all of them were Type B and only two cases within them were Type 2. This result indicates that hospitals construct new building in extra sites without demolishing old buildings if the age difference is less than 30 years. On the contrary, eight cases out of nine old hospital buildings over 40 years were demolished (Type 2) and in eight cases, they constructed new buildings on vacant lots of old buildings.

Discussion on construction era

Twenty-five hospitals were sorted in chronological order of old buildings' construction era (Table 10.23).

Table 10.22 Hospital type according to building age

Hospital Name (Gray: Public Sector)	No. of Beds	Type of Building	Type of Site	Type of Growth and Change	Building Age Difference
Kurashiki Central Hospital	1,166	B	2	B2	69
Osaka Red Cross Hospital	1,021	A	2	A2	68
St. Luke's International Hospital	520	A	2	A2	59
Osaka National Hospital	694	B	2	B2	56
Yokote Municipal Hospital	229	A	2	A2	49
Otemae Hospital	400	A	2	A2	49
Tottori Prefectural Kousei Hospital	304	A	1	B2	45
Kyoto Medical Center	600	A	2	A2	44
NTT Medical Center Tokyo	665	A	2	A2	44
Toho University Omori Medical Center	948	B	1	B1	40
Aichi Medical University Hospital	1,014	B	1	B1	40
Tokyo Metropolitan Bokutoh Hospital	772	B	2	B2	37
Spinal Injury Center	150	A	1	A1	36
Japanese Red Cross Medical Center	708	A	1	A1	33
Yokohama Municipal Citizen's Hospital	650	B	2	B2	31
Aichi Cancer Center	500	A	1	A1	30
Nihonmatsu Hospital	160	A	1	A1	30
NTT East Izu Hospital	196	B	2	B2	28
Asahi Rosai Hospital	250	B	1	B1	28
Osaka International Cancer Institute	500	B	1	B1	24
Tokyo Medical University Hachioji Medical Center	610	B	1	B1	21
Juntendo University Urayasu Hospital	653	B	1	B1	20
Chiba Emergency Medical Center	100	B	1	B1	18
Musashino Red Cross Hospital	611	B	2	B2	18
Takarazuka City Hospital	446	B	1	B1	14

Table 10.23 Hospital type according to completion year of old building

Hospital Name (Gray: Public Sector)	No. of Beds	Type of Building	Type of Site	Type of Growth and Change	Completion Year of Old Building
Kurashiki Central Hospital	1,166	B	2	B2	1923
St. Luke's International Hospital	520	A	2	A2	1933
Osaka Red Cross Hospital	1,021	A	2	A2	1937
Otemae Hospital	400	A	2	A2	1955
NTT East Izu Hospital	196	B	2	B2	1956
NTT Medical Center Tokyo	665	A	2	A2	1956
Osaka National Hospital	694	B	2	B2	1958
Kyoto Medical Center	600	A	2	A2	1959
Yokote Municipal Hospital	229	A	2	A2	1960
Yokohama Municipal Citizen's Hospital	650	B	2	B2	1960
Asahi Rosai Hospital	250	B	1	B1	1960
Tokyo Metropolitan Bokutoh Hospital	772	B	2	B2	1962
Tottori Prefectural Kousei Hospital	304	A	1	A1	1963
Nihonmatsu Hospital	160	A	1	A1	1963
Toho University Omori Medical Center	948	B	1	B1	1964
Aichi Cancer Center	500	A	1	A1	1965
Aichi Medical University Hospital	1,014	B	1	B1	1974
Japanese Red Cross Medical Center	708	A	1	A1	1976
Osaka International Cancer Institute	500	B	1	B1	1977
Spinal Injury Center	150	A	1	A1	1978
Chiba Emergency Medical Center	100	B	1	B1	1979
Tokyo Medical University Hachioji Medical Center	610	B	1	B1	1981
Musashino Red Cross Hospital	611	B	2	B2	1981
Juntendo University Urayasu Hospital	653	B	1	B1	1984
Takarazuka City Hospital	446	B	1	B1	1984

What is notable is that 11 out of 12 hospitals built before 1962 were Type 2 while 12 out of 13 hospitals built after 1963 were Type 1. This means that the earlier the old buildings were constructed, the easier they are to be demolished when new buildings are constructed to replace them. Of course, older buildings may not be capable of accommodating required functions after new buildings are in use, one of the biggest reason being that the concept of growth and change was not taken into consideration when those older buildings were designed. According to the drawings we examined, new buildings were spread throughout hospital sites in 16 cases completed before 1970, while buildings are arranged in a compact way in nine cases after 1970. This difference suggests that the growth and change concept directly influenced Japanese hospital design.

Conclusions

We overviewed the history of growth and change in Japan and gained perspective on the application of related methodologies in Japan and overseas, through reviewing published literature and architectural drawings. While the number of overseas hospital cases in our study are limited, similar methodologies are adopted in successive periods all over the world. It is interesting that methodologies derived from John Weeks's proposal appear to have spread simultaneously. While we notice there are some limitations to our research, such as that some methodologies like "Extra Site Space" might have been so conventional that architects do not think it necessary to mention their use, we hope this study adds to the understanding of the importance of planning for long-lived hospital design.

Case study: growth and change of the University of Tokyo Teaching Hospital

Literature and interview survey

Regarding the University of Tokyo Teaching Hospital, its history has been discussed in various books (Medical School of the University of Tokyo, 1967) and thesis studies (Okada, 2005; Torisu, 1999). Elements of growth and change had been extracted from these sources and rearranged in chronological order to see why the growth and change concept was necessary and how it was realized.

Interviews with Professor Yasumi Yoshitake of Architecture at the University of Tokyo (1916–2003) and Professor Makoto Ito of Architecture at Chiba University (1927–2010) had been carried out in the previous thesis. In addition to architectural professors, Mr Haruki Hakomori (1950-) at the Administration Section of the hospital was interviewed in order to include administrative aspects.

Outline of hospital operations

The origin of this hospital dates back to the Otamagaike smallpox vaccination center, established in 1858. Moved once or twice in Tokyo, it began hospital work in the current location in 1876. They have delivered medical services with an educational and research focus for over 140 years.

The University of Tokyo Teaching Hospital is situated at 7-3-1 Hongo, Bunkyo-ku, Tokyo Japan. The owner is The University of Tokyo (National University Corporation). The hospital has 1,163 inpatient beds, serves 2,962 outpatients per day, and 17,072 ER patients per year, and houses 37 diagnostic departments.

Characteristics of the process of growth and change

One of the biggest characteristics of the hospital is that its ownership changed in 2004 from a National University to a National University corporation. The main budget allocated by the Japanese government decreased each year since 2004, so that they are required to earn money from running the hospital to pay for growth and change. Another characteristic is that they are part of the University's Medical School. While the hospital construction budget is a fiscal investment and uses loans they must repay, the Medical School construction budget is covered by the national tax.

In addition, because of this relationship, projects for growth and change are affected not only by Medical School building plans but also by the priorities of other schools in the University. Therefore its decision-making processes are complicated and fairly long compared with private hospitals. In such projects, the first step is to formulate growth and change ideas which are transferred to the Building and Repairs section of the University to make architectural drawings. The University Department of Architecture may become involved at this stage. The University submits the drawing for a budget request to the Education Ministry along with a supplementary documentation or rationalization of the educational philosophy, as the buildings in question also serve educational purposes. Since the project could be totally or partially rejected at every step, long-term and ambitious projects are difficult to be approved.

Outline of the process of growth and change

Discussion of the process of growth and change is based on the available literature sources. Due to this, the process is divided into seven historic periods from the viewpoint of drastic changes of hospital architecture at the University of Tokyo (Figure 10.1).

Early Hongo Era (1876–1900)
Pavilion Ward Era (1900–1924)
Professor Uchida Era (1924–1952)
Professor Yoshitake Era (1952–1968)
Small Refurbishment Era (1968–1982)
Redevelopment Era (1982–2006)
PFI (Private Finance Initiative) Era (2006-Present)

Early Hongo Era (1876–1900)

At the time the University of Tokyo was established in 1877, there was only a Faculty of Medicine, whose teaching hospital buildings were the so-called "pavilion type," consisting of three parallel wooden single-story buildings. The hospital site stood on the south side of Sanshiro Pond where the Medical School buildings are now located. The main building of the Medical School was Western-style wooden architecture of two stories built in 1876 when the Medical School moved to Hongo. However, the building was moved again in the same campus in 1911 when the new hospital pavilion building construction started. The building was reduced in size and its symbolic clock tower was removed on this occasion; it was then converted into the University's Historiography Department.

Pavilion Ward Era (1900–1924)
A new campus plan to reduce the Medical School and enlarge the hospital site was drawn up when other schools began moving to the Hongo campus in 1900. The reason was that the hospital was expected to expand because of the increasing medical demand. New hospital buildings had to be built in the vacant lot generated by destroying some part of the existing pavilion-style Medical School buildings; thus the hospital buildings spontaneously followed the pavilion style. This made sense in terms of ventilation and lighting because the long side of each building was facing south. Consequently, the hospital layout inherited the genes of the early Hongo Era. New Medical School building construction was completed as planned while the hospital building remained unfinished because of the Great Kanto Earthquake in 1923.

Professor Uchida Era (1924–1952)
Although not only the hospital building but also the entire campus was severely damaged by the 1923 earthquake, Engineering Building No. 2 was safe, even though it was under construction. The architect was Professor Yoshikazu Uchida, Department of Architecture, Faculty of Engineering who was also involved in designing the hospital's psychiatric ward at that time. The University assigned him to become chief manager of the Building and Repairs Section as a concurrent post from 1924 to 1938 in order to put him in charge of the campus restoration project. He took on this difficult role on condition that the series of design projects would be counted as a part of the classes of architectural education.

The basic concept of the campus planning included several elements. 1) Each building would have a non-flammable SRC (steel reinforced concrete) structure with a central courtyard space; 2) buildings would be arranged along the central campus axis; and 3) building facades would be unified in "Uchida Gothic" using brown "scratched tile" which was suggested by the Building and Repairs Section requiring rational and low-cost architecture. The hospital site was divided in three by three blocks with a large central courtyard. The main entrance was set in the middle block facing the main street, flanked on each side by surgery and internal medicine blocks. As the hospital was designed as a part of the University campus, the main entrance moved from the south to the east side.

While the drawing was persuasive, the problem was the construction process. As vacant site space was severely limited, Professor Uchida designed the very necessary rooms in the first phase, with the idea to connect them to other buildings in a later phase. Some buildings were completed with exposed reinforcing bars for future connection, but they were never used. These isolated buildings created difficulties later because they were too new to be demolished, according to the National University accounting system. World War II interrupted the project during the construction of the surgery building, after the completion of outpatient and internal medicine buildings. Reconstruction of the surgery building became the main theme of the next phase.

Professor Yoshitake Era (1952–1968)

The basic concept of post-war projects was the centralization of the hospital administration system – imported from the United States – and the diagnosis and treatment functions. Professor Uchida's original planning concept had to change because it had been based on a decentralized system.

Professor Yoshitake started new projects with young medical doctors in 1952 when the budget was approved. At the same time, he lectured on hospital administration at the then National Institute of Hospital Administration (present National Institute of Public Health) to hospital directors. Among them was Professor Misawa, the director of the University of Tokyo Teaching Hospital. This relationship enabled Professor Yoshitake to ask Professor Misawa to document every demand from all departments and to calculate the total required floor area. However, the result was that the large central courtyard planned by Professor Uchida was the only place to build the new central treatment building (Figure 10.2). Ironically, the surrounding building designed by Professor Uchida was too strong to demolish because his design put special emphasis on seismic resistance learned from the Great Kanto Earthquake.

As not only centralization, but also the old surgery building whose operating theaters were equipped with drafty wooden windows were pressing issues, these two functions were planned to merge into one building. In 1957, the central treatment building piggybacking surgery was completed. This was the first centralized healthcare building realized in Japan.

According to Professor Makoto Ito at Chiba University, then a graduate student of Professor Yoshitake and having worked on the project, this planning was not really a "master plan" but just a hand-drawn H-shape building outline without room arrangements because of the limited fiscal budget allocated for steel structure construction. Unlike during the Uchida Era, Professor Yoshitake was working under the Building and Repairs Section whose short-sighted budget process left all the project design work to Professor Yoshitake's teaching studio. As graduate students had played a central role in designing with young medial doctors, there had been mistakes such as a steel beam that was installed but that had to be cut and replaced.

Designing operating theaters was also irregular because each of the four theaters was in a different style. One adopted an egg-shape interior following the example of Saint-Lô Hospital in France. Another introduced air conditioning against the Building and Repairs Section's intention. The interior of all theaters were finished with inexpensive veneer walls in prospect of future change.

In 1964, a six-story central patient ward was completed, designed by the Building and Repairs Section with cantilever beams expecting future extension like the Uchida Era project. No extension was ever realized.

Another patient ward building, the north patient ward, was planned and built in 1968 as an 11-story high tower by Professor Yoshitake in order not only to shrink the building footprint but also reduce the size of nursing units in accordance with the latest hospital management theory. Other ambitious ideas like double-loaded corridor planning, wooden interior finishing, and many single-bed rooms were also realized in the tower. However, three floors have been vacant for 27 years despite the fact that there are older patient wards still in use around the newer bed tower. This extraordinary situation was mainly caused by nurses' objections; they were required to provide more night shifts in the new nursing unit size (40 beds per unit) using a constant number of staff determined by national university regulations. Unfortunately, this conflict was used as a pretext for the student movement that emerged at the time with a lasting effect on the successive phase.

Even while the north patient tower was running dysfunctionally, the hospital was designing the new south patient ward plan in 1972, in order to expand the central treatment department by accommodating the piggybacked surgery ward. Additionally, they were planning a new outpatient building in order to empty existing outpatient buildings for more central treatment expansion.

As an aside, the Building and Repairs Section building, where Professor Yoshitake was working, was located in the converted building that originally housed the Historiography Department. This historic building from 1876 was disassembled and rebuilt to the University's botanical garden in 1969 and now serves as the architecture museum.

Small Refurbishment Era (1968–1982)

Because the Education Ministry did not allow a new budget for the University during the north patient tower malfunction, neither building extensions nor reconstruction proceeded in the 1970s while arguments about the master plan continued. The University campus master plan committee was established in 1974 after Professor Yoshitake left the university. The committee included the successor Professor Shigebumi Suzuki, who planned to solve the old outpatient building problems in the hospital area. Final hospital redevelopment planning was determined in 1980, in which new buildings would be constructed in sequence: first, the central treatment department, then the outpatient department, and finally the patient ward.

Redevelopment Era (1982–2006)

The Education Ministry did not release the budget on the hospital redevelopment due to the north patient tower malfunction. As a result, in 1982 the hospital planned the solution to the vacant bed problem (finally solved in 1996 in a different way) and established the Future Planning Office under the Administration Section while commissioning Okada and Associates to make a master plan. Since the architect Shin'ichi Okada (who studied under Professor Yoshitake) learned from the failure of Professor Uchida and Yoshitake projects that the master plan is not a panacea, he advocated what he called a "system master plan." The concepts were: 1) to first design permanent corridors; 2) to lay out buildings to avoid blocking the corridor; and 3) to enable building designs to be changed by unexpected demands in future. These ideas are reminiscent of Professor Yoshitake's unfinished operation theater.

The "system master plan" designed in 1982 was different from the one in 1980 in the sequence of construction order (Figure 10.3). The central treatment building would be constructed first, followed by the patient ward and outpatient building. There was increased pressure at that time to respect the old "Uchida Gothic" buildings – especially to preserve their facades facing the main street.

At the same time, the hospital was planning to redevelop the branch hospital separately from the main hospital. However, they decided to merge the branch into the main hospital to respect the Education Ministry's intention. This conclusion produced a new master plan accommodating 1,301 beds, enabled by using the "system master plan" which had a spatial margin to absorb the unexpected branch hospital. Furthermore, as its budget was allocated solely on the main hospital, the central treatment building was divided into two buildings constructed in different years. The "system master plan" worked again and finally redevelopment resumed after 14 years.

While the Future Planning Office promoted the construction of the central treatment building I, the patient ward, outpatient building, and treatment building II after the redevelopment launched, ruins of a feudal lord's castle were found during site excavation, and its investigation was expected to be expanded into the future patient ward site. Then the construction sequence of the patient ward and the outpatient building was exchanged and the central treatment building I was finally completed in 1987. The outpatient building construction had to wait until 1991 because of the unsolved hospital merger.

Since new projects for the 21st century emerged in hospital planning in 1990s, everyone noticed that the ongoing master plan assumed a floor area of 92 m^2 (990 ft^2) per bed, automatically calculated by the Education Ministry considering the number of departments, beds, outpatients, and residents. The hospital vigorously discussed this area allowance with the ministry and was given approval in 1996 to increase the floor area to 124 m^2 (1,334 ft^2) per bed, which later became the Ministry's standard. The 15-story high patient ward was completed in 2000 and this floor area increase accelerated an endowed project "the 22nd Century Medical Center" which resulted in a two-floor extension in 2006 on top of the planned seven-story high central treatment II building. Eventually, the redevelopment project was finished and each building's entrance was moved to the south, the original direction as planned 140 years ago.

The patient ward II construction project, included in the latest master plan, was postponed because all the National Universities had transformed into independent administrative units in 2004.

PFI (Private Finance Initiative) Era (2006–present)

After the transformation mentioned above, every university was eager to introduce private funds. The University of Tokyo Teaching Hospitals were

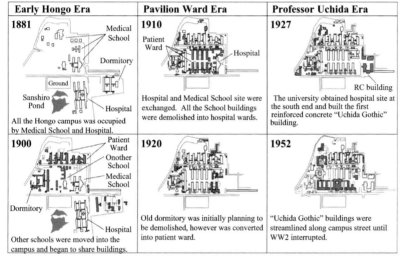

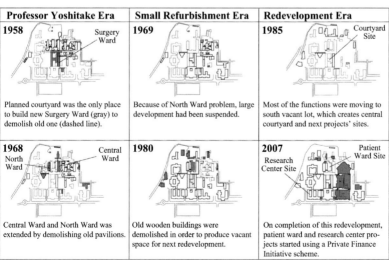

Figure 10.3
Hospital site at each era (NORTH to the left).

not an exception. A patient ward II PFI project started in 2013 with scheduled completion in 2018, and other hospital PFI projects are ongoing.

Conclusion

The University of Tokyo Teaching Hospital had encountered internal or external confusion such as university rearrangement, the Kanto Great Earthquake, World War II and the student movements in the middle of Early Hongo Era, Pavilion Ward Era, Professor Uchida Era, and Professor Yoshitake Era and these incidents led each project to be changed or stopped. As a leading hospital, not only medical demand but also larger changes promoted or rejected its growth and change plans.

Professor Uchida realized the three by three block arrangement because of disaster recovery. However, he had to leave the old pavilions due to the war. Since Professor Yoshitake inherited the three by three strongly constructed buildings, it could be said that his major achievement is limited to the reconstruction of the old pavilions. The redevelopment master plan was successfully completed in 2006 for the first time, brushing off many political changes. This took 24 years since the adoption of the "system master plan," and 54 years since Professor Uchida's plan.

In 2006, the University's symbolic "Iron Gate," which was removed in 1918, was reconstructed on the 150th anniversary of the Medical School, and opened the campus to the community again. The layers of memories represented by this reconstruction at the long-established Medical School appear without architects' intentions, but are nevertheless an important part of community life.

References

Architectural Institute of Japan (1960, December). *Kenchiki Sekkei Siryo Shusei (In Japanese)*. Tokyo: Maruzen.

Ito, M (1965, December). The Shape of Future Hospitals (In Japanese). *Architecture and Society*, 46(12).

Kenchiku Bunka Editorial Office (1949, February). About Chain System Hospital (In Japanese). *Kenchiku Bunka*, (27).

Medical Affairs Office of the Ministry of Health and Welfare (1950, July). Guideline of Hospital Site Acquisition and Its Architectural Design (In Japanese). *BYOIN*, 3(1).

Medical School of the University of Tokyo (1967). *The Centenary History of Medical School of the University of Tokyo (In Japanese)*. Tokyo: The Centenary Association of Medical School of the University of Tokyo.

Mori, R and M Koike (1899, May). *New Hygiene: Second Edition (In Japanese)*. Tokyo: Nankodo Shoten.

Nightingale, F (1859). *Notes on Hospitals*. London: John W. Parker and Son.

Okada, S (2005, June). *Meaning of the System of Hospital Architecture (In Japanese)*. Tokyo: Shokokusha.

Osuga, Y (1951, August). Divided Building for General Hospital in Middle or Small Cities (In Japanese). *BYOIN*, 5(2).

Takamatsu, M (1923, September). About Hospital Architecture (In Japanese). *The Japanese Journal of Medical Instrumentation*, 1(5).

Takemiya, K, A Kakehi, and K Okamoto (2016, March). Study Report on the Growth and Change of Hospital Architecture: Japan Institute of Healthcare Architecture Research Project in 2015 (In Japanese) Tokyo: Japan Institute of Healthcare Architecture.

Torisu, R (1999, March). *A Research on the Change of Hospital: Case Study of the University of Tokyo Teaching Hospital.* Master Thesis of Architecture, Tokyo: University of Tokyo.

Tsuboi, N (1874, February). Design and Knowledge of Hospital Architecture (In Japanese). *IJI ZASSHI*, (6).

Watanabe, Y (1887, January). Hospital Design Method (In Japanese). *Journal of Architecture and Building Science*, 1(1).

Weeks, J and Y Nagasawa (Translator) (2000, September). Were Hospitals Able to Correspond to "Growth and Change?": A Verification on Northwick Park Hospital (In Japanese). *BYOIN*, 59(9).

Yamashita, T (2003, April). A Verification of "Growth and Change" in Hospitals (In Japanese). *BYOIN*, 62(4).

Yanagisawa, M (1969, September). Growth and Change of Hospital Architecture (In Japanese). *The Current Medicine*, 17(1).

Yoshitake, Y et al. (1962, June). *Hospital: Kenchikugaku Taikei <35> (In Japanese)*. Tokyo: Shokokusha.

Index

Page numbers in *italics* refer to figures. Page numbers in **bold** refer to tables.

Academic Medical Centers (AMCs) 54, 55–56
access system 46
Accident, Emergency and Surgical Center "INO" 47–49
accountability 55
adaptability/adaptations 64–65, 69, 71–72, 82, 84–85, 114, 140–141, 145, 147–148, 159–160
area availability 17, *17*, 20
autonomy of individual units 6–7
AZ Groeninge hospital 108–122, *111*, *114*, *116*, *117*

Baecker, Dirk 28
Banner Estrella Medical Center 71–90
Banner Ironwood 79
Base Buildings 2–4, 93, 127, 135
Baumschlager Eberle Architekten 111–112, 113–114
boundary friction 102, 104
Brecht, Bertolt 28
bridge connections 45–46, 48
budgeting process 130, *132*, 134
building components, partition of 17, *17*
building lines 43–45
building use, length of 63

capacity analysis 126, *128*, 129–130
change: design for 108–122; planned for 91–106; planning for 71–90; tools for planning 140–162
connection level 45, 48
consumerism 55
contractor, selecting 132
cost reduction, pressure for 55
Counter Clockwise, The Power of Possibility (Langer) 27–28
Creating Capabilities (Nussbaum) 27
crop rotation 43, 49

demographics 55
density 42
design adaptations 85, 89
"Design and Construction of General Hospitals" (Shaffer) 167
Design for Change 108–122
design phase 134
disentanglement 43
drawings survey 173, 178, 180
"duffle coat" strategy *see* loose-fit strategy
du Prie construction company 133–134

easements 7
electrical system/capacity 67, 135–136
embedding services 118–120
expansion faces 77

facade, load-bearing 117–118, *117*, *118*
facilities development, dynamic 54–70
Facility Guidelines Institute (FGI) 79, 81–82, 85, 90
feasibility 130
Febelarch 117
first-hand experience test 142, 148
fit-out 2, 3–4, 10, 93, 102, 127, 135
fixtures 8–9
flexibility 17, *17*, 41, 72, 109
floor plates, changes in 66–67
floor-to-floor dimensions 67, 68
Flüchtlingsgespräche (Brecht) 28
furniture, fixtures and equipment (FF&E) 93, 127, 135

196

Index

generality 109, 114–115
gravitation 47
Green Deals 108
green spaces and routes 43
grid spacing 67, 68
growth and change concept 167, 180–182, 188
Guidelines for Design and Construction of Hospitals and Outpatient Facilities (FGI) 81–82, 85, 90
Guntern, Gottlieb 28
Gyproc CableStud 125, 135, *136*

Habraken, John 112, 118
Hakomori, Haruki 187
Hamdi, N. 109
Healthcare Facility Design for Flexibility (Kendall et al.) 135
"health village" 111
height development 45
Hendrickx, Hendrik 110
HENN Architects 32–53
Het Vliethuys 125–139, *126*, *127*, *128*, *137*
hidden design 19–20
hospice, transformation to 125–139
hospital buildings, growth and changes of 164–194
hospitals, Base Buildings and 4–5
HVAC system 136, 138
"Hygiene theory in the Navy and Army" (Tsuboi) 164–165

indeterminate architecture 145
infrastructure model 1–10, *5*
Initial Outfitting and Transition 4
innovation 18
INO 21–22
inpatient buildings 58–60, **59**
Inselspital University healthcare campus 32–53, *33–34*, *38*
interconnection 43
interfaces between levels 102, 104
Ito, Makoto 167, 187, 190

Japanese hospitals: case study on 187–194; construction era and 185–186; growth and change in 167–168, **168**, 170, 180–182; historical survey of 164–167, **165**; methodologies within 168–173, **169**, **170**, *171*, *172*, **173**, **174–180**, **181–186**; site locations 182–184

Kaiser Permanente 79
kneading dough 36, 42
Kroll, Lucien 109

La MéMé 109
Langer, Ellen 27–28
Lariboisière Hospital 165
legal implications of infrastructure model 7
life history test 141–142, 147
Llewelyn-Davies, Richard 167
loose-fit strategy (also "duffle coat" strategy) 145, 152–153
Lunder Building 58, 60, 63, 67–69

market incentives 55
MAS (master plan for the urban area of Bern's University Hospital) 25–26, 29–30
Massachusetts General Hospital (MGH) 54–70
mass housing 92
McMaster University Health Sciences Centre (MHSC) 143–144, *143*, 161
mechanical capacity 67, 68
MEP infrastructure 55, 56, 58, 60, 62–63, 68–69, 73
Misawa, Professor 190
Monte Carlo simulation 155–156, 158
Mori, Ogai (Rintaro) 165–166
multi-strategy buildings 145

NBBJ 71–90
New Hygiene (Mori) 165–166
Nightingale, Florence 165
Northwick Park Hospital (NPH) 144–153, *145*, *146*, *149*, 161, 167
Notes to Hospitals (Nightingale) 165
Nussbaum, Martha 27

Ogawa, Takehiko 167
Okada, Shin'ichi 192
Open Building approach 91–106, 108–122, 125–139; *see also* System Separation (SYS)
open space 41–42
Operating Concept 15, *16*, 19
operating rooms 60, 67
Oresunder Hospital 166
Organizational Concept 15, *16*, 19
Organizational Master Plan 46–47, *47*, 48
Organization Und Management (Baecker) 28
OSAR Architects 111–112

Index

Osuga, Yanagi 167
outpatient buildings 60–61, **61**

paradigm shift 13–14
Paradoxes of Planning, The (Westin) 28
personal property 8
practice patterns, changing 55
preventive building design 13–30
Primary System (PS) 17–18, 19, 20, *23*, 93, 98
Process Concept 15, *16*
property, types of 8–9
prospective evaluation 142–144, 148–151, *150*, **151**, *152*, 153–162

real property versus real estate 8–9
reinvestment cycles 64
renovation versus new construction 65–66
retrospective evaluation 141–142, 146–148, 161
risks 20, 157–158
road systems *27*
room sizes, increases in 67

Sammy Ofer Heart Building 93–106, *94*, *101*, *103*
schematic design options *96*
science and technology, in healthcare 54–55
Secondary System (SS) 17–18, 19, 20, *23*, 93, 98
Seiler, Anna 34
Sennett, Richard 28
separation walls 135
Shaffer, Marshall 167
Sharon, Arad 95, 98
shopping malls 2–3
simulation, prospective evaluation using 153–161, **154**, **155**, *156*, *157*, *158*, **159**, 162
SmithGroup 79, 81, 82, 89–90
soft space 69, 84
space fields 72, *73*, 79, 84
spatial concept 115–117
Spatial Master Plan 46–47, 48, 49–51
Spirit of Creativity, The (Guntern) 28
"Study Report on the Growth and Change of Hospital Architecture" (Takemiya et al.) 164
subtractive approach 76
Supports: An Alternative to Mass Housing (Habraken) 92
survival test 141, 146–147

sustainability 21
Sustainable Master Plan 46–47
system master plan 192
System Separation (SYS) 13–30, 91, 95, *97*; *see also* Open Building approach

Takamatsu, Masao 166
technical concept 118–120, *119*
technical infrastructure 46
Tel Aviv Sourasky Medical Center 91–106
temporality 109
tendering principles 130, 132
territorial hierarchy 7
Tertiary System (TS) 17–18, 19, 20, 93, 98
3D modeling 130, 134
"Time-Space" project 22
trade fixtures 8–9
Tumor and Organ Center 49, 51

Uchida, Yoshikazu 189–190, 194
uncertainty 112–113
unified control architecture 5
United States Defense Health Agency 4
Université de Louvain-la-Neuve 109
University of Tokyo Teaching Hospital 187–194, *193*
urban quarters 36, 41
user flows 76–77
user participation 9–10
Uses of Disorder, The (Sennett) 28
utility systems, infrastructure model and 7

Van Der Meeren, Willy 109, 110
Van Reeth, Bob 109
Vermolen, Hilde 111, 112, 113, 121
vonRoll (university building) 22–25, *24*
Vrije Universiteit Brussel 109, 110

Weeks, John 144–145, *145*, 148, 152–153, 167, 172–173, 187
Westin, Sara 28
Wright, Frank Lloyd 5

Yanagisawa, Makoto 164, 167
Yawkey's "Nine Commandments" 61–62, **62**
Yoshitake, Yasumi 167, 187, 190–192, 194

Ziss, Ranni 98